From Financial Crisis to Stagnation

The U.S. economy today is confronted with the prospect of extended stagnation. This book explores why. Thomas I. Palley argues that the Great Recession and the destruction of shared prosperity are due to flawed economic policy over the past thirty years. One flaw was the growth model adopted after 1980 that relied on debt and asset price inflation to fuel growth instead of wages. The second flaw was the model of globalization that created an economic gash. Financial deregulation and the house price bubble kept the economy going by making ever more credit available. As the economy cannibalized itself by undercutting income distribution and accumulating debt, it needed larger speculative bubbles to grow. That process ended when the housing bubble burst. The earlier post–World War II economic model based on rising middle-class incomes has been dismantled, while the new neoliberal model has imploded. Absent a change of policy paradigm, the logical next step is stagnation. The political challenge we face now is how to achieve paradigm change.

Thomas I. Palley is an economist living in Washington, D.C. He is currently an associate of the Economic Growth Program of the New America Foundation in Washington, D.C. He was formerly chief economist with the U.S.-China Economic and Security Review Commission. Prior to joining the Commission, he served as director of the Open Society Institute's Globalization Reform Project and as assistant director of Public Policy at the AFL-CIO. Dr. Palley is the author of *Plenty of Nothing: The Downsizing of the American Dream and the Case for Structural Keynesianism* (1998) and *Post Keynesian Economics* (1996). He has published in numerous academic journals and written for the *Atlantic Monthly*, *American Prospect*, and *Nation* magazines. His numerous op-eds are posted on his Web site, www.thomaspalley.com. He holds a BA from Oxford University and an MA in International Relations and a PhD in Economics from Yale University.

From Financial Crisis to Stagnation

*The Destruction of Shared Prosperity
and the Role of Economics*

THOMAS I. PALLEY

CAMBRIDGE UNIVERSITY PRESS
Cambridge, New York, Melbourne, Madrid, Cape Town,
Singapore, São Paulo, Delhi, Mexico City

Cambridge University Press
32 Avenue of the Americas, New York, NY 10013-2473, USA

www.cambridge.org
Information on this title: www.cambridge.org/9781107612464

First published 2012
First paperback edition 2013

A catalog record for this publication is available from the British Library.

Library of Congress Cataloging in Publication Data
Palley, Thomas I., 1956–
From financial crisis to stagnation : the destruction
of shared prosperity and the role of economics / Thomas I. Palley.
p.   cm.
Includes bibliographical references and index.
ISBN 978-1-107-01662-0 (hardback)
1. United States – Economic conditions – 2009– 2. United States – Economic
policy. 3. Recessions – United States. 4. Financial crises – United
States. 5. Global Economic Crisis, 2008–2009. I. Title.
HC106.84.P35   2011
330.973–dc23   2011027047

ISBN 978-1-107-01662-0 Hardback
ISBN 978-1-107-61246-4 Paperback

We shape our tools and they in turn shape us.

Marshall McLuhan, *Understanding Media:*
The Extensions of Man
(New York: McGraw Hill, 1964)

Contents

.

Figures

Tables

Preface

The U.S. economy and much of the global economy are now languishing in the wake of the Great Recession and confront the prospect of extended stagnation. This book explores how and why we got to where we are and how we can escape the pull of stagnation and restore shared prosperity.

The focus of the book is ideas. Marshall McLuhan (1964), the famed philosopher of media, wrote: "We shape our tools and they in turn shape us." Ideas are disembodied tools and they also shape us.

The underlying thesis is that the Great Recession and the looming Great Stagnation are the result of fatally flawed economic policy. That policy derives from a set of economic ideas. The implication is that avoiding stagnation and restoring shared prosperity will require abandoning the existing economic policy frame and the ideas on which it is based and replacing them with a new policy frame based on a new set of ideas.

This book is very different from other books on the crisis in its placement of ideas and politics at the very core. Existing discussion leaves economics to economists and politics to political scientists. That division results in radical misunderstanding. Ideas are always politically rooted, and that holds especially clearly for economic ideas. Consequently, fully understanding a particular economic idea requires understanding its political roots.

If ideas have political roots, there will inevitably be political opposition to a change of ideas. It is not just economic policy that is politically contested; so too are the ideas that provide the justification for policy. This contrasts with the dominant view among economists, who believe theory is apolitical and politics only enters with policy. That is wrong. Politics is about what kind of theory to use and how to use it (policy), and the idea that the best theory wins is a political fiction pushed by the political winners.

The arguments presented in the book are not complex, but that does not mean they are grasped easily. This is because engrained habits of thought continually reassert themselves, particularly the denial of politics and ideology. As Keynes (1936) wrote in the preface to his *General Theory*: "The ideas which are expressed so laboriously are extremely simple and should be obvious. The difficulty lies, not in the new ideas, but in escaping from the old ones, which ramify, for those brought up as most of us have been, into every corner of our minds" (p. viii).

Peeling the Onion of Misunderstanding

It is always difficult to change people's minds because people like to stick with ideas with which they are comfortable and familiar. That is human psychology. But even when people are open to change, the task of persuasion is difficult – and the current task is especially so, being many-layered, like peeling an onion of misunderstanding.

With regard to the phenomenon of the Great Recession, there is a need to offer an alternative explanation. In addition, there is a need to say what is wrong with orthodox accounts, of which there are many.

However, there is a deeper problem. The structural Keynesian account of the Great Recession presented in the book rests on different economic theory. That means there is the prior task of opening readers' minds to this different theory.

Even after this, there is a further layer of complexity, particularly with regard to the question of what must be done to restore shared prosperity. Today's dominant economic theory (often referred to as neoclassical economics) is rooted in a social philosophy about the relation of individuals, markets, and society. That social philosophy is neoliberalism, and it is almost impossible to challenge orthodox economic theory and policies without addressing the failings of this social philosophy. Absent an understanding of those failings, readers are likely to be drawn ineluctably back to the neoliberal framing of the economy and prescriptions that are at the root of the problem.

This leads to a final difficulty, namely that there is a sociology of the economics profession that serves to defend neoliberal economic orthodoxy and obstruct alternative understandings. That sociology is obscured by the economists' use of the rhetoric of scientific truth, and exposing it is, therefore, also part of the task of persuasion.

Acknowledgments

I thank my mother, Claire Palley, and my wife, Margarita Cereijido, for encouraging me to write this book and keeping me at it. I also thank Ron Blackwell, who has been a friend, mentor, and colleague from whom I have long benefited intellectually and who has always generously shared his insights and understandings; Sherle Schwenninger of the New America Foundation for supporting (intellectually and financially) prior work that has been included in this book as Chapter 4; Robert Pollin and Stephanie Seguino, who read the manuscript and offered many valuable suggestions; and Scott Parris of Cambridge University Press for his willingness to publish a book that so openly challenges the conventional wisdom. Lastly, I thank the production team at Newgen and the copyediting team at PETT Fox, Inc., for their help in typesetting and editing the manuscript.

PART I

ORIGINS OF THE GREAT RECESSION

1

Goodbye Financial Crash, Hello Stagnation

This book is about the financial crash of 2008 and the Great Recession that followed. It also predicts the Great Recession will be followed by a Great Stagnation during which the unemployment rate will remain high, wages will stagnate, and a general sense of economic disquiet will prevail.

This is not a tight numeric forecast, but rather a prediction about directional tendency based on current economic policies in the United States and other countries. There will undoubtedly be months when the news is good and months when it is bad, but the general tendency will be one of stagnation and failure to recover shared prosperity. Growth will continue, but it will be growth with unnecessary high unemployment. Moreover, growth will be slower than what could be achieved in a full-employment economy.

Though difficult to predict, the stock market may even do well. First, stagnation will result in low interest rates and that tends to be good for stock values. Second, high unemployment will pressure wages in favor of profits. Third, many companies may be able to make profits from their operations in emerging market economies where the consumer credit cycle looks like it may rev up. But, regardless of how the stock market performs, a strong stock market should not be confused with shared prosperity. Stock ownership is enormously concentrated among the wealthy, and ordinary working families depend on wage and salary income.

In effect, the Great Recession has created a wounded economy in which large segments of society risk permanent exclusion from prosperity. Even though policy makers succeeded in preventing the financial crisis from spiraling into a second Great Depression, they have failed to fix the underlying structural failings that led to the crisis. That is why the economy is wounded and why the prognosis is one of stagnation.

This gloomy economic outlook reflects the fact that the private sector and global economy is beset by economic weakness and contradiction created by thirty years of market fundamentalist policy. Much of the global economy is now debt-saturated and short of demand. In this environment, stagnation is the default condition and the existing policy mix of expansionary monetary and fiscal policy will be insufficient to jump-start sustainable growth with shared prosperity.

It does not have to be this way. A flawed economic paradigm created the current condition and as long as it prevails, the prospect is for stagnation. If the paradigm can be replaced, then prosperity can be restored. The great lesson of the twentieth century is that shared prosperity is made and not found. The right economic structure based on the right policies produces shared prosperity, as happened in the generation after World War II. A wrong economic structure based on wrong economic policies produces exclusion and stagnation, as happened in the 1930s and is happening again.

Core Thesis

The core thesis of the book is that the roots of the financial crisis of 2008 and the Great Recession can be traced to a faulty U.S. macro-economic paradigm that has its roots in neoliberalism, which has been the dominant intellectual paradigm. One flaw in the paradigm was the growth model adopted after 1980 that relied on debt and asset price inflation to drive demand in place of wage growth linked to productivity growth. A second flaw was the model of engagement with the global economy that created a triple economic hemorrhage of spending on imports, manufacturing job losses, and off-shoring of investment.

The combination of stagnant wages and the triple hemorrhage from flawed globalization gradually cannibalized the U.S. economy's income and demand-generating process that had been created after World War II on the back of the New Deal. However, this cannibalization was obscured by financial developments that plugged the growing demand gap.

Financial deregulation and financial excess are central parts of the story, but they are not the ultimate cause of the crisis. Financial developments contributed significantly to the housing bubble and the subsequent crash. However, they served a critical function in the new model, their role being to fuel demand growth by making ever larger amounts of credit easily available. Increasing financial excess was needed to offset the increasing negative effects of the model of growth and global economic engagement that undermined the demand-generating process on which the U.S. economy depended.

This process might have gone on for quite a while longer. However, between 2001 and 2007, the flawed model of global economic engagement accelerated the cannibalization process – which is where China becomes such an integral part of the story. This created the need for a huge bubble that only housing could provide, and when it burst, it pulled down the entire economy because of the housing bubble's massive dependence on debt.

Finance plays a critical role within this explanation of the financial crisis and the Great Recession, but it is not the prime cause. Persistent financial expansion kept the process going far longer than it would otherwise. Absent this expansion, the economy would have tumbled into stagnation long ago because of its contradictions. However, the price of keeping the economy going in this fashion was a deeper crash. Rather than coming to a slow grinding halt, extended financial excess meant when the contradictions finally asserted themselves, the economy exploded in financial pyrotechnics. It also means more prolonged stagnation because of the burden of accumulated debt.

The old post–World War II growth model based on rising middle-class incomes was dismantled by the market fundamentalist revolution of the late 1970s and early 1980s. The financial crisis of 2008 signaled the implosion of the market fundamentalist model. That has created the opening for a new paradigm that the book labels "structural Keynesianism."

Economic Policy and the Metaphor of Pump Priming

The underlying economic policy problem can be thought of in terms of the metaphor of a well in which the flow of water represents economic activity. Expansionary monetary and fiscal policy "prime the pump" by stimulating demand. That creates spending and jobs, triggering a multiplier effect in the economy.

The problem with pump-priming policy is it only works if there is water in the well, and the well is now dry. That implies existing policy will not succeed.

If the well is dry, we need to drill a new well. That means building a new economy based on a new economic paradigm. The challenge is to rebuild the income and demand-generating process, which have been corroded by thirty years of market fundamentalism. Only this can generate the self-sustaining private-sector growth needed to eliminate mass unemployment and restore shared prosperity.

History, Politics, and Where to Begin

One of the great challenges writing a book on the economic crisis is choosing where to begin the story. The financial crisis and the Great Recession are part of history, and history is a continuum. For many economists, the focus is the housing price bubble that burst in 2006, and the housing price bubble clearly played a major role in the crisis. However, this book argues that the origins of the crisis are to be found long before the housing price bubble. Moreover, the bubble was a logical outcome when viewed in the context of a longer historical narrative about the U.S. economy.

Most accounts of the crisis take a relatively short horizon. That makes telling the story easier. First, a shorter period means a simpler story with fewer factors to take into account. Second, events are more recent and therefore fresher in readers' memories. Third, there may also be political motives in attributing the crisis to recent events. In particular, Democrats would like to pin the blame on the Bush administration of 2001–2009.

In this author's view, the Bush administration was not the cause. It certainly played along by embracing the policies that caused the crisis. However, the ultimate cause lies in the failure of the market fundamentalist paradigm that was adopted in the late 1970s and early 1980s.

The important implication is that political support in the United States for the paradigm has been bipartisan. That also holds in Europe where "new" social democrats have moved closer to their conservative counterparts. In the United States, there certainly have been different shades of support, and a significant segment of the Democratic Party always opposed the market fundamentalist paradigm. However, the politically dominant New Democrat wing of the Democratic Party has always supported it and still does.

There are several lessons from these brief political observations. First, the economy is not a "natural" phenomenon. Instead, it is made and shaped by economic policy.

Second, the policy adopted reflects the economic views of the winners, and those views in turn reflect the economic interests of the winners. That also holds for academic economics. Universities and economics departments are part of society and they therefore reflect society's dominant view that is shaped by society's winners. Except for economists, this is something most social scientists recognize and acknowledge.

Third, changing economic policy involves putting new ideas in place via politics. This is a two-step agenda: winning the war of ideas and winning the political battle. One without the other does not produce change. That is the historical tragedy of the Obama administration.

Fourth, the fact that neoliberal economics has captured both sides of the political aisle (Republican and New Democrat) makes it extremely difficult to dislodge. This difficulty operates at two levels. First, the two parties masquerade as if engaged in a titanic economic policy struggle when in reality both have supported a common paradigm. That masquerade is confusing to the public and crowds out political space for a true alternative. Second, the United States has an entrenched two-party political system with limited room for political competition via new entry. That is because of the "first past the post," winner-take-all electoral system. Putting the two difficulties together creates a real bind. Even if the public were to see through the political masquerade, it would have nowhere to go.

This political system is very durable, but it is not indestructible. The problem is it will only give way under extreme events that impose significant economic suffering and hardship. Moreover, if it does give way, there are no guarantees about the subsequent outcome. Thus, the forces of reaction, who argue for a doubling-down of the market fundamentalist policies that have already failed us so badly, could win. Those forces may also be accompanied by other political forces of intolerance and hate.

In this regard, the experiences of the 1930s in Europe and the United States hold important lessons about the political dangers that could accompany the Great Stagnation. Although fascism only prevailed in Europe, there were powerful similar forces in the United States in the form of the German American Bund, the Liberty League, the America First movement, and the Klu Klux Klan. Popular history provides a comforting narrative about the overwhelming triumph of FDR's politics and economics of the New Deal. The historical record is far more complex and ominous.

2

The Tragedy of Bad Ideas

In his famous essay on the Bengal famine of 1943, Nobel Prize–winning economist Amartya Sen (1982) argues famines occur because of political inequalities built into the mechanism for distributing food. The great Ukraine famine of 1932–33 in Stalin's Soviet Union also had political roots, as did the late 1950s Great Leap Forward famine in Mao's communist China. The greatest tragedies are human-made and are rooted in bad ideas.

The same holds for the financial crash of 2008, the Great Recession, and the looming Great Stagnation, which are the product of flawed economic ideas, implemented through economic policy, in the service of particular economic and political interests. Keynes (1936) was aware of this power of ideas as he struggled to win acceptance of the ideas in his *General Theory*: "(T)he ideas of economists and political philosophers, both when they are right and when they are wrong, are more powerful than is commonly understood. Indeed, the world is ruled by little else. Practical men, who believe themselves to be quite exempt from any intellectual influences, are usually the slave of some defunct economist" (p. 383). The tragedy of bad economic ideas is that once they grab hold of society's imagination, it becomes nearly impossible to persuade people to abandon them. Instead, the ideas must be lived through and disproved by experience. This may now have happened to neoliberalism, with the crisis creating an opportunity to implement a new set of economic ideas.

Ironically, this power of ideas and the role of crisis in creating opportunity for change was fully understood by the great neoliberal economist, Milton Friedman (1962, 2002):

"There is enormous inertia – a tyranny of the status quo – in private and especially government arrangements. Only a crisis – actual or perceived – produces

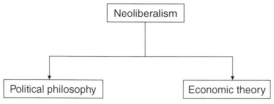

Figure 2.1. The structure of neoliberalism.

real change. When that crisis occurs the actions that are taken depend on the ideas that are lying around" (pp. xiii–xiv).

He went on further to describe the role of economists as follows:

"... to develop alternatives to existing policies, to keep them alive and available until the politically impossible becomes possible" (p. xiv).

Friedman exploited the social and economic dislocations of the 1970s to push his policy agenda. Even though he was a purveyor of faulty ideas, he was a brilliant polemicist and intellectual strategist. The intellectual revolution he fathered is still with us, but the financial crash of 2008 and the Great Recession have finally created an opportunity for a sensible counterrevolution.

The Origins and Logic of Neoliberalism

The flawed idea that has dominated economic policy making for the past thirty years, to the exclusion of almost all else, is neoliberalism. As illustrated in Figure 2.1, neoliberalism is a way of thinking about society that embodies both a political philosophy and an economic theory. The reference to "liberalism" reflects an intellectual lineage that connects with nineteenth-century economic liberalism associated with Manchester, England. The Manchester system was predicated on laissez-faire economics and was closely associated with the free-trade movement of that era.

Modern neoliberalism comes in European and American versions that have subtle but important differences. The European strain is principally associated with the work of Austrian economists Friedrich von Hayek and Ludwig von Mises, who impressed deeply British Prime Minister Margaret Thatcher. It sees the economy as historical and indeterministic. Markets are essential but they are also always and everywhere imperfect.

On the political side, Hayek (1944) argued for a market system on the grounds that state-directed centrally planned systems inevitably suppress freedom. That is because centrally planned systems diminish freedom of decision making and choice.

On the economic side, Hayek (1945) identified the benefits of the market system in terms of its decision-making capacity. The underlying economic problem is decision making and resource allocation in a world of radically imperfect and incomplete information. No central planner could conceivably make efficient decisions in such an environment. Instead, the best thing is to settle for the market mechanism based on decentralized choice and decision making, guided by the self-interest of individuals and the profit-making desire of firms. The market mechanism is the best available, but it is never perfect, because the nature of the problem being solved denies the possibility of a perfect solution.

The American strain centers on the Chicago School of economics, its two most prominent exponents being Milton Friedman and George Stigler. For American neoliberals, the economy is deterministic and well described by the mathematical formulations of neoclassical economics. Markets – now described as free markets – are also essential, but they are seen through the lens of "perfection." Moreover, perfect markets, or a close approximation thereof, are claimed to characterize real-world capitalism.

In the hands of the American Chicago School, neoliberalism morphed into a philosophy of market fundamentalism, changing the quality of the argument. Hayek's (1944) *Road to Serfdom* argued market economies are essential for freedom because centrally planned economies inevitably produce oppression. Friedman (1962) made a more affirmative argument whereby freedom of choice is the essence of freedom, and markets facilitate free choice. However, along with this reframing of the political case for markets, Friedman initiated a tradition that replaced European neoliberalism's watchful skepticism of government with animus to government.

With regard to economics, Friedman also replaced the European view of the inherent limits of the market system dictated by the nature of the economic problem, with a view of perfect markets. This intellectual shift was facilitated by American economists' proclivity to mathematical treatments that neatly solved economic problems – an instance of methodology acting as boss rather than servant, redefining the phenomenon rather than investigating it.

The American Chicago School claims real-world market economies produce roughly efficient (so-called Pareto optimal) outcomes, defined as outcomes where one cannot make someone better off without making someone else worse off. The implication is that government should stay out of the picture because public policy cannot improve market outcomes.

Chicago School economists acknowledge the existence of market failures – such as monopoly, natural monopoly, externalities, and provision of public goods. However, these are viewed as relatively rare and of small scale. Moreover, government intervention is claimed to usually make the economy worse off because of bureaucratic incompetence, capture of regulators by special interests, and political distortions.[1] The conclusion is that market failures are relatively rare, and most of the time even market failure is not a justification for government intervention because the costs of government failure exceed those of market failure. Instead, society should aim for minimalist government – a night watchman state – that only provides national defense, protects property and person, and enforces contracts.

Furthermore, not only does the American tradition advocate minimalist government, but it goes a step further and looks to weaken government by subjecting it to market discipline. This has been particularly apparent in the project of globalization. Unrestricted international movement of production and financial capital disciplines and disempowers government by diminishing national policy effectiveness

---

[1] The government-failure argument began with Milton Friedman and Anna Schwartz's (1963) government-incompetence hypothesis that blamed the Federal Reserve for turning a recession into the Great Depression via inappropriate policy response. Friedman (1961) also argued that government policy suffered from fundamental implementation problems owing to time lags in taking action and those lags resulted in policy that was destabilizing rather than stabilizing. These early arguments were then bolstered by arguments about bureaucratic failure (Niskannen, 1971), regulatory capture (Stigler, 1971), and rent-seeking behavior (see, for example, Tullock, 1967; Krueger, 1974). By the 1980s, the idea of the benevolent but incompetent public official had been replaced by the self-interested public official (Barro and Gordon, 1983).

and curtailing policy space. These erosions in turn hollow out democracy by shrinking the feasible set of social arrangements. All of this is justified with neoliberal rhetoric about empowering markets, which are the source of freedom. However, the reality is that it empowers capital by giving capital the option of exit that can be used to discipline government and labor. Because power is relative, the algebra of power implies an increase in the power of capital means a decline in the power of the state and workers.

Among Chicago School extremists, animus to government now extends beyond shrinking and weakening government to sabotaging government (Palley, 2006a; Galbraith, 2008). The thinking is that government failure, even if by design, will persuade people that government cannot work.

This newer strain of thinking explains why many American conservatives have been so casual about large budget deficits although nominally opposed to them. Conservatives' de facto embrace of deficits reflects a long-term strategy aimed at financially hamstringing government, known as "starve the beast."[2] The logic is large tax cuts and unfunded increases in military spending increase the national debt and interest payments thereon, ultimately limiting government financially. At the end of the day, the rich will have received both tax cuts and interest payments on the debt, and government is also forced to shrink.

In sum, American neoliberal thinking consists of a combination of idealization of markets and animus to government, and over the past thirty years it has substantially dominated politics and economic policy. Such thinking, supported by the economic and political interests that benefitted from it, pushed a remaking of economic policy along lines that ultimately caused the crisis. This remake included the deregulation movement and opposition to modernizing financial market regulation; the retreat from macroeconomic policy aimed at full employment; the attack on New Deal reforms that leveled the labor market playing field and provided protections against economic insecurity; and corporate globalization that integrated economies without regard to social and economic standards.

---

[2] See Bartlett (2007) for a discussion of the origins of the "starve the beast" metaphor. Bartlett, B., "Starve the Beast: Origins and Development of a Budgetary Metaphor," *The Independent Review*, 12 (no. 1), pp. 5–26.

Microeconomic Critiques of Neoliberalism

Modern neoliberal economics is subject to multiple critiques. One form is microeconomic critique that is an internal critique in the sense that it challenges the logic of the Chicago school on its own theoretical grounds.

The Massachusetts Institute of Technology (MIT) School of economics, founded by Paul Samuelson, argues that real-world economies are afflicted pervasively by market failures – including monopoly power, externalities associated with problems like pollution, and an inability to supply public goods such as street lighting or national defense. Moreover, it also holds that government can successfully remedy market failure, and that the Chicago argument of government failure is overstated. Thus, government failure can be prevented by good institutional design that makes government transparent, accountable, and subject to democratic political competition. Policy interventions that address market failures can therefore often make everyone better off. That said, the MIT School's critique of the Chicago School is one of degree rather than kind, as both schools share a common analytical framework.

The Keynesian Critique of Neoliberalism

A second completely different and more fundamental critique is the Keynesian critique, which states that market economies may not be able to generate full employment. However, as illustrated in Figure 2.2, the Keynesian critique is divided into "textbook Keynesianism" and "Structural Keynesianism." This distinction is not widely recognized and it is critical to the argument of this book, because textbook Keynesianism is a more modest critique.

Textbook Keynesianism takes the economic system as given and looks to patch problems. Philosophically, it is closely connected to MIT microeconomics in that it sees economic downturns as the result of temporary disturbances that take time to adjust to because of market frictions that prevent prices and wages adjusting immediately. These frictions are a form of market failure, which connects textbook Keynesianism to MIT microeconomics. The role of policy is to temporarily step in and assist the adjustment process.

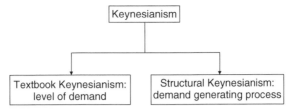

Figure 2.2. Different strands of Keynesianism.

Structural Keynesianism focuses on the economic institutions and arrangements needed to make the economy work. For much of the time, a patch is enough, but there are times when a patch will not work and deeper changes to the system are needed because of structural problems. That is the situation today.

Both textbook Keynesianism and Structural Keynesianism start with two basic Keynesian propositions. First, the level of economic activity depends on the level of demand. If there is not enough demand in the economy, firms will not have the incentive to create full employment. Second, there are times when market economies are short of demand and the market system is unable to generate sufficient demand.

Modern mainstream economics dismisses by assumption Keynesian concerns about inadequate demand. Instead, it begins with the image of a barter economy in which, absent impediments to exchange, all mutually beneficial trades are realized because rational economic agents want to obtain the benefits of exchange. That is the foundation of the Chicago School's claims about market economies being optimal and generating full employment.

Keynesianism challenges this view. It argues the economy is a monetary economy marked by fundamental uncertainty regarding the future, and it is also peopled by emotional human beings who are motivated by the ebb and flow of animal spirits.

In a monetary economy, aggregate demand (i.e., the total demand for goods and services in an economy) can be reduced when people delay spending plans in response to fluctuating animal spirits. They wait out their fears about an uncertain future by holding money.

Under such conditions, a market system may be unable to restore a level of aggregate demand sufficient to ensure full employment. Whereas lower prices work to increase demand in an individual market, that does not work for an entire economy in which money and debt are used extensively. This is because a fall in the general price level increases the burden of debts, causing cutbacks in spending. It also causes defaults that can wreck the banking system and upend financial markets. Deflation (the prospect of falling prices) may further encourage people to delay spending because buyers expect lower future prices.

Textbook Keynesianism recognizes the central role of aggregate demand in determining economic activity. Its focus is the "level of aggregate demand," and recessions are explained as the result of temporary shortages of demand. When an economy goes into recession, textbook Keynesianism recommends applying a policy patch that temporarily increases demand. This includes measures like lower interest rates to stimulate private spending and increased government spending or tax cuts that increase the budget deficit. Under normal conditions, these pump-priming policies can speed up the return to full employment.

Structural Keynesianism adds additional concerns with underlying "demand generating process," which is the product of the economic system. Its process perspective is dynamic and is also concerned with income distribution. Recessions can be due to temporary declines in private-sector demand, but they can also be due to failings in the underlying demand-generating process. If the system is faulty, it can suffer from persistent lack of demand. In this event, the economy will experience prolonged stagnation and even depression as happened in the 1930s and may now be happening again. It is this idea of "systemic" versus "temporary" demand shortage that distinguishes structural Keynesianism from textbook Keynesianism.

Taking its lead from the great Polish economist Michal Kalecki, Structural Keynesianism adds concern with income distribution that affects the level of demand. High-income households tend to save proportionately more so that increased income inequality can lead to too much saving and demand shortage.

The concern with income distribution in turn leads to concern with the institutions and arrangements that affect income distribution via their impact on workers' bargaining power. The stability of the demand-generating process is also affected by the arrangements governing the financial sector, which connects with the work of economist Hyman Minsky and leads to concerns about financial regulation.

The structural Keynesian focus on the economy's demand-generating process goes to the heart of the current problem and explains why the Great Recession is different from recent recessions. Thirty years of neoliberal policy have fundamentally undermined the demand-generating process in the U.S. economy. The net result is the economy is suffering from a systemic shortage of demand due to deep-rooted problems in the demand-generating process, which market forces cannot solve.

The Unfreedom Critique

The microeconomic and Keynesian critiques have profound consequences. First, they undermine neoliberalism's claims about the economic efficiency of markets. Second, they challenge its political claims about the relation between markets and freedom.

Neoliberalism advertises itself as a philosophy of freedom, and freedom provides the political justification for an unfettered market system on the grounds that unfettered markets promote freedom. Given this, to oppose unfettered markets is implicitly to oppose freedom. Furthermore, given that according to the American Chicago School, unfettered markets produce a free lunch by maximizing economic well-being, to oppose unfettered markets is also to reject a free lunch.

The flaw in the argument is that unfettered market economies do not work the way that Milton Friedman and his colleagues claim. This means they do not deliver a free lunch, nor do they automatically promote freedom.

The great failing of the economics profession has been its acceptance of the basic description of market economies provided by the Chicago School. Once that was done, the game was up. If unfettered markets produce roughly efficient economic outcomes and also promote freedom, who could possibly be against that?

The microeconomic and Keynesian critiques show that unfettered markets do not work the way the Chicago School claims. This means following Chicago policy recommendations can be an economic disaster – which is what the financial crash and the Great Recession have shown once again.

Keynes (1936) identified the economic limits of the market system when he wrote of unemployment:

When 9,000,000 men are employed out of 10,000,000 willing and able to work, there is no evidence that the labor of these men is misdirected. The complaint against the present system is not that these 9,000,000 men ought to be employed on different tasks, but that tasks should be available for the remaining 1,000,000 men. It is in determining the volume, not the direction, of actual employment that the existing system has broken down. (p. 379)

In short, for Keynes, the economic problem was that the system only created nine million jobs when ten million wanted to work. Today, we are seeing this economic problem again.

This economic failure of unfettered markets in turn has negative consequences for freedom, which undermines the claim that laissez-faire automatically promotes freedom. This is because unfettered markets tend to increase income inequality and often produce financial crisis and high unemployment. That is the evidence from thirty years of market fundamentalist policy.[3] Income inequality, unemployment, and economic deprivation in turn hollow out and caricature freedom by removing the means to enjoy it. In the language of Amartya Sen (1999, p. xii), unemployment and economic deprivation are forms of "unfreedom."

Massive income and wealth inequality also have profound political consequences because they tilt political power in favor of the rich. Because part of democratic freedom is the enjoyment of political freedom through the democratic system, this shift in power to the rich implicitly reduces the power of the rest. To paraphrase George Orwell, it creates a world in which some are freer than others – a form of political unfreedom.

Introducing the concept of unfreedom radically changes the assessment of the relation between markets and freedom. Although markets promote the freedom of many, they can also increase the unfreedom of others. Consequently, unfettered markets can reduce overall freedom.

---

[3] See Milanovic, B. [2007]. *Worlds Apart: Measuring International and Global Inequality*, Princeton, NJ: Princeton University Press.

The fundamental policy challenge is how to balance this conflict. Promoting the freedom of some may increase the unfreedom of others, whereas remedying the unfreedom of some may infringe the freedom of others.

Neoliberal thinking ignores this problem by denying the conceptual legitimacy of unfreedom and giving zero policy weight to remedying unfreedom. This makes for powerful rhetoric, because the assumption that unfreedom does not exist means unfettered markets can only increase freedom. However, it is only this assumption that produces the rabbit of freedom out of the market fundamentalist hat.

Not only does market fundamentalism increase unfreedoms of millions; it can also pose a threat to the freedom of all. The enjoyment of freedom ultimately rests on political rights that are socially enforced, and it is here that unemployment and economic deprivation are the greatest danger. Ultimately, people will only value a system that values them. If the system does not value them, then they may cease to value it and turn against it.

Market fundamentalism creates a system that does not value people – a society in which "you are on your own." That can work in times of prosperity, but it is unlikely to hold up in times of prolonged economic hardship and insecurity. Under such conditions, there can easily be a turn to the politics of intolerance that scapegoats particular ethnic and racial groups, or even a turn to authoritarian politics that attacks the freedom of all.

In sum, neoliberalism is blind to the issues of unfreedom, the conflict between freedom and unfreedom, and the need for an economic system that is politically embedded in a sustainable way. These were the critical issues identified by Karl Polyani (1944) in his analysis of the failings of nineteenth-century capitalism that led to early-twentieth-century fascism. Ironically, although claiming to promote freedom, neoliberalism's denial and suppression of these issues make it a threat to freedom, directly by promoting unfreedom and indirectly by promoting political alienation.

The End of History, Again?

Following the fall of the Berlin Wall in 1989, political economist Francis Fukuyama (1992) wrote a book titled *The End of History and the*

Last Man. The thesis was that the fall of the Wall marked the absolute triumph of liberal market democracy over communism and authoritarian centrally planned economies because it showed the latter did not work.[4]

China's economic success and growing appeal as an economic model, despite being an authoritarian state, suggest Fukuyama's claims were overstated. Instead, the fall of the Wall marked the end of a chapter of history.

Viewed in this more modest light, the Great Recession may mark the end of another chapter. The financial crisis and Great Recession may be to American capitalism what the fall of the Berlin Wall was to the Soviet system. In hindsight, it may mark the end of the era of unbound neoliberalism that is behind the tragedy of the Great Recession.

Nothing is certain in history – or to quote Yogi Berra, "It aint over till it's over." There remains the possibility of political reaction that produces a doubling-down of market fundamentalism that strips away the remaining elements of the New Deal and the welfare state. If that happens, the tragedy of bad ideas will persist and shared prosperity will become a relic.

But there also exists the opening for a new course based on different ideas about market capitalism. Under that new course, markets will remain a critical mechanism, but nested in a set of institutions that create a stable demand-generating process, curb financial excess and excessive income inequality, provide for basic economic security, and prevent adverse global competition that produces a global race to the bottom. That is the structural Keynesian alternative presented in the second half of this book.

[4] Fukuyama, F. [1992]. *The End of History and the Last Man*, New York: Free Press.

3

Overview

Three Perspectives on the Crisis

The financial crisis and Great Recession have inflicted enormous economic harm and suffering. They are complex and controversial events, and how they are explained will greatly affect the future economic course and prospects. That is because the selected explanation will affect how policy makers respond. With so much at stake, this has triggered contested debate, with different political and economic interests advancing differing explanations.

This book offers a particular explanation, but to help readers understand the full logic and significance of the argument, it is worth summarizing the debate. Broadly speaking, there exist three different perspectives, and each is linked to a political point of view. That alone is significant as it illustrates the inevitable and unavoidable close connection between politics and economic analysis.

That is the nature of economics. One may wish it otherwise, but the reality is that the richness and complexity of economic events means events can support different theories and explanations. That does not mean anything goes, but it does mean there can exist multiple explanations, each consistent with the facts. This in turn compels choosing an explanation – which means accepted economic truth is as much the result of persuasion as it is of scientific endeavor.

Figure 3.1 illustrates the competing explanations examined in the book. There are two basic perspectives: the neoliberal and structural Keynesian. The neoliberal perspective can also be termed the mainstream or orthodox perspective because it currently dominates the economics profession.

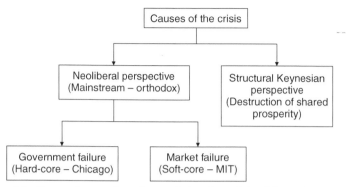

Figure 3.1. Competing explanations of the financial crisis and the Great Recession.

The neoliberal perspective is subdivided into a hard-core *government failure* hypothesis and a soft-core *market failure* hypothesis. Within the United States, the hard-core government failure hypothesis is politically associated with the Republican Party. Among academic economists, it is associated with the University of Chicago, Stanford University, and the University of Minnesota. The soft-core market failure hypothesis is politically associated with New Democrats and Third Way Democrats, which includes the Obama administration. Among academic economists, it is principally associated with MIT and Princeton University.

The structural Keynesian *destruction of shared prosperity* hypothesis advocated by this book is politically associated with Labor Democrats, trade unions, and progressives. However, it has no representation in major research universities, reflecting the absence of Keynesian economics within the mainstream of the economics profession.

The neoliberal government failure and market failure hypotheses adopt a narrow-lens interpretation of the crisis, whereas the structural Keynesian destruction of shared prosperity hypothesis adopts a broad-lens interpretation. The narrow-lens approach views the crisis as being due to some combination of monetary policy failure, regulatory failure, and faulty business practices within the financial sector. The broad-lens approach views it as resulting from generalized failure of the current economic policy paradigm. That failure includes regulatory failure, but it also includes failure of macroeconomic policy toward employment and income distribution and failure of international economic policy.

The Hard-Core Government Failure Perspective

The government failure perspective maintains the crisis is rooted in the housing bubble and its subsequent bursting. The housing bubble is in turn a result of a combination of failed monetary policy and failed regulatory policy, with the focus being bad interest rate policy and excessive government intervention in the housing market.[1]

During the last recession, the Federal Reserve pushed its target interest rate to 1 percent, a level not seen since the recession of 1958. The previous recession officially ended in November 2001, and hard-core market fundamentalists argue the Federal Reserve mistakenly continued lowering its policy interest rate long after. Thus, the federal funds rate only bottomed in July 2003, when it hit 1 percent, and it was then held at that level until June 2004. According to the hard-core hypothesis, the result was that interest rates were set too low for too long. Moreover, once the Fed started raising rates, it did so only very gradually, in quarter-point increments over a three-year period. This created a loose monetary background that drove the housing price bubble.

A second hard-core argument is regulatory failure resulting from a fragmented regulatory structure that splits authority between the Federal Reserve, the Securities and Exchange Commission (SEC), the Federal Deposit Insurance Corporation (FDIC), the Commodity Futures Trading Commission (CFTC), the Office of Thrift Supervision (OTS), and state regulation of insurance companies. This allowed dangerous lending and underwriting practices to slip through the cracks, giving rise to massive loan and investment losses that only became evident when the bubble burst.

A third argument is Congressional intervention in credit markets caused the crisis. One intervention was Congress's support for the giant mortgage securitization firms, Fannie Mae and Freddie Mac. These firms were given an implicit government guarantee on their debts that lowered their funding costs, thereby supposedly allowing them to underwrite the subprime mortgage disaster and the housing boom.[2]

---

[1] See Taylor, J.B. [2009], "How Government Created the Financial Crisis," *Wall Street Journal*, Monday, February 3, A.19.

[2] See Calomiris, C.W. and P.J.Wallison [2008], "Blame Fannie Mae and Congress for the Credit Mess," *Wall Street Journal*, Tuesday, September 23, A.29.

Another Congressional distortion was the Community Reinvestment Act (CRA) of 1977 that aimed to increase homeownership among disadvantaged communities. This compelled banks to make loans to persons (mainly minorities) living in inner-city areas, who could not afford the loans. That lending then fueled the housing price bubble and drove subsequent high rates of default.[3]

The Soft-Core Market Failure Perspective

The soft-core market failure perspective also maintains that regulatory failure was a major contributory factor. However, while accepting the hard-core argument of regulatory fracture, the soft-core perspective reverses the nature of the regulatory failure and argues that financial market regulation was too weak. Rather than doing too much, government did too little. This inadequacy allowed excessive leverage and risk taking by banks and financial firms, which fueled the housing price bubble.[4]

A second factor emphasized by the market failure perspective is incentive pay structures within financial firms. These pay structures emphasized commissions on transactions and bonuses paid out of profits. That encouraged brokers and bankers to engage in loan pushing rather than good lending because every new loan was a transaction that earned a commission and generated profits. Brokers and bankers therefore got paid immediately, whereas defaults and loan losses only surfaced later and there was no claw-back of compensation.

The incentive pay structure for individuals dovetailed with the securitized lending business model adopted by banks and financial firms – also known as the "originate to distribute" model. Under this new business model, firms make loans, bundle them in mortgage-backed

---

[3] See Husock, H. [2008], "The Financial Crisis and the CRA," *City Journal of the Manhattan Institute*, October 30, http://www.city-journal.org/2008/eon1030hh.html

[4] See Group of Thirty [2009], "Financial Reform: A Framework for Financial Stability," Washington DC, report issued January 15. It is ironic that Third Way New Democrats endorse inadequate regulation as the principal cause of the crisis, as the policy of deregulation and opposition to regulation was supported by President Clinton's New Democrat administration. The Clinton Administration twice reappointed Alan Greenspan, perhaps the leading opponent of financial regulation, as Chairman of the Federal Reserve. It also opposed regulation of the credit default swap market that has played an important role in propagating the crisis. See Goodman, P.S. [2008], "The Reckoning: Taking a Hard Look at the Greenspan Legacy," *New York Times*, October 9.

securities, and then sell those mortgage-backed securities to pension funds, insurance companies, and other investors.

There are two important features of the "originate to distribute" model. First, because lenders do not retain the loans and mortgages they originate, profits are earned on the securitization fee rather than loan interest paid over the duration of the loan. Second, because originators do not retain any interest in the loans and mortgages, they have a reduced incentive to ensure the credit quality of the borrower is initially sound.

The combination of employees' incentive pay structure and the "originate to distribute" business model together created a disastrous incentive structure within firms. Under the "originate to distribute" model, firms maximize profits by loan pushing, as that maximizes fees. This pleases both myopic shareholders and top management that draws a significant portion of its remuneration from stock options. Simultaneously, individual employees are incentivized to loan push, as their pay is maximized by maximizing transactions. In this fashion, the new business model encouraged reckless lending, and economists and regulators completely failed to see this. That failure is epitomized by former Federal Reserve Chairman Alan Greenspan's admission (October 23, 2008) to the House Committee of Government and Reform: "I made a mistake in presuming that the self-interests of organizations, specifically banks and others, were such as that they were best capable of protecting their own shareholders and their equity in the firms."

A third factor emphasized by market failure advocates is soft fraud. Thus, as part of loan pushing, brokers may have misrepresented loan terms and also promoted risky adjustable-rate products with attractive teaser interest rates that were followed by higher rates that made the product more costly and unaffordable. At the same time, brokers and firms relaxed standards and vigilance, encouraging loose lending – epitomized by so-called infamous "No Doc NINJA" loans (no documents, no income, no job or assets). This relaxation may have encouraged a culture of fraud in which both borrower and lender mutually participated, with the permissiveness of lenders facilitating fraud by borrowers. This role of fraud is delightfully and ironically captured by John Kenneth Galbraith (1954) in his classic, *The Great Crash, 1929*:

To the economist embezzlement is the most interesting of crimes. Alone among the various forms of larceny it has a time parameter. Weeks, months, or years may elapse between the commission of the crime and its discovery. (This is a period, incidentally, when the embezzler has his gain and the man who has been embezzled, oddly enough, feels no loss. There is a net increase in psychic wealth.) At any given time there is an inventory of undiscovered embezzlement in – or more precisely not in – the country's businesses and banks. This inventory – it should perhaps be called the bezzle – amounts at any moment to many millions of dollars. It also varies in size with the business cycle. (pp. 152–53)

Such fraudulent practices were facilitated by the hoopla surrounding homeownership, which was peddled as a sure route to riches – as evidenced by the 2006 book, *Why the Real Estate Boom Will Not Bust – And How You Can Profit From It: How to Build Wealth in Today's Expanding Real Estate Market*, written by David Lereah who was then Chief Economist of the National Association of Home Builders. With everyone believing house prices could only go up, there was little to worry about if loans were granted a little loosely because they would always have backing collateral.

A final causal factor emphasized by both Alan Greenspan and current Federal Reserve Chairman Ben Bernanke is global financial imbalances (i.e., the large U.S. trade deficit).[5] The argument is that the large trade deficit caused massive financial inflows into the United States, which pushed interest rates down, thereby fermenting the housing price bubble. Global financial imbalances rather than mistaken Federal Reserve monetary policy were therefore to blame for too-low interest rates – which conveniently gets the Federal Reserve off the hook.

The Destruction of Shared Prosperity Perspective

The third approach is the structural Keynesian destruction of shared prosperity perspective. It agrees with market failure arguments regarding fractured and inadequate regulation, faulty incentive structures, and fraud. However, it also views these arguments as insufficient for explaining the crisis. A housing price bubble and financial crash of the

---

[5] See Bernanke, B.S. [2010a], "Causes of the Recent Financial and Economic Crisis," Testimony before the Financial Crisis Inquiry Commission, Washington, DC, September 2; and Greenspan, A. [2009], "The Fed Didn't Cause the Housing Bubble," *Wall Street Journal*, March 11.

scale experienced require a larger macroeconomic explanation and cannot be explained solely by microeconomic market failures, most of which have been around for a long time.

From a structural Keynesian perspective, the triggering macroeconomic cause of the crisis was the weak economic recovery and fragile expansion after the recession of 2001.[6] This weakness was significantly due to the trade deficit and acceleration of offshoring of production owing to globalization. The trade deficit sucked in imports that displaced domestic production and jobs, while the acceleration of production offshoring resulted in factory closures and diversion of new investment spending. The major cause of these developments was flawed U.S. international economic policy.

As a result, the United States never experienced a full recovery in manufacturing and business investment spending after the recession of 2001. That explains the extended period of so-called jobless recovery that lasted into 2003, and it meant continuous downward pressure on labor markets, which contributed to wage stagnation.

The weak exit from recession contributed to persistent fears the economy would stall and fall back into recession. That caused the Fed to lower rates to 1 percent in July 2003 and to keep them at that low level until June 2004, which succeeded in sustaining the economic expansion but only at the cost of causing the housing price bubble.

Government failure proponents blame the Federal Reserve's policy of excessively low interest rates for causing the bubble. On the surface, the critique is right and low interest rates were indeed the proximate cause of the bubble. However, digging deeper, the Fed was justified in keeping rates low owing to legitimate fears that the economy would have fallen back into recession.

That points to the deep underlying cause of the bubble, namely the growing structural weakness of aggregate demand and job creation in the U.S. economy. This weakness necessitated low interest rates and ongoing asset price inflation (a process that began in the 1980s) to keep the economy growing. However, that in turn begs the question of the reasons for the increasing underlying weakness in the U.S.

---

[6] See Palley, T.I. [2006b] "The Weak Recovery and Coming Deep Recession," *Mother Jones*, March 17, and Palley, T.I. [2008a] "America's Exhausted Growth Paradigm," *The Chronicle of Higher Education*, April 11.

aggregate demand generation process. Answering that question leads back to neoliberal changes in the U.S. economic policy paradigm after 1980, which is the subject of the next chapter.[7]

Why Interpretation Matters: Policy Implications

In the wake of the Great Recession and its aftermath, economic policy makers now confront two challenges. First, there is a need to jump-start the economy and begin the process of repairing the labor market and recovering the jobs that have been lost. Second, there is a need to ensure renewed growth, but it must be growth that delivers shared prosperity. The three different perspectives described earlier give rise to very different recommendations regarding how to meet these policy challenges, which is why the debate is so important.

The Hard-Core Government Failure Policy Response

The hard-core government failure perspective argues for financial regulatory consolidation combined with deregulation that eliminates the Community Reinvestment Act (1977) and privatizes the mortgage giants, Fannie Mae and Freddie Mac. To the extent that temporary fiscal stimulus is needed, it should take the form of permanent tax cuts as this incentivizes the supply side of the economy. The budget deficit, which will be worsened by tax cuts, is to be closed later by cutting Social Security payments and Medicaid. Finally, the Federal Reserve should adopt an inflation-targeting regime conducted through a so-called Taylor rule that sets interest rates by formula.

The Soft-Core Market Failure Policy Response

The soft-core market failure perspective argues for strengthening financial regulation, including regulatory consolidation. A principal focus of regulatory reform has been on "soft" measures like increasing

---

[7] For a more extensive discussion see Palley, T.I. [1998a], *Plenty of Nothing: The Downsizing of the American Dream and the Case for Structural Keynesianism*, Princeton, NJ: Princeton University Press, and Palley, T.I. [2002b] "Economic Contradictions Coming Home to Roost? Does the U.S. Face a Long Term Aggregate Demand Generation Problem?" *Journal of Post Keynesian Economics*, 25 (Fall), 9–32.

financial transparency by making products like derivatives trade through clearing markets. Additionally, there is support for a regulatory body tasked with watching the financial system's overall financial stability. The belief is that the financial crisis was due to lack of transparency that impeded markets and regulators from correctly assessing risks, including systemic risk.

Among more aggressive market failure proponents there is also support for quantitative regulation, which has been out of fashion for twenty-five years, to go along with regulation aimed at enhanced transparency. These quantitative regulations include measures to limit allowable leverage for financial firms; requirements that banks retain some part of loans that they originate; and reforms of incentive pay. However, in general, these types of reforms tend to have greater support from structural Keynesians.

The market failure perspective also supports temporary fiscal stimulus along traditional textbook Keynesian lines. However, whereas the Republican government failure perspective advocates fiscal stimulus via tax cuts, the New Democrat market failure perspective tends to argue for increased government spending on the grounds that it has a bigger multiplier effect on economic activity. Also, temporary spending programs are viewed as having less of an adverse effect on the long-run budget deficit. That is because it is easier to repeal temporary spending programs than tax cuts because the latter expose politicians to the unpopular political charge of raising taxes.

Judging by the partisan rancor of political discourse, it would be easy to think that the hard-core government failure (Republican) and soft-core market failure (New Democrat) perspectives were worlds apart. However, the reality is that they have much in common. That highlights an important feature of the current political arrangement, which appears to offer far greater choice than is actually available. This appearance serves an important role, blocking political space for real choice by pretending real choice is already on offer.

Both the hard-core and soft-core perspectives believe that after the crisis is over, there will be a need for budget discipline that will require reducing Social Security and Medicaid benefits. Most importantly, both perspectives see no need for larger structural changes regarding the economic paradigm. In their view, the economy is undergoing an unusually deep recession that has created a large output gap.

However, there is nothing intrinsically wrong with the underlying economic growth paradigm. Policy should therefore help the economy close the output gap, but thereafter growth should be able to continue as before.

The Structural Keynesian Policy Response

The structural Keynesian destruction of shared prosperity perspective shares the soft-core market failure view on a need for stronger regulation and fiscal stimulus. However, it is more in favor of quantitative financial regulation (i.e., balance-sheet regulation for financial firms) and more supportive of larger fiscal stimulus that puts greater emphasis on spending rather than tax relief.

However, the defining difference with the market failure perspective concerns the macroeconomic model of growth and global economic engagement. From a structural Keynesian perspective, the recession is not simply a deep recession with high unemployment. Instead, the financial crisis represents the exhaustion of the economic paradigm that has driven the U.S. economy for the past thirty years.

For the past generation, U.S. economic growth has been fueled by asset price inflation and rising debt. The financial crisis has shown this pattern to be unsustainable, and the implication is that the U.S. economy needs a new growth model. Zero interest rates, massive financial injections by the Federal Reserve, and large deficit-financed fiscal stimulus may be able to temporarily stabilize the economy, but they cannot generate long-term growth with shared prosperity.

In the recessions of 1981, 1991, and 2001, the "patch" of monetary easing and fiscal stimulus worked because the neoliberal growth model was still intact. Asset prices still had room to rise, and households and corporations had room to borrow. That space has now been used up. The implication is that the United States has reached the limits of debt-led growth and its growth model is broken.

Although emergency Keynesian policies succeeded in putting in place a floor for the economy, the United States will still find itself stuck in extended stagnation. Failure to restore growth then risks producing an unpredictable political backlash, because fiscal and monetary stimulus is being sold as a growth tonic when in reality all it can do is stabilize the economy and limit further deterioration.

The Importance of Opening Debate

Owing to their political dominance, the government failure (Republican) and market failure (New Democrat) perspectives have been widely aired. However, the structural Keynesian (Labor Democrat) perspective has been little discussed, reflecting its relative lack of effective political representation. That is short-changing the debate about the financial crisis and Great Recession.

From a structural Keynesian perspective, the extraordinary policy actions of 2008 and 2009 prevented a catastrophic depression, but the economy is now trapped in a stagnation that promises to be prolonged. The only way out is the fundamental restructuring of economic policy. However, that is off the table because of the continued monopoly of the hard-core neoliberal government failure and soft-core neoliberal market failure perspectives. Cracking that monopoly and opening the debate about the causes of the crisis is therefore a matter of public import.

4

America's Exhausted Paradigm

Macroeconomic Causes of the Crisis

The current financial crisis is widely recognized as being tied to the bursting of the housing price bubble and the debts accumulated in financing that bubble. Most commentary has therefore focused on market failure in the housing and credit markets. But what if the housing price bubble developed because the economy needed a bubble to ensure continued growth? In that case, the real cause of the crisis would be the economy's underlying macroeconomic structure. A focus on the housing and credit markets would miss that.

Despite the relevance of macroeconomic factors for explaining the financial crisis, there is resistance to such an explanation. In part, this is because such factors operate indirectly and gradually, whereas microeconomic explanations that emphasize regulatory failure and flawed incentives within financial markets operate directly. Regulatory and incentive failures are specific, easy to understand, and offer a concrete "fixit" agenda that appeals to politicians who want to show they are doing something. They also tend to be associated with tales of villainy that attract media interest (such as Bernie Madoff's massive Ponzi scheme, or the bonus scandals at AIG and Merrill Lynch). Finally, and perhaps most importantly, a microeconomic focus does not challenge the larger structure of economic arrangements, whereas

This chapter (Palley, 2009a) was originally commissioned by the New America Foundations' Economic Growth Program whose permission to use it is gratefully acknowledged. The original report is available at http://www.newamerica.net/ publications/policy/america_s_exhausted_paradigm_macroeconomic_causes_ financial_crisis_and_great_recession. An abbreviated version of that paper was published in *Empirica*, 38 (1), 2011.

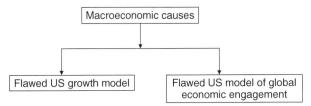

Figure 4.1. Macroeconomic causes of the economic crisis.

a macroeconomic focus invites controversy by placing these matters squarely on the table.

However, an economic crisis of the current magnitude does not occur without macroeconomic forces. That means the macroeconomic arrangements that have governed the U.S. economy for the past twenty-five years are critical for explaining the crisis. As illustrated in Figure 4.1, two factors in particular have been important. The first concerns the U.S. economic growth model and its impact on the pattern of income distribution and demand generation. The second concerns the U.S. model of global economic engagement and its impact on the structure of U.S. economic relations within the global economy.

The macroeconomic forces unleashed by these twin factors have accumulated gradually and made for an increasingly fragile and unstable macroeconomic environment. The brewing instability over the past two decades was visible in successive asset bubbles, rising indebtedness, rising trade deficits, and business cycles marked by initial weakness (so-called jobless recovery) followed by febrile booms. However, investors, policy makers, and economists chose to ignore these danger signs and resolutely refused to examine the flawed macroeconomic arrangements that led to the cliff's edge.

The Flawed U.S. Growth Model

Economic crises should be understood as a combination of proximate and ultimate factors. The proximate factors represent the triggering events, whereas the ultimate factors represent the deep causes. The meltdown of the subprime mortgage market in August 2007 triggered the current crisis, which was amplified by policy failures such as the decision to allow the collapse of Lehman Brothers. However, a crisis of the magnitude now being experienced requires a facilitating macroeconomic environment. That macroeconomic environment has been a long time in the making and can be traced back to the election of Ronald Reagan in 1980, which symbolized the inauguration of the era of neoliberal economics.

The Post-1980 Neoliberal Growth Model

The impact of the neoliberal economic growth model is apparent in the changed character of the U.S. business cycle.[1] Before 1980, economic policy was designed to achieve full employment, and the economy was characterized by a system in which wages grew with productivity. This configuration created a virtuous circle of growth. Rising wages meant robust aggregate demand, which contributed to full employment. Full employment in turn provided an incentive to invest, which raised productivity, thereby supporting higher wages.

After 1980, with the advent of the new growth model, the commitment to full employment was abandoned as inflationary, with the result that the link between productivity growth and wages was severed. In place of wage growth as the engine of demand growth, the new model substituted borrowing and asset price inflation. Adherents of the new orthodoxy made controlling inflation their primary policy concern, and set about attacking unions, the minimum wage, and other worker protections. Meanwhile, globalization brought increased foreign competition from lower-wage economies and the prospect of offshoring of employment.

The new neoliberal model was built on financial booms and cheap imports. Financial booms provide consumers and firms with collateral to support debt-financed spending. Borrowing is also sustained by financial innovation and deregulation that ensures a flow of new financial products, allowing increased leverage and widening the range of assets that can be collateralized. Meanwhile, cheap imports ameliorate the impact of wage stagnation, thereby maintaining political support for the model. Additionally, rising wealth and income inequality makes high-end consumption a larger and more important component of economic activity, leading to the development of what Ajay Kapur, a former global strategist for Citigroup, termed a "plutonomy."

---

[1] See Palley, T.I. [2005a], "The Questionable Legacy of Alan Greenspan," *Challenge* 48 (November–December): 17–31.

These features have been visible in every U.S. business cycle since 1980, and the business cycles under presidents Reagan, Bush *père*, Clinton, and Bush *fils* have robust commonalities that reveal their shared economic paradigm. Those features include asset price inflation (equities and housing); widening income inequality; detachment of worker wages from productivity growth; rising household and corporate leverage ratios measured respectively as debt/income and debt/equity ratios; a strong dollar; trade deficits; disinflation or low inflation; and manufacturing-sector job loss.

The changes brought about by the post-1980 economic paradigm are especially evident in manufacturing-sector employment (see Tables 4.1 and 4.2). Before 1980, manufacturing-sector employment rose in expansions and fell in recessions, and each expansion tended to push manufacturing-sector employment above its previous peak.[2] After 1980, the pattern changes abruptly. In the first two business cycles (between July 1980 and July 1990), manufacturing-sector employment rises in the expansions but does not recover its previous peak. In the two most recent business cycles (between March 1991 and December 2007), employment in this sector not only fails to recover its previous peak, but actually falls over the entirety of the expansions.[3]

---

[2] The 1950s are an exception because of the Korean War (June 1950–July 1953), which ratcheted up manufacturing employment and distorted manufacturing employment patterns.

[3] Defenders of the neoliberal paradigm argue that manufacturing has prospered, and the decline in manufacturing employment reflects healthy productivity trends. As evidence, they argue that real manufacturing output has increased and remained fairly steady as a share of real GDP. This reflects the fact that manufacturing prices have fallen faster than other prices. However, this is owing in part to hedonic "quality adjustment" statistical procedures that count improved information technology embodied in manufactured goods as increased manufacturing output. It is also due to increased use of cheap imported components that are not subject to the same hedonic statistical adjustments. As a result, the real cost of imported inputs is understated, and that has the effect of making it look as if real manufacturing output is higher. The stark reality is that the nominal value of manufacturing output has fallen dramatically as a share of nominal GDP. The United States has also become more dependent on imported manufactured goods, with imported manufactured goods making up a significantly increased share of total manufactured goods purchased. Moreover, U.S. purchases of manufactured goods have risen as a share of total U.S. demand, indicating that the failure lies in U.S. production of manufactured goods, which has lost out to imports. See Bivens, J. [2004], "Shifting Blame for Manufacturing Job Loss: Effect of Rising Trade Deficit Shouldn't Be Ignored," *EPI Briefing Paper* No. 149, Washington, DC: Economic Policy Institute.

Table 4.1. *Manufacturing Employment by Business Cycle,*
October 1945–January 1980

Trough	Employment (Millions)	Peak	Employment (Millions)	Change
October 1945	12.5	November 1948	14.3	1.8
October 1949	12.9	July 1953	16.4	3.5
May 1954	15.0	August 1957	15.9	0.9
April 1958	14.5	April 1960	15.7	1.2
February 1961	14.8	December 1969	18.6	3.8
November 1970	17.0	November 1973	18.8	1.8
March 1975	16.9	January 1980	19.3	2.4

Sources: National Bureau of Economic Research, Bureau of Labor Statistics and author's calculations.

Table 4.2. *Manufacturing Employment by Business Cycle,*
July 1980–December 2007

Trough	Employment (Millions)	Peak	Employment (Millions)	Change
July 1980	18.3	July 1981	18.8	0.5
November 1982	16.7	July 1990	17.7	1.0
March 1991	17.1	March 2001	16.9	−0.2
November 2001	15.8	December 2007	13.8	−2.0

Sources: National Bureau of Economic Research, Bureau of Labor Statistics and author's calculations.

Accompanying this dramatic change in the pattern of real economic activity was a change in policy attitudes, perhaps most clearly illustrated by the attitude toward the trade deficit. Under the earlier economic model, policy makers viewed trade deficits as cause for concern because they represented a leakage of aggregate demand that undermined the virtuous circle of growth. However, under the new model, trade deficits came to be viewed as semi-virtuous because they helped control inflation and because they reflected the choices of consumers and business in the marketplace. According to neoliberal economic theory, those choices represent the self-interest of economic agents, the pursuit of which is good for the economy. As a result, the trade deficit was allowed to grow steadily, hitting new peaks as a share of GDP in each business cycle after 1980. This changed pattern is illustrated in Table 4.3, which shows the trade deficit as a share of GDP at each business cycle peak.

Table 4.3. *The U.S. Goods Trade Deficit by Business Cycle Peaks, 1960–2007*

Peak Year	Trade Deficit ($ Millions)	GDP ($ Billions)	Trade Deficit/ GDP (%)
1960	3,508	526.4	0.7
1969	91	984.6	0.0
1973	1,900	1,382.7	0.1
1980	−25,500	2,789.5	−0.9
1981	−28,023	3,128.4	−0.9
1990	−111,037	5,803.1	−1.9
2001	−429,519	10,128.0	−4.2
2007	−819,373	13,807.5	−5.9

Sources: Economic Report of the President (2009) and author's calculations.

Table 4.4. *Hourly Wage and Productivity Growth, 1967–2006 (2007 Dollars)*

Period	Productivity Growth	Hourly Wage Growth	Productivity-Wage Gap
1967–73	2.5%	2.9%	−0.4
1973–79	1.2	−0.1	1.3
1979–89	1.4	0.4	1.0
1989–2000	1.9	0.9	1.0
2000–06	2.6	−0.1	2.7

Source: Michel et al. (2009).

The effect of the changed growth model is also evident in the detachment of wages from productivity growth, as shown in Table 4.4, and in rising income inequality, as shown in Table 4.5. Between 1979 and 2006, the income share of the bottom 40 percent of U.S. households decreased significantly, while the income share of the top 20 percent increased dramatically. Moreover, a disproportionate part of that increase went to the 5 percent of families at the very top of income-distribution rankings.

The Role of Economic Policy

Economic policy played a critical role in generating and shaping the new growth model, and the effects of that policy boxed in workers.[4]

---

[4] In an earlier book, I analyzed in detail how economic policy has impacted income distribution, unemployment, and growth (*Plenty of Nothing: The Downsizing of the*

Table 4.5. *Distribution of Family Income by Household
Income Rank, 1947–2006*

Year	Bottom 40%	Next 40%	Next 15%	Top 5%
1947	16.9%	40.1%	25.5%	17.5%
1973	17.4	41.5	25.6	15.5
1979	17.0	41.6	26.1	15.3
1989	15.2	40.2	26.7	17.9
2000	14.1	38.1	26.6	21.1
2006	13.5	38.0	27.0	21.5

Sources: Mishel et al. (2009) and author's calculations.

The new model can be described in terms of a neoliberal policy box (see Figure 4.2), the four sides of which are globalization, small government, labor market flexibility, and retreat from full employment. Workers are pressured on all four sides, and it is this pressure that has led to the severing of the wage/productivity growth link.[5]

Globalization, in part spurred by policies encouraging free trade and capital mobility, means that American workers are increasingly competing with lower-paid foreign workers. That pressure is further increased by the fact that foreign workers are themselves under pressure owing to the so-called Washington Consensus development policy, sponsored by the International Monetary Fund (IMF) and the World Bank, which forces them into the same box as American workers. Thus, not only do these policies undermine demand in advanced countries; they also put pressure on demand in developing countries by pressuring workers there too. This is clearly evident in China, which has been marked by rising income inequality and a sharp decline in the

American Dream and the Case for Structural Keynesianism [Princeton, NJ: Princeton University Press, 1998a]). The metaphor of a box is attributable to Ron Blackwell of the AFL-CIO.

[5] There is a deeper political economy behind the neoliberal box, which has been termed "financialization." See Epstein, G. [2001], "Financialization, Rentier Interests, and Central Bank Policy," unpublished manuscript, Department of Economics, University of Massachusetts, Amherst, MA, December; and Palley, T.I. [2008b], "Financialization: What It Is and Why It Matters," in *Finance-led Capitalism: Macroeconomic Effects of Changes in the Financial Sector*, ed. Eckhard Hein, Torsten Niechoj, Peter Spahn, and Achim Truger (Marburg, Germany: Metroplis-Verlag). The policy agenda embedded in the box is driven by financial markets and corporations who are now joined at the hip, with corporations pursuing a narrow financial agenda aimed at benefiting top management and financial elites.

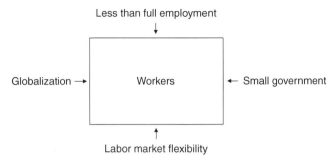

Figure 4.2. The neoliberal policy box.

consumption-to-GDP ratio.[6] The net result of global implementation of neoliberal orthodoxy is the promotion of deflationary global economic conditions.

Small-government policies undermine the legitimacy of government and push privatization, deregulation, and light-touch regulation. Although couched in terms of liberating the economy from detrimental governmental interference, small-government policies have resulted in the erosion of popular economic rights and protections. This is exemplified by the 1996 reform of U.S. welfare rights. Moreover, the government's administrative capacity and ability to provide services have been seriously eroded, with many government functions being outsourced to corporations. This has led to the creation of what the economist James Galbraith (2008) terms the "predator state," in which corporations enrich themselves on government contracts while the outsourced workers employed by these corporations confront a tougher work environment.

Labor market flexibility involves attacking unions, the minimum wage, unemployment benefits, employment protections, and employee rights. This is justified in the name of creating labor market flexibility, including downward wage flexibility, which, according to orthodox economic theory, is supposed to generate full employment. Instead, it has led to wage stagnation and widening income inequality.

Abandonment of full employment means having the Federal Reserve emphasize the importance of keeping inflation low over maintaining

---

[6] See International Monetary Fund [2006], "People's Republic of China: Staff Report for the 2006 Article IV Consultation," Washington, DC.

full employment. This switch was promoted by the economics profession's adoption of Milton Friedman's (1968) notion of a natural rate of unemployment.[7] The theoretical claim is that monetary policy cannot affect long-run equilibrium employment and unemployment, so it should instead aim for a low and stable inflation rate. In recent years, that argument has been used to push the adoption of formal inflation targets. However, the key real-world effect of the natural-rate theory has been to provide the Federal Reserve and policy makers with political cover for higher actual unemployment, which has undermined workers' bargaining power regarding wages.[8]

The Neoliberal Bubble Economy

The implementation of neoliberal economic policies destroyed the stable virtuous-circle growth model based on full employment and wages tied to productivity growth, replacing it with the current growth model based on rising indebtedness and asset price inflation. Since 1980, each U.S. business cycle has seen successively higher debt-to-income ratios at the end of expansions, and the economy has become increasingly dependent on asset price inflation to spur the growth of aggregate demand.

Table 4.6 shows the rising household-debt-to-GDP ratio and rising nonfinancial business-debt-to-GDP ratio under the new growth model. Compared to the period between 1960 and 1981, the period between 1981 and 2007 saw enormous increases in the debt-to-GDP ratios of both the household and nonfinancial corporate sectors.

Table 4.7 shows the rising household debt service ratio, measured as a ratio of debt service and financial obligations to disposable personal income. That this ratio trended upward despite declining nominal interest rates is evidence of the massively increased reliance on debt by households.

Table 4.8 shows the pattern of house price inflation over the past twenty years.[9] This table is revealing in two ways. First, it shows the extraordinary scale of the 2001–06 housing price bubble. Second, it

---

[7] The natural rate of unemployment is also referred to as the NAIRU or nonaccelerating inflation rate of unemployment.

[8] See Palley, T.I. [2007a], "Seeking Full Employment Again: Challenging the Wall Street Paradigm," *Challenge*, 50 (November–December), 14–50.

[9] S&P/Case-Shiller index data is only available from 1987.

Table 4.6. *Household Debt-To-GDP and Nonfinancial Corporation Debt-To-GDP Ratios by Business Cycle Peaks, 1960–2007*

Year	GDP ($ billions)	Household Debt (H) ($ billions)	H-to-GDP	Nonfinancial Corporate Debt (C) ($ billions)	C-to-GDP
1960	526.4	215.6	0.41	201.0	0.38
1969	984.6	442.7	0.45	462.0	0.47
1973	1,382.7	624.9	0.45	729.5	0.53
1981	3,128.4	1,507.2	0.48	1662.0	0.53
1990	5,803.1	3,597.8	0.62	3,753.4	0.65
2001	10,128.0	7682.9	0.76	6,954.0	0.69
2007	13,807.5	13,765.1	1.00	10,593.7	0.77

Sources: FRB Flow of Funds Accounts and author's calculations.

Table 4.7. *Household Debt Service and Financial Obligations Ratio (DSR)*

Year	1980.q3	1991.q3	2001.q4	2007.q4
DSR (%)	10.9	12.0	13.4	14.3

Source: Federal Reserve Board.

Table 4.8. *CPI Inflation and Home Price Inflation Based on the S&P/Case-Shiller National Home Price Values Index*

Period	1987.q1– 1990.q1	1990.q1– 1995.q1	1995.q1– 2001.q1	2001.q1– 2006.q1
Home price inflation (%)	6.7	0.6	5.7	10.9
Average CPI inflation (%)	4.5	3.5	2.5%	2.5
Excess house inflation (%)	2.2	–2.9	3.2	8.4

reveals the systemic role of house price inflation in driving economic expansions. Over the last twenty years, the economy has tended to expand when house price inflation has exceeded consumer price index (CPI) inflation. This was true for the last three years of the Reagan expansion. It was true for the Clinton expansion. And it was true for the Bush Sr. expansion. The one period of sustained housing price stagnation was between 1990 and 1995, which was a period

Table 4.9. *Personal Savings Rate (PSR)*

Period	1960	1969	1973	1980	1981	1991	2001	2007
PSR (%)	7.3	7.8	10.5	10.0	10.9	7.3	1.8	0.6

Source: Economic Report of the President (2009), table B-30.

Table 4.10. *Brief History of The Federal Funds Interest Rate, June 1981–January 2010*

	High	Low
June 1981	19.10%	
December 1992		2.92%
November 2001	6.51	
May 2004		1.00
July 2007	5.26	
December 2008		0.16

Source: Board of Governors of the Federal Reserve.

of recession and extended jobless recovery. This is indicative of the significance of asset price inflation in driving demand under the neoliberal model.

Along with rising debt ratios, households progressively cut back on their savings rates, as shown in Table 4.9. This reduction provided another source of demand.

Lastly, disinflation and the space it created for lower nominal interest rates were also critical for the new paradigm. In recessions and financial upheavals, U.S. economic policy makers were quickly able to restore growth by lowering interest rates and opening the spigot of credit. This pattern is captured in Table 4.10, which shows three long cycles governing the Federal Reserve's federal funds interest rate over the period between 1981 and 2010.

Given the initial high interest rates in 1981, the Federal Reserve had enormous space to lower rates each recession, and in recovery, rates were raised but by not as much. It was this process that lay behind the so-called Great Moderation and the perceived success of monetary policy. However, the reality was that the Federal Reserve was consuming the disinflation dividend (i.e., the Fed was using up the policy space provided by lower inflation to lower interest rates). That could not last forever, and in the Great Recession it has finally hit the zero lower bound to nominal interest rates.

In sum, the new growth paradigm put in place after 1980 involved squeezing worker incomes, squeezing household saving rates, raising debt levels, persistent asset price inflation in excess of CPI inflation, and reliance on ever lower nominal interest rates. This logic made it economically unsustainable. That is because the economy was eventually going to hit constraints imposed by debt ceilings, pushing the saving rate to zero, inflating asset prices to bubble levels, and hitting the nominal interest rate floor.

Although intrinsically unsustainable, the paradigm lasted far longer than expected because of the ability to raise debt limits, and squeeze saving rates lower and push asset prices higher than imagined. That is the real significance of financial innovation and deregulation that contributed to these extension mechanisms.

Viewed from this angle, financial innovation and deregulation did not cause the crisis. The neoliberal paradigm was always going to fail owing to its internal contradiction, but financial innovation and deregulation kept the model going longer. However, the sting in the tail is that rather than simply grinding to a slow stop, this extension resulted in the accumulation of large financial imbalances. Consequently, when these extension mechanisms eventually exhausted themselves, the result was an implosion that took the form of a financial crisis capable of producing a far bigger and more dangerous collapse.[10]

The Flawed Model of Global Economic Engagement

Although prone to instability (i.e., to boom and bust), the neoliberal growth model might have operated successfully for quite a while

---

[10] This means the crisis is not a pure "Minsky" crisis. Hyman Minsky (1992, 1993) saw crises as the result of endogenous financial instability that developed over time. However, the current crisis is a crisis of the neoliberal paradigm. That paradigm fostered financial instability as a way of sustaining itself. Consequently, when the crisis hit, it took on the appearance of a classic Minsky crisis, but its real roots lie in the neoliberal model. For a more extensive discussion of this issue, see Palley, T.I. [2010a], "The Limits of Minsky's Financial Instability Hypothesis as an Explanation of the Crisis," *Monthly Review* (April), 28–43.

longer were it not for a U.S. economic policy that created a flawed engagement with the global economy. This flawed engagement undermined the economy in two ways. First, it accelerated the erosion of household incomes. Second, it accelerated the accumulation of unproductive debt – that is, debt that generates economic activity elsewhere rather than in the United States.

The most visible manifestation of this flawed engagement is the goods trade deficit, which hit a record 6.4 percent of GDP in 2006. This deficit was the inevitable product of the structure of global economic engagement put in place over the past two decades, with the most critical elements being implemented by the Clinton administration under the guidance of Treasury secretaries Robert Rubin and Lawrence Summers. That eight-year period saw the implementation of the North American Free Trade Agreement (NAFTA), the adoption after the East Asian financial crisis of 1997 of the "strong dollar" policy, and the establishment of permanent normal trade relations (PNTR) with China in 2000.

These measures cemented the model of globalization that had been lobbied for by corporations and their Washington think tank allies. The irony is that giving corporations what they wanted undermined the new model by surfacing its contradictions. The model would likely have eventually slumped because of its own internal dynamic, but the policy triumph of corporate globalization accelerated this process and transformed it into a financial crash.

The Triple Hemorrhage

Flawed global economic engagement created a "triple hemorrhage" within the U.S. economy. The first economic hemorrhage, long emphasized by Keynesian economists, was the leakage out of the economy of spending on imports. Household income and borrowing was significantly spent on imports, creating incomes offshore rather than in the United States. Consequently, borrowing left behind a debt footprint but did not create sustainable jobs and incomes at home.

The second hemorrhage was the leakage of jobs from the U.S. economy as a result of offshore outsourcing, made possible by corporate globalization. Such offshoring directly reduced the number of higher-paying manufacturing jobs, cutting into household income. Moreover, even when jobs did not move offshore, the threat of offshoring could be used to secure lower wages, thereby dampening wage growth and helping sever wages from productivity growth.[11]

The third hemorrhage concerned new investment. Not only were corporations incentivized by low foreign wages, foreign subsidies, and undervalued exchange rates to close existing plants and shift their production offshore; they were also incentivized to shift new investment offshore. That did double damage. First, it reduced domestic investment spending, hurting the capital-goods sector and employment therein. Second, it stripped the U.S. economy of modern industrial capacity, disadvantaging U.S. competitiveness and reducing employment that would have been generated to operate that capacity.

A further unanticipated economic leakage from the flawed model of global engagement concerns energy prices. Offshoring of U.S. manufacturing capacity has often involved the closing of relatively energy-efficient and environmentally cleaner production and its replacement with less efficient and dirtier foreign production. In addition, the shipping of goods from around the world to the U.S. market has compounded these effects.[12] These developments added to energy demand and contributed to the 2005–08 increase in oil prices, which added to the U.S. trade deficit and effectively imposed a huge tax (paid to OPEC) on U.S. consumers. Additionally, 2008 saw a bubble in oil prices as speculative excess migrated from financial markets to commodity markets.[13]

The flawed model of global economic engagement broke with the old model of international trade in two ways. First, instead of having roughly balanced trade, the United States has run persistent large trade deficits. Second, instead of aiming to create a global marketplace

[11] See Bronfenbrenner, K. [2000],*Uneasy Terrain: The Impact of Capital Mobility on Workers, Wages, and Union Organizing*, Report prepared for the United States Trade Deficit Review Commission, Washington, DC, September; and Bronfenbrenner, K. and S. Luce[2004], *The Changing Nature of Corporate Global Restructuring: The Impact of Production Shifts on Jobs in the U.S., China, and Around the Globe*, Report prepared for the U.S.-China Economic and Security Review Commission, Washington, DC, October.

[12] See Peters, G.P., J.C. Minx, C.L. Weber, and O. Edenhofer [2011], "Growth in Emission Transfers Via International Trade from 1990 to 2008," Center for International Climate and Environmental Research, Oslo, Norway, March 29.

[13] See Masters, M.W. and A.K. White [2008], "The Accidental Hunt Brothers: How Institutional Investors are Driving up Food and Energy Prices," Special Report, July 31, http://www.accidentalhuntbrothers.com.

in which U.S. companies could sell their products, its purpose was to create a global production zone in which U.S. companies could operate. In other words, the main purpose of international economic engagement was not to increase U.S. exports by creating a global market place. Rather, it was to create a global production zone from which U.S.-owned production platforms in developing countries could supply the American market, or from which U.S. corporations could purchase cheaper imported inputs.

As a result, at the bidding of corporate interests, the United States joined itself at the hip to the global economy, opening its borders to an inflow of goods and exposing its manufacturing base. This was done without safeguards to address the problems of exchange rate misalignment, systemic trade deficits, or the mercantilist policies of trading partners.

NAFTA

The creation of the new system took off in 1989 with the implementation of the Canada-U.S. Free Trade Agreement that established an integrated production zone between the two countries. The 1994 implementation of NAFTA (North American Free Trade Agreement) was the decisive next step. First, it fused Canada, the United States, and Mexico into a unified North American production zone. Second, and more importantly, it joined developed and developing economies, thereby establishing the template U.S. corporations wanted.

NAFTA also dramatically changed the significance of exchange rates. Before, exchange rates mattered for trade and the exchange of goods. Now, they mattered for the location of production. That, in turn, changed the attitude of large U.S. multinational corporations (MNCs) toward the dollar. When U.S. companies produced domestically and looked to export, a weaker dollar was in their commercial interest, and they lobbied against dollar overvaluation. However, under the new model, U.S. corporations looked to produce offshore and import into the United States. This reversed their commercial interest, making them proponents of a strong dollar. That is because a strong dollar reduces the dollar costs of foreign production, raising the profit margins on their foreign production sold in the United States at U.S. prices.

NAFTA soon highlighted this new dynamic, because Mexico was hit by a financial crisis in January 1994, immediately after the

Table 4.11. *U.S. Goods Trade Balance with Mexico before and after NAFTA ($Billions)*

1991	1992	1993	1994	1995	1996	2000	2005	2007
2.1	5.4	1.7	1.3	−15.8	−17.5	−24.5	−49.7	−74.6

Source: U.S. Census Bureau.

implementation of the free-trade agreement. To U.S. corporations, which had invested in Mexico and planned to invest more, the peso's collapse versus the dollar was a boon as it made it even more profitable to produce in Mexico and reexport to the United States. With corporate interests driving U.S. economic policy, the peso devaluation problem went unattended – and in doing so it also created a critical precedent.

The effects of NAFTA and the peso devaluation were immediately felt in the U.S. manufacturing sector in the form of job loss, diversion of investment, firms using the threat of relocation to repress wages, and an explosion in the goods trade deficit with Mexico, as shown in Table 4.11. Whereas prior to the implementation of the NAFTA agreement, the United States was running a goods trade surplus with Mexico, immediately afterward, the balance turned massively negative and kept growing more negative up to 2007.

These features helped contribute to the jobless recovery of 1993–96, although the economy was eventually able to overcome this with the stock market bubble that launched in 1996, the emergence of the Internet investment boom that morphed into the dot-com bubble, and the tentative beginnings of the housing price bubble, which can be traced back to 1997. Together, these developments spurred a consumption and investment boom that masked the adverse structural effects of NAFTA.

The Response to the East Asian Financial Crisis
The next fateful step in the flawed engagement with the global economy came with the East Asian financial crisis of 1997, which was followed by a series of rolling financial crises in Russia (1998), Brazil (1999), Turkey (2000), Argentina (2000), and Brazil (2000). In response to these crises, Treasury Secretaries Rubin and Summers adopted the same policy that was used to deal with the 1994 peso crisis, thereby

creating a new global system that replicated the pattern of economic integration established with Mexico.[14]

Large dollar loans were made to the countries in crisis to stabilize their economies. At the same time, the collapse of their exchange rates and the appreciation of the dollar was accepted and institutionalized in the form of a "strong dollar" policy.[15] This increased the buying power of U.S. consumers, which was critical because the U.S. consumer was now the lynchpin of the global economy, becoming the buyer of first and last resort.[16]

The new global economic architecture involved developing countries exporting their production to the United States. Developing countries embraced this export-led growth solution to their development problem and were encouraged to do so by the IMF and the World Bank. For developing countries, the new system had a number of advantages, including the ability to run trade surpluses that allowed them to build up foreign exchange holdings to defend against capital flight; providing demand for their output, which led to job creation; and providing access to U.S. markets that encouraged MNCs to redirect investment spending toward them. The latter was especially important as it transferred technology, created jobs, and built up developing countries' manufacturing capacity.

U.S. multinationals were also highly supportive of the new arrangement as they now gained global access to low-cost export production platforms. Not only did this mean access to cheap foreign labor, but the overvalued dollar lowered their foreign production costs, thereby

[14] It cannot be overemphasized that the policies adopted by Treasury Secretaries Robert Rubin and Lawrence Summers reflected the dominant economic paradigm. As such, Rubin and Summers had the support of the majority of the U.S. political establishment, the IMF and the World Bank, Washington's premier think tanks, and the economics profession.

[15] China had already gone this route with a large exchange rate devaluation in 1994. Indeed, there is reason to believe that this devaluation contributed to hatching the East Asian financial crisis by putting other East Asian economies under undue competitive pressures and diverting foreign investment from them to China.

[16] The strong-dollar policy was also politically popular, constituting a form of exchange rate populism. Boosting the value of the dollar increased the purchasing power of U.S. consumers at a time when their wages were under downward pressure due to the neoliberal model. Households were under pressure from globalization, yet at the same time they were being given incentives to embrace it. This is why neoliberalism has been so hard to tackle politically.

Table 4.12. *U.S. Goods Trade Balance ($Billions)*

1995	1996	1997	1998	1999	2000
−174.2	−191.0	−198.4	−248.2	−347.8	−454.7

Source: U.S. Census Bureau.

Table 4.13. *U.S. Goods Trade Balance with Pacific Rim Countries ($ Billions)*

1995	1996	1997	1998	1999	2000
−108.1	−101.8	−121.6	−160.4	−186.0	−215.4

Source: U.S. Census Bureau.

further increasing profit margins. Large importers, like Wal-Mart, also supported this arrangement. Furthermore, many foreign governments offered subsidies as an incentive to attract foreign direct investment (FDI).

In effect, the pattern of incentives established by the response to the East Asian financial crisis encouraged U.S. corporations to persistently downsize their U.S. capacity and shift production offshore for import back to the United States. This created a dynamic for progressively eroding U.S. national industrial capacity, while foreign economies were encouraged to steadily expand their capacity and export their way out of economic difficulties.

As with NAFTA, the adverse effects of this policy were visible almost immediately. As shown in Table 4.12, the goods trade deficit took a further leap forward, surging from $198.4 billion in 1997 to $248.2 billion in 1998, and rising to $454.7 billion in 2000. In addition, as shown in Table 4.13, there was a surge in imports from Pacific Rim countries. Part of the surge in the trade deficit was due to the boom conditions sparked by stock market euphoria, the dot-com bubble, and housing price inflation, but the scale of the trade deficit surge also reflects the flawed character of U.S. engagement with the global economy.

The proof of this claim is that manufacturing employment started falling despite boom conditions in the U.S. economy. Having finally started to grow in 1996, manufacturing employment peaked in

March 1998 and started declining three full years before the economy went into recession in March 2001. That explains why manufacturing job growth was negative over the entirety of the Clinton expansion – a first in U.S. business cycle history.

As with NAFTA, these adverse effects were once again obscured by positive business cycle conditions. Consequently, the Clinton administration dismissed concerns about the long-term dangers of manufacturing job loss. Instead, the official interpretation was that the U.S. economy was experiencing – in the words of senior Clinton economic policy advisers Alan Blinder and Janet Yellen – a "fabulous decade" significantly driven by policy.[17] According to the ideology of the decade, manufacturing was in secular decline and destined for the dustbin of history. The old manufacturing economy was to be replaced by a "new economy" driven by computers, the Internet, and information technology.

China and Permanent Normal Trading Relations (PNTR)
Although disastrous for the long-run health of the U.S. economy, NAFTA-style corporate globalization plus the strong-dollar policy was extremely profitable for corporations. Additionally, the ultimate costs to households were still obscured by the ability of the U.S. economy to generate cyclical booms based on asset price inflation and debt. That provided political space for a continued deepening of the global engagement model, the final step of which was to incorporate China as a full-fledged participant.

Thus, corporations now pushed for the establishment of permanent normal trading relations with China, which Congress enacted in 2000. That legislation in turn enabled China to join the World Trade Organization (WTO), which had been established in 1996.

---

[17] See Blinder, A.S. and J.L. Yellen [2001], *The Fabulous Decade: Macroeconomic Lessons from the 1990s*, New York: Century Foundation Press. To the extent there was concern in the Clinton administration about manufacturing, it was about the hardships for workers regarding job dislocations. Additionally, there was political concern that produced some sweet talk (i.e., invitations to policy consultations) aimed at placating trade unions. However, there was no concern that these outcomes were due to flawed international economic policy. Not only did this policy failure contribute to eventual disastrous economic outcomes, it may well have cost Vice President Al Gore the 2000 presidential election. The Clinton administration's economic advisers may have downplayed the significance of manufacturing-sector job loss, but blue-collar voters in Ohio did not.

Table 4.14. *U.S. Goods Trade Balance with China before and after PNTR ($ Billions)*

1998	1999	2000	2001	2002	2003	2004	2005	2007
56.9	−68.7	−83.9	−83.1	−103.1	−124.1	−161.9	−201.5	−256.2

Source: U.S. Census Bureau.

The significance of PNTR was not about trade, but rather about making China a full-fledged part of global production arrangements. China had enjoyed access to the U.S. market for years, and its entry into the WTO did generate some further tariff reductions. However, the real significance was that China became a fully legitimate destination for foreign direct investment. That is because production from China was now guaranteed permanent access to the U.S. market, and corporations were also given internationally recognized protections of property and investor rights.

Once again the results were predictable and similar to the pattern established by NAFTA, although the scale was far larger. Aided by a strong dollar, the trade deficit with China increased dramatically after 2001, growing at a rate of 25 percent per annum and jumping from $83.1 billion in 2001 to $201.5 billion in 2005 (see Table 4.14). Moreover, there was also massive inflow of foreign direct investment into China so that it became the world's largest recipient of FDI in 2002 – a stunning achievement for a developing country.[18] So strong was China's attractiveness as an FDI destination that it not only displaced production and investment in the United States, but also displaced production and investment in Mexico.[19]

According to academic and Washington policy orthodoxy, the new global system was supposed to launch a new era of popular shared prosperity. Demand was to be provided by U.S. consumers. Their spending was to be financed by the "new economy" based on information technology and the globalization of manufacturing, which would drive higher productivity and income. Additionally, consumer spending could be financed by borrowing and asset price inflation, which was sustainable because higher asset prices were justified by increased productivity.

[18] "China Ahead in Foreign Direct Investment" [2003], *OECD Observer*, No. 237, May.
[19] See Greider, W. [2001], "A New Giant Sucking Sound," *The Nation*, December 13.

This new orthodoxy was enshrined in what was termed the "New Bretton Woods Hypothesis," according to which the global economy had entered a new golden age of global development, reminiscent of the postwar era.[20] The United States would import from East Asian and other developing economies, provide FDI to those economies, and run large trade deficits that would provide the demand for the new supply. In return, developing countries would accumulate financial obligations against the United States, principally in the form of Treasury securities. This would provide them with foreign exchange reserves and collateral that was supposed to make investors feel secure. China was to epitomize the new arrangement.[21]

The reality is that the structure of U.S. international engagement, with its lack of attention to the trade deficit and manufacturing, contributed to a disastrous acceleration of the contradictions inherent in the neoliberal growth model. That model always had a problem regarding sustainable generation of demand because of its imposition of wage stagnation and high income inequality. Flawed international economic engagement aggravated this problem by creating a triple hemorrhage that drained consumer spending, manufacturing jobs, and investment and industrial capacity. This, in turn, compelled even deeper reliance on the unsustainable stopgaps of borrowing and asset price inflation to compensate.

As for developing economies, they embraced the post-1997 international economic order. However, in doing so they tied their fate to the U.S. economy, creating a situation in which the global economy was flying on one engine that was bound to fail. Consequently, far from creating a decoupled global economy, it created a linked economy characterized by a concertina effect: When the U.S. economy crashed in 2008, other economies began weakening in its wake.

[20] See Dooley, M.P., D. Folkerts-Landau, and P. Garber [2003], "An Essay on the Revised Bretton Woods System," Working Paper 9971, Cambridge, MA: National Bureau of Economic Research, September; and Dooley, Folkerts-Landau, and Garber [2004], "The US Current Account Deficit and Economic Development: Collateral for a Total Return Swap," Working Paper 10727, Cambridge, MA: National Bureau of Economic Research, August.

[21] For a critique of the New Bretton Woods hypothesis, which explains why it was unsustainable, see Palley, T.I. [2006c], "The Fallacy of the Revised Bretton Woods Hypothesis: Why Today's System Is Unsustainable and Suggestions for a Replacement," Public Policy Brief No. 85, The Levy Economics Institute of Bard College.

America's Exhausted Macroeconomic Paradigm

The twin macroeconomics factors of an unstable growth model and of flawed global economic engagement were put in place during the 1980s and 1990s. However, their full adverse effects took time to build, and the chickens only came home to roost in the 2001–07 expansion. From that standpoint, the Bush administration is not responsible for the financial crisis. Its economic policies can be criticized for mean-spiritedness and a greater proclivity for corporate favoritism, but they represented a continuation of the policy paradigm already in place. The financial crisis, therefore, represents the exhaustion of that paradigm rather than being the result of specific policy failures on the part of the Bush administration.

In a nutshell, the U.S. implemented a new growth model that relied on debt and asset price inflation. As the new model slowly cannibalized itself and became weaker, the economy needed larger speculative bubbles to grow. The flawed model of global engagement accelerated the cannibalization process, thereby creating the need for a huge bubble that only housing could provide. However, when that bubble burst, it pulled down the entire economy because of the bubble's massive dependence on debt.

In many regards, the neoliberal paradigm was already showing its limits in the 1990s. An extended jobless recovery marked the business cycle of the 1990s when the term was coined, and the subsequent 1990s boom was accompanied by a stock market bubble and the beginnings of significant house price inflation.

The recession of 2001 saw the bursting of the stock market and dot-com bubbles. However, although investment spending was hit hard, consumer spending was largely untouched, owing to continued household borrowing and continued moderate increases in home prices. Additionally, the financial system was largely unscathed, because the stock market bubble involved limited reliance on debt financing.

Yet, despite the relative shallowness of the 2001 recession and aggressive monetary and fiscal stimulus, the economy languished in a second extended bout of jobless recovery. The critical factor was the trade deficit and offshoring of jobs resulting from the model of globalization that had been decisively implemented in the 1990s. This

Table 4.15. *U.S. Manufacturing-Sector Employment (Millions)*

1997	1998	1999	2000	2001	2002	2003	2005	2007
17.42	17.56	17.32	17.26	16.44	15.26	14.51	14.32	13.88

Source: Economic Report of the President (2009), table B-46.

drained spending, jobs, and investment from the economy, and also damped down wages by creating job insecurity.

The effects are clearly visible in the data for manufacturing employment. As noted earlier, manufacturing employment peaked in March 1998, shortly after the East Asian financial crisis and three years before the economy went into recession. Thereafter, manufacturing never really recovered from this shock and continued losing jobs throughout the most recent expansion (see Table 4.15).

The sustained weakness of manufacturing effectively undermined economic recovery, despite expansionary macroeconomic policy. According to the National Bureau of Economic Research, the recession ended in November 2001, when employment was 130.9 million. Two years later (November 2003), total employment was 130.1 million – a decrease of 800,000 jobs. Over this period, manufacturing lost 1.5 million jobs, and total manufacturing employment fell from 15.83 million to 14.32 million.

Failure to develop a robust recovery, combined with persistent fears that the economy was about to slip back into recession, prompted the Federal Reserve to lower interest rates. Beginning in November 2000, the Fed cut its federal funds rates significantly, lowering it from 6.5 to 2.1 percent in November 2001. However, the weakness of the recovery drove the Fed to cut the rate still further, pushing it to 1 percent in July 2003, where it was held until June 2004.

Ultimately, the Federal Reserve's low-interest-rate policy succeeded in jump-starting the economy by spurring a housing price boom, which in turn sparked a construction boom. That boom became a bubble, which burst in the summer of 2007. What is important about this history is that the economy needed an asset price bubble to restore full employment, just as it had needed the stock market and dot-com bubbles to restore full employment in the 1990s.

Given the underlying structural weakness of the demand-generating process, which had been further aggravated by flawed globalization, a bubble was the only way back to full employment. Higher asset prices were needed to provide collateral to support borrowing that could then finance spending.

A housing bubble was particularly economically effective for two reasons. First, housing ownership is widespread so the consumption wealth effects of the bubble were also widespread. Second, higher house prices stimulated domestic construction employment by raising prices above the cost of construction. Moreover, the housing bubble was a form of "house price populism" that benefitted incumbent politicians who could claim credit for the fictitious wealth created by the bubble.

The Federal Reserve is now being blamed by many for the bubble,[22] but the reality is that it felt compelled to lower interest rates for fear of the economy falling back into recession. Additionally, inflation – which is the signaling mechanism the Federal Reserve relies on to assess whether monetary policy is too loose – showed no indication of excess demand in the economy. Indeed, all the indications were of profound economic weakness and demand shortage. Finally, when the Federal Reserve started raising the federal funds interest rates in mid-2004, the long-term rate that influences mortgages changed little. In part this may have been because of recycling of foreign country trade surpluses back to the United States, but the real cause likely was expectations of weak future economic conditions that kept the lid on long-term interest rates.

This reality is confirmed by a look back at the expansion of 2001–07 compared to other expansions. By almost all measures it ranks as the weakest business cycle since World War II. Table 4.16 shows "trough to peak" and "peak to peak" measures of GDP growth, consumption growth, investment spending growth, employment growth, manufacturing employment growth, profit growth, compensation growth, wage and salary growth, change in the unemployment rate, and change in the employment/population ratio of this business cycle relative to other postwar cycles. The 2001–07 cycle ranks worst in seven of the ten measures and second-worst in two other measures. If the comparison is restricted to the four cycles lasting twenty-seven quarters or

---

[22] See Taylor, J.B. [2009], "How Government Created the Financial Crisis," *Wall Street Journal*, February 9.

Table 4.16. *Rank of Last Business Cycle Relative to Cycles since World War II (1 = Best; 10 = Worst)*

	Expansion Only (1 = Best, 10 = Worst)	Full Cycles (1 = Best, 10= Worst)	Full Cycles (1 = Best, 4= Worst)
	All	All	Cycles lasting more than 27 quarters
Number of cycles	10	10	4
Rank of 2001–07 cycle			
GDP growth	10	8	4
Consumption growth	9	9	4
Investment growth	10	9	4
Employment growth	10	9	4
Manufacturing-sector employment growth	10	10	4
Profit growth	4	2	1
Compensation growth	10	9	4
Wage and salary growth	10	9	4
Change in unemployment rate	9	5	4
Change in employment/ population ratio	10	10	4

Sources: Bivens, J., and J. Irons[2008], "A Feeble Recovery: The Fundamental Economic Weaknesses of the 2001–07 Expansion," EPI Briefing Paper No. 214, Washington, DC: Economic Policy Institute, December; and author's calculations.

more, the 2001–07 cycle is worst in nine of ten measures and best in one measure – profit growth. This weak performance occurred despite a housing price and credit bubble of historic proportions. That is the clearest evidence possible of the structural weakness of the U.S. macroeconomic model and why a bubble was needed to sustain growth.

This structural weakness is the heart of the matter, but as yet, policy makers and the economics profession are unwilling to acknowledge it. The refusal to change paradigms means the economy will likely be unable to escape the pull of stagnation. That is because stagnation is the logical next stage of the model.

5

The Role of Finance

Chapter 4 described how the flawed U.S. model of growth and global economic engagement created conditions that inevitably tended to stagnation. It is now time to fill in the role of finance, which plays a critical part in explaining why the contradictions of the neoliberal model took so long to surface and why they surfaced in the form of a financial crisis.

Figure 5.1 illustrates the structural Keynesian explanation of the Great Recession, which involves three elements: a flawed growth model, a flawed model of global engagement, and a flawed model of financial markets. These three elements interacted in a specific way. The model of global economic engagement exacerbated the weaknesses inherent in the growth model. Balanced against this, the model of financial markets provided support for growth but at the cost of increasing financial fragility (indebtedness) combined with increasingly inflated asset prices (e.g., the housing price bubble).

In effect, the model of growth and global engagement eroded the foundations of the real economy while the model of financial markets simultaneously created a "Wile E. Coyote" economy that ran off the cliff. Financial exuberance kept the economy running in thin air for a considerable time, but participants eventually realized there was no ground beneath them. At that stage, financial markets turned pessimistic and then completely froze with the collapse of Lehman Brothers in September 2008. Thereafter, the fundamentally deteriorated structure of the real economy asserted itself and now drives the economic outlook.

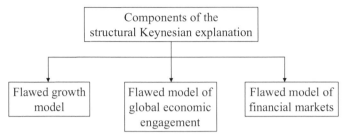

Figure 5.1. The structural Keynesian explanation of the Great Recession.

This analysis of events is subtly different from the conventional narratives of left and right. The story from the right is that the crisis was purely financial. However, if that were true, growth and full employment should have rebounded once the financial system was stabilized and credit flows restored. The story from the left is that the worsening of income distribution caused the crisis. However, the reality is that income distribution was deteriorated long in advance and the crisis only happened when financial markets realized they were running on thin air. Only after the financial crisis did the full depressing effects of deteriorated income distribution kick in to hold the economy down despite massive fiscal and monetary stimulus.

The Role of Finance

The basic thesis with regard to finance is as follows. The flawed models of growth and global engagement undermined the foundations of the economy (i.e., the manufacturing base and the process of income and demand generation). That created a growing demand shortfall relative to demand needed to sustain full employment, and this shortfall was filled via financial markets.

In the 1980s, the shortfall was filled by massive federal budget deficits, a stock market boom, rising home prices, and rising debt. The 1990s saw more of the same, with large budget deficits in the first half of the decade, followed by an accelerated rise in stock prices, housing prices, and private debt. Additionally, there was the new phenomenon of the Internet bubble. The 2000s saw the housing price bubble that pushed financial excess deep into the economy, as houses are the most widely owned asset, the largest asset of most households, and the asset that is easiest to borrow against.

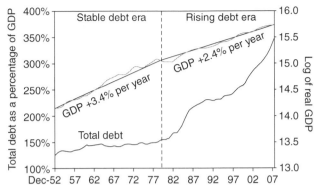

Figure 5.2. Total domestic debt and growth, 1952–2007.
Source: Grantham (2010).

This process of finance filling the demand gap is captured in Figure 5.2, which shows the path of real GDP and total debt as a percent of GDP.[1] The neoliberal era formally kicks off in 1980 and is associated with slower annual real GDP growth than the preceding Keynesian period (2.4 percent vs. 3.4 percent). It is also marked by a continuous and accelerating increase in total domestic debt. This debt does not increase growth. Instead, it helps maintain growth in the face of the depressing tendencies of the neoliberal models of growth and global economic engagement.

The massive increase in debt was necessary to stave off the tendency to stagnation inherent in the neoliberal model. It was accomplished by financial deregulation, financial innovation, and increased risk taking by borrowers, lenders, and investors. This is where finance enters the picture, and the catalog of financial deregulation and innovation over the period between 1980 and 2008 is striking.

Four landmark pieces of legislation pushing financial deregulation were:

- The Depository Institutions Deregulation and Monetary Control Act (1980), which allowed commercial banks to pay interest on checkable deposits.

---

[1] See Grantham, J. [2010], "Night of the Living Fed," *GMO Quarterly Letter*, October. Total debt consists of the debt of the nonfinancial and domestic financial sectors as provided by the Federal Reserve in its quarterly flow-of-funds accounts.

- The Garn–St.Germain Depository Institutions Act (1982), which deregulated the saving & loan industry and allowed banks to provide adjustable-rate mortgages.
- The Riegle-Neale Interstate Banking and Branching Efficiency Act (1994), which repealed restrictions on the creation of nationwide commercial banks.
- The Gramm-Leach-Bliley Act (1999), which repealed the Glass–Steagall Act (1933) and parts of the Bank Holding Act (1956) and allowed the combination of investment banks, commercial banks, and insurance companies under one roof.

The general thrust of legislation was to break down boundaries between financial institutions and combine their activities on grounds that it increased competition, increased the supply of finance, and there were synergies that increased efficiency and lowered costs of providing finance. The agenda also promoted national financial institutions that were far larger in size, pooled risks across regions, and had greater access to finance.

This legislative agenda aimed at expanding the supply of finance was supported by a similar expansive regulatory agenda. Federal Reserve policy makers, guided by the economics profession, shifted to an exclusive focus on interest rates and abandoned concern about the quantity and allocation of credit. This shift was reflected in the abandonment of quantitative regulation of balance sheets; the decline in the significance of bank reserve requirements; refusal to use instruments like stock margin requirements to tamp down speculation; and refusal to use existing powers of credit control.

A similar shift was seen in other regulatory agencies. In 1998, Treasury Secretaries Rubin and Summers, in combination with Federal Reserve Chairman Alan Greenspan, successfully blocked regulation of derivatives. The Commodities Futures Modernization Act of 2000 exempted derivatives from regulation and allowed them to be traded almost entirely free of regulation in so-called over-the-counter markets. In 2004, the SEC passed its net capital exemption rule that reduced the amount of capital Wall Street's largest brokerage houses had to hold, and it also allowed investment banks to adopt self-regulation with regard to assessing the value of their capital at risk. An immediate consequence of the rule was a surge in investment bank leverage, and debt-to-equity ratios rose from around 15 to 1 in 2004 to over 30 to 1 by 2008.

The overarching thrust of policy was to remove regulatory constraints and increase the elasticity of the supply of finance. The argument was that consenting adults in credit markets know best and their decisions also produce the best outcomes for the economy as a whole.

Another significant policy change was the promotion of defined-contribution pension arrangements (such as individual retirement accounts and 401[k] plans) in place of traditional defined-benefit arrangements. Rather than receiving a fixed monthly payment as under the old arrangements, retirement income was now made to depend on workers' success as individual investors.

In addition to increasing the uncertainty of retirement income, the spread of these new plans had two important consequences. First, it raised the salience and significance of financial markets for households, creating a new culture of speculation and greed epitomized by the 1987 movie *Wall Street*. Second, it meant pensions were now structured as a personal asset that could serve as collateral and be borrowed against.

The environment created by these new policies both spurred financial innovation and gave room for financial innovations to have large impacts. One critical development was continued growth of the commercial paper market and money market mutual funds, which had taken off in the late 1970s in response to the high inflation rates of that decade. This development was absolutely critical to financing of investment banks and the shadow (or parallel) banking system.

The commercial paper market enabled companies to get financing by selling short-term notes with a maturity of less than one year. These notes were bought by money market mutual funds, which were attractive to traditional bank depositors because they paid a higher interest rate than bank deposits. Consequently, depositors began to shift out of traditional bank deposits into money markets. The commercial paper market–money market fund nexus thus set in train a dynamic whereby investment banks and the shadow banking system grew at the expense of traditional commercial banks.

Another innovation in the 1980s was the junk bond market that allowed less creditworthy corporations to raise finance. This market was also critical in developing the concept of leveraged buyouts and fueled the leveraged buyout boom of the 1980s. It also contributed to development of investor appetite for high-yield, riskier securities that were to become part of the landscape of the housing price bubble.

With regard to the housing market, there were a series of innovations. A first change was the gradual easing of loan-to-value conventions. In the 1960s and 1970s, the convention was to restrict mortgages to 3.5 times before-tax income, and mortgage servicing costs (interest, taxes, and insurance) were limited to one-third of income. Beginning in the 1980s, these standards were progressively relaxed. By the end of the bubble they had all but disappeared, as reflected in infamous subprime NINJA (no income, no job or assets) mortgages and 105 percent mortgages that lent more than the value of the home. This relaxation process gave homebuyers access to progressively more mortgage credit, which served to drive up housing prices. It also exposed lenders to huge losses.

A second innovation was the development of home equity loans that allowed households to borrow against accumulated home equity. As the housing price bubble developed after 1996 and housing prices rose, this innovation effectively turned houses into ATMs.

A third critical innovation was the development of mortgage-backed securities (MBS). Traditionally, banks had held on to mortgage loans until they were fully repaid. Now, banks bundled mortgages together as part of a single security and sold shares in that security. This process of bundling and resale prevented banks from becoming "loaned up" and gave them a steady stream of finance for new lending. It also made mortgages more liquid because they could be sold on, which attracted more financing for mortgage lending. Lastly, MBS diversified risk by pooling mortgages and then selling them to distant Wall Street investors. However, they also spread risk, and the claimed diversification properties may have encouraged complacency about risk, which was significantly reassembled among large buyers of MBS.[2]

Yet another innovation was collateralized debt obligations (CDOs) that went a step further than simple MBS. Individual mortgages and debts were bundled into a single trust entity that, in turn, issued

---

[2] See Rajan, R.G. [2005], "Has Financial Development Made the World Riskier?" Paper presented at the Jackson Hole Conference of the Kansas City Federal Reserve Bank, http://www.kc.frb.org/publicat/sympos/2005/PDF/Rajan2005.pdf

securities (i.e., bonds) to investors. As the trust received cash payments on the underlying mortgages and debts, they were passed on to CDO bondholders. Moreover, the trust could issue many different classes of bonds. For example, the bonds could be structured (i.e., "tranched") so that cash payments would first flow to one class of bonds (i.e., tranche A), then if surplus cash remained, it would flow to the next tranche (i.e., tranche B), and so on. In this way a CDO could engineer a pool of low-rated (junk) mortgages and debt into bonds (i.e., tranches) with ratings ranging from noninvestment grade up to AAA. The importance of the CDO innovation was that it transformed underlying toxic loans into AAA loans. That enticed a far larger class of investors to buy them, thereby expanding the supply of finance for the bubble.

Such financial engineering was also used to justify taking on more risk and paying higher prices. The claim was that such engineering created new financial assets with different risk-return properties. According to portfolio theory, this increased portfolio diversification possibilities, justifying higher prices for the underlying junk that went into the engineered assets. It also supposedly reduced risk, thereby justifying taking on new replacement risk.

Another innovation was credit default swaps (CDSs), which are unregulated tradable insurance contracts on debt that pay off in the event of default. Their value is that they give owners the ability to insure against extreme outcomes, thereby limiting risk on a particular investment holding and thereby enabling taking on additional risk on some other investment. CDS pricing also provides the market with information about the likelihood of a company defaulting.

However, with CDS came two unrecognized dangers. First, CDS gave a false sense of security. Insurance contracts are only as good as the underlying insurer. This is where AIG and the 1998 decision not to regulate derivatives, including CDS contracts, become relevant. AIG sold billions of dollars of CDS insurance and booked the premium income, but it then could not meet its CDS obligations when they came due in the crash. That meant many companies were holding worthless insurance, rendering their financial positions weaker. A second and graver problem was that investors were allowed to buy CDS protection on bonds they do not own. That is like buying life insurance on someone else's life, which is well known to create moral hazard problems: You have an incentive to secretly murder the insured person to collect the insurance. A similar incentive prevailed on Wall Street, so that rival banks were likely buying CDS insurance on the likes of Bear Stearns and Lehman Brothers. Those purchases sent a signal that investors thought these companies were likely to go belly up, which in turn drove up the price of their funding, creating a self-fulfilling prophecy.

A final development was simple regulatory avoidance. Effective regulations limit what companies can do, which means they are costly to companies (ineffective regulations are not costly to companies because they do not limit what companies can do). Consequently, companies have an incentive to avoid regulations to avoid restrictions and costs.

Regulatory avoidance played an important role in financial markets over the past thirty years. One instance was the emergence of the shadow banking system. Because commercial banking is regulated, lenders had an incentive to establish bank-like firms (shadow banks) that were unregulated. Rather than funding themselves with traditional deposits, shadow banking firms obtained finance via the commercial paper market, selling their paper to money market funds. This structure avoided costly regulation associated with taking deposits, and these shadow banks also escaped costly capital requirements.

Another instance was the emergence of structured investment vehicles (SIVs), such as got Citibank into trouble. To escape costly regulation, commercial banks set up unregulated subsidiaries (SIVs) that invested in mortgage-backed securities. These subsidiaries financed themselves via the commercial paper market, using the fact that they were subsidiaries of large commercial banks to access credit at preferential low rates. This arrangement enabled commercial banks to shovel MBS and CDOs into their SIVs, finance the SIV cheaply, and pocket the differential between the interest rate received on MBS and CDOs and the lower rate paid on commercial paper. However, when the price of MBS and CDOs started failing, the cost of bailing out their SIVs began to pull down the sponsoring commercial bank – which is how Citibank almost failed.

In effect, SIVs were the way in which regulated commercial banks tried to participate in the shadow banking system's profit bonanza. That participation increased the supply of mortgage financing for housing, commercial real estate lending, and consumer lending. It also exposed the entire regulated banking system to tremendous risk because the commercial banks were ultimately liable for their SIVs should anything go wrong – as eventually happened.

A final factor driving increase in the supply of finance and risk taking was changed psychology and perceptions of market participants. This squarely connects the crisis to Hyman Minsky's (1992, 1993) financial instability hypothesis. Minsky's fundamental insight was that in financial markets, success breeds excess, which breeds failure. Success drives market participants to become overconfident and also to believe that the world has changed permanently for the better, so that they can take yet more risk and make even greater profits.

Moreover, these changes in psychology and perception affect all market participants, including regulators (and economists). This is critical because it explains why market discipline tends to gradually break down. Not only are borrowers infected, but so too are lenders and regulators. That means both market discipline and regulatory discipline can weaken progressively.[3]

Periods of boom promote optimism and memory loss regarding past crashes, as well as change business culture. Regulators are also taken in by the same mechanisms. Thus, business cycle expansions often generate chatter about "the death of the business cycle." In the 1990s, the chatter was about the "new economy," of which Federal Reserve Chairman Alan Greenspan was a big supporter.[4] In the 2000s, the chatter was about the "great moderation," and Federal Reserve Chairman Ben Bernanke was a big believer in this.[5]

Moreover, there are evolutionary mechanisms that lock in proclivity to risk taking via success and promotion. Thus, managers and entrepreneurs who make profits come to dominate. Since risk takers tend to make more profit, cautious investment managers and entrepreneurs will tend to fall behind over time and the population of managers and entrepreneurs will be increasingly dominated by high rollers.[6] This process is reported by Zakaria (2008):

Boykin Curry, managing director of Eagle Capital, says "For 20 years, the DNA of nearly every financial institution had morphed dangerously. Each

---

[3] See Palley (2009b [2011a]).
[4] See Greenspan (2000).
[5] See Bernanke (2004).
[6] This mechanism has similarities with the noise-trader mechanism described by De Long et al. (1990).

time someone pressed for more leverage and more risk, the next few years proved them 'right.' These people were emboldened, they were promoted and they gained control over even more capital. Meanwhile, anyone in power who hesitated, who argued for caution, was proved 'wrong.' The cautious types were increasingly intimidated, passed over for promotion. They lost their hold on capital."

In sum, the combination of a constant stream of innovations and deregulation, changing psychology and belief, and changing business and regulatory culture created what seemed to be a perpetual-motion financial machine. The new machine supported ever-increasing asset prices and borrowing that plugged the demand shortfall created by the flawed neoliberal model of growth and global economic engagement.

On the lending side, the new machine was characterized by an increasingly elastic supply of finance driven by financial innovations, increased appetites for risk, regulatory avoidance, and removal of regulatory constraints. It was also driven by financial engineering that created a belief that risk had been permanently lowered. This belief increased enormously the willingness of investors to buy the financial assets created by lenders.

On the borrowing side, the new machine created a constantly increasing pool of supposedly creditworthy borrowers. The progressive relaxation of lending standards made more and more credit available, which drove up both house and commercial real estate prices, and higher housing prices then served as an ATM for consumer spending via home equity loans. The trend of higher house and commercial real estate prices in turn increased the attractiveness of real estate as an asset class, attracting yet more money from both investors and homeowners.

However, perpetual-motion machines do not exist in the real world or in finance. Although it ran for an awfully long time, the new system was in fact akin to a Ponzi scheme. The longer it ran, the more fragile and costly it became.

The Mechanics of the Crash

It is now time to reconstruct the mechanics of the financial crash of September 2008. These mechanics are the direct product of the system of finance that was allowed to develop in the thirty years prior to the crash. That system became increasingly corrupted and fragile with the approval of regulators and the Federal Reserve.

This observation is germane to Chairman Greenspan's challenge to his critics to show where he was wrong on decisions he made as Federal Reserve chairman.[7] His errors were not with regard to setting of interest rates. Instead, they were regarding his opposition to financial regulation and quantitative monetary policy and his strong support of the broader neoliberal economic policy paradigm. Greenspan's attitudes and misunderstanding of the state of credit markets are succinctly captured in the following quote from April 2005, just fifteen months before the house price bubble burst:

"With these advances in technology, lenders have taken advantage of credit-scoring models and other techniques for efficiently extending credit to a broader spectrum of consumers. The widespread adoption of these models has reduced the costs of evaluating the creditworthiness of borrowers, and in competitive markets, cost reductions tend to be passed through to borrowers. Where once more-marginal applicants would simply have been denied credit, lenders are now able to quite efficiently judge the risk posed by individual applicants and to price that risk appropriately. These improvements have led to rapid growth in subprime mortgage lending; indeed, today subprime mortgages account for roughly 10 percent of the number of all mortgages outstanding, up from just 1 or 2 percent in the early 1990s."[8]

Figure 5.3 describes the main ingredients that went into making the financial crisis. They were flawed incentives within the system of lending; excessive leverage among lenders; and mismatch of funding maturities among lenders.

To understand how these pieces fit together to create a financial doomsday machine, it is necessary to understand the financial business model that came to characterize the shadow banking sector and Wall Street. At the base of the model lies a system of flawed incentives whereby brokers and bankers were paid via commissions and bonuses from profits. That system of payment created an incentive to

---

[7] Interview with Kelly Evans of the *Wall Street Journal*, January 7, 2011.

[8] Greenspan, A. [2005], "Consumer Finance," Remarks at the Federal Reserve System's Fourth Annual Community Affairs Research Conference, Washington, DC, April 8. Thanks to Willem Buiter at ft.com/maverecon for the quotation.

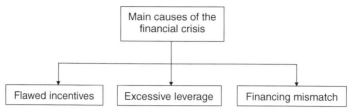

Figure 5.3. Main causes of the financial crisis.

push loans rather than engage in sound lending. That is because more transactions increased commission income and profits.

The new system of incentives was intimately tied to the development of mortgage-backed securities (MBS), CDOs, and the shadow banking system. Recall, under the old traditional banking system, banks made loans and mortgages and held on to them until they were repaid. That pattern gave banks an incentive to engage in sound lending as they bore the costs of default.

The emergence of MBS and CDOs fundamentally changed that. Now, instead of holding on to mortgages and loans, banks made loans and then sold them for bundling in MBS and CDOs. This process became known as the "originate to distribute" model. The critical feature is that profits are booked when the loan is sold. That sets up an incentive for brokers and bankers to make as many loans as possible, thereby maximizing commissions and profits. If loans subsequently sour, they are long gone from the books, having been bundled and sold as part of an MBS.

This incentive to loan push infected the whole chain of dealing beginning with real estate brokers, through mortgage brokers, insurance brokers, assessors, ratings agencies and bankers. Thus, MBS and the "originate to distribute" business model it spawned removed a critical market discipline. Borrowers are frequently overly optimistic and willing to extend themselves (especially in real estate) because they can declare bankruptcy. That places the onus on lenders to impose market discipline and make sound loans. The "originate to distribute" fundamentally undercut that market discipline all down the line, from the housing project in Las Vegas to the Lehman Brothers' board room on Seventh Avenue in Manhattan. Everyone on the lending side of the transaction had an incentive to see that the deal went through so as to collect commissions, fees, and bonuses.

The second critical failing was excessive leverage (defined as the debt-to-equity ratio) among banks, particularly the Wall Street investment banks. Equity capital is the most expensive form of capital, and return on equity (i.e., profits relative to equity) is a standard metric of bank performance. Banks, therefore, have a double incentive to keep their equity funding as low as possible, and instead to rely on debt financing. Consequently, banks instinctively pushed their debt-to-equity ratios up, and Wall Street's investment banks were given space to go even further by the SEC's 2004 net capital exemption ruling.

The critical implication is that leverage creates financial fragility. Consider a leverage ratio (debt-to-equity) of 30 to 1 so that every $31 of asset holdings is financed with $30 of debt and $1 of equity. In that case, a 3.4 percent decline in asset prices will cause $1 of losses, which entirely wipes out equity, rendering a bank insolvent. Such declines are totally within the realm of ordinary, yet Wall Street investment banks adopted extraordinary leverage ratios, with the full approval of regulators and the Federal Reserve. That explains why they were so quickly wiped out when the property bubble burst and defaults started rolling in.

The third critical ingredient was maturity mismatch of financing, particularly in the shadow banking system and Wall Street investment banks. Banking always involves a maturity mismatch in that banks take deposits that can be withdrawn on demand and they use that money to make longer-term loans. This potentially exposes banks to sudden withdrawals by depositors that they are unable to meet.

In the past, this danger gave rise to the problem of bank runs, when depositors, seeing one bank cannot meet withdrawals, start trying to withdraw from all banks.[9] The 2008 financial crisis created an analogue of the traditional bank run problem.[10] Rather than financing themselves

---

[9] For commercial banks, the bank run problem has been solved by the Federal Reserve's discount window and by deposit insurance provided by the Federal Deposit Insurance Corporation (FDIC). The discount window enables solvent banks to get cash from the Federal Reserve to meet a sudden spate of withdrawals. Banks can also borrow cash on the federal funds market – a market for lending "cash." Meanwhile, depositors at untroubled banks have no incentive to withdraw because their deposits are guaranteed by the FDIC.

[10] See Gorton, G.B. [2008], "The Panic of 2007," paper presented at "Maintaining stability in a changing financial System," a symposium sponsored by the Federal Reserve Bank of Kansas City, held in Jackson Hole, WY, August 21–23.

with deposits, the shadow banking system and Wall Street investment banks financed their activities via the commercial paper market. Thus, rather than taking small deposits, they borrowed large sums for short periods of time – usually with a maturity from thirty days to one year. They used these sums to issue mortgages or buy MBS and CDOs.

This pattern of financing created the potential for problems similar to bank runs. In the event that commercial paper market lenders lost confidence in a bank, they could refuse to roll over their financing, forcing the bank to repay its commercial paper borrowings and thereby pushing the bank into insolvency. That, in turn, exposed the whole system, because a generalized collapse of confidence could quickly develop, causing commercial paper funding to dry up for all banks – which is exactly what happened in late 2008 after the collapse of Lehman Brothers. With the shadow banks and Wall Street investment banks lacking access to the Federal Reserve's discount window and with the commercial paper market lacking an analogue of FDIC insurance, the commercial paper market completely froze as lenders lost confidence in all banks.

We are now in a position to assemble the full mechanics of the financial crisis. The sequence of events took years to play out, and one can think of the economy as being engaged in a long-running, accelerating Ponzi scheme centered on real estate. Ponzi frauds involve using the contributions of new investors to pay off generously earlier contributors, thereby making the scheme attractive to yet more investors. As with all Ponzi schemes, the crash happened extraordinarily rapidly once investors recognized there was no "there" there.

Moreover, the sequence played out in a repeated fashion, beginning with the smaller, most risky parts of the shadow banking system; then moving along the spectrum, consuming larger and larger, more recognized names; and finally consuming Wall Street's investment banks and large commercial banks like Citigroup. It was only stopped by the rescue actions of the U.S Treasury and the Federal Reserve, which essentially granted the financial system unlimited access to Treasury and Federal Reserve financing.

The basic sequence of events is described in Figure 5.4. It begins with toxic loans produced by the "originate to distribute" model of banking, with its flawed lending incentives. This first stage took years and was characterized by an accelerating buildup of toxic loans.

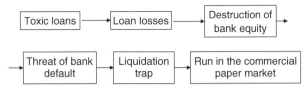

Figure 5.4. The stylized sequence of events leading to the financial crisis of 2008.

Once those loans started to default en masse, the result was the destruction of bank equity. Given their high leverage ratios, this left banks insolvent and raised the threat of default. This is also where speculation in the CDS markets kicked in because adverse speculation that signaled an increased default probability could create self-fulfilling prophecy by causing the supply of credit to a bank to vanish overnight.

The CDS market also caused additional problems through margin calls because insurers were required to post additional margin monies (i.e., collateral) as default risk rose. This created a cash squeeze, forcing asset sales that further drove down asset prices. Margin call squeezes also impacted the hedge funds that had borrowed to buy MBS and CDOs, and they impacted the stock market, as many investors had borrowed money to buy stocks.

This created a "liquidation trap" in which falling asset prices triggered margin calls, forcing more asset sales, causing yet lower prices and additional margin calls. The meltdown syndrome was then further aggravated by mark-to-market accounting rules requiring financial firms to value certain assets at market prices. That meant falling asset prices caused immediate mark-to-market losses that imperiled firms' financial standing even though the cash flows from the assets were unchanged. Furthermore, as asset prices kept falling, hedge funds reduced trading, thereby making markets thinner and raising bid-ask spreads, which increased potential losses.[11]

The final stage was a run in the commercial paper market, as lenders lost confidence in banks and refused to roll over their loans. This last stage is where the maturity mismatch of financing kicks in, because much of the shadow banking and the SIVs of commercial

---

[11] The evaporation of trading volumes is explored in Dodd, R. [2007], "Subprime: Tentacles of a Crisis," *Finance and Development*, 44 (4), December.

banks were financed with short-term borrowing that had to be constantly rolled over.

Once underway, the September 2008 financial crisis triggered a four-fecta of negative forces that stopped the economy dead in its tracks and revealed the deep weaknesses that had been papered over by the bubble. First, the financial crisis froze credit markets and eviscerated confidence, both with regard to regular business relationships and with regard to the future. Second, all the standard business cycle mechanisms immediately went into deep reverse, with asset prices, credit availability, spending, and employment all collapsing. Third, the economy was left burdened with the economic detritus of the bubble-distorted expansion. This included huge debt burdens, a tidal wave of mortgage foreclosures, an overbuilt real estate sector, and a bloated financial sector. Fourth, the economy was stripped of the credit expansion and asset price inflation mechanism that had offset the neoliberal model of growth and global economic engagement, leaving it stuck with a structurally flawed income- and demand-generating process.

Global Transmission of the Crisis

Finance also played an important role in the global transmission of the crisis, and this role was far greater than in past recessions because of financial globalization that has integrated national financial markets. Prior to the Great Recession, there had been much chatter among economists about "decoupling" – the idea that emerging markets could keep growing even if the United States slipped into recession. This would have marked a historic break because in the past, when the United States sneezed, developing countries tended to catch a cold. However, as with other ideas, decoupling turned out to be a false hypothesis. Instead, when the U.S. economy crashed, other economies started crashing in a chain reaction.

The channels of global transmission are shown in Figure 5.5. The first major channel was trade, which has always been an important international transmission channel. As the U.S. economy slowed, that reduced imports, which are other countries' exports, thereby lowering economic activity globally. However, because of reliance by many countries on export-led growth focused on the U.S. market, the trade channel was more virulent. This shows how globalization can amplify

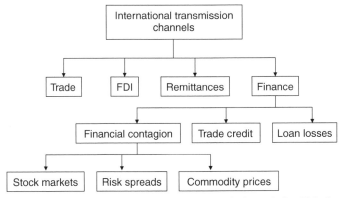

Figure 5.5. The channels of international transmission of the U.S. financial crisis.

transmission mechanisms and it explains why world trade collapsed at the fastest rate since the Great Depression of 1929.[12]

Before the crisis, the global economy was undermining the U.S. economy via the triple hemorrhage of the trade deficit, job offshoring, and investment offshoring. After the crisis, the process reversed, and contraction of the U.S. economy started undermining the global economy.

A second channel was foreign direct investment (FDI). As multinational companies saw their exports from developing countries fall, the need for investment spending aimed at expanding productive capacity in those countries was reduced.

A third channel, which was particularly important to Central America, was remittances. Over the past three decades, there has been a flood of immigration into the United States from Mexico and other Central American countries, and these immigrants send large remittances back to support families remaining there. With the increase in U.S. unemployment, these remittances shrank considerably.

The fourth channel was finance, and it has several subchannels, as shown in Figure 5.5. One subchannel was financial contagion. Thus, as the U.S. stock market fell with the collapse of confidence, other countries' stock markets started falling in tandem. The realization that the United States had been subject to a real estate bubble

---

[12] See Eichengreen, B. and K. O'Rourke [2009], "A Tale of Two Depressions," *VoxEU. org*, July 3.

made investors in Ireland and Spain realize these countries also had property bubbles.

A second contagion effect was via risk spreads, and premiums required for riskier borrowers rose dramatically. In Eastern Europe, there was effectively a sudden stop of capital flows. Iceland was the first country to go bankrupt and provided an indicator of things to come. Its banking system had become a de facto SIV that borrowed short term to finance MBS and CDO purchases. Now, it could not roll over its financing, pushing Iceland into default, and its default in turn ricocheted into the UK economy, which had been a big lender to Iceland. This reflects the chain nature of financial systems so that default by a borrower in turn puts lenders at risk.

A third contagion effect operated via commodity prices. As the bubble ran its course, more and more speculative finance started chasing commodities, causing a commodity price bubble in 2007–08, which benefited commodity exporting countries. With the financial crisis, these speculative flows reversed, causing commodity prices to tumble, now to the disadvantage of commodity exporters. Moreover, the decline was amplified by the collapse in real economic activity that put additional downward pressure on commodity prices.

Another channel whereby finance transmitted the crisis was trade credit. International trade relies on short-term credit to finance exports and imports. The freezing up of credit markets froze trade credit too, creating a financial channel that multiplied the decline in global trade.

The third and most enduring financial channel was losses on U.S. investments held by foreign banks. This channel has been especially important in Europe because European banks (particularly German, British, Belgian, and Dutch) had been big buyers of Wall Street toxic issues. In part, these purchases reflected recycling of Europe's trade surpluses, providing another channel whereby trade imbalances played into destabilizing the global economy. However, European banks also made large speculative purchases of Wall Street MBS and CDOs financed with short-term dollar borrowings. Consequently, they too were caught by the freezing of the U.S. commercial paper market, leaving them short of dollar funding. This explains why the Federal Reserve entered into massive foreign currency swap arrangements with the European Central Bank. Without that swap, Europe's banks might have defaulted on their dollar borrowings, which in turn would have brought down the U.S. banking system.

The investment losses of European banks in turn compelled European governments to bail out their banking systems. Those bailouts, in combination with budget deficits caused by recession, have in turn contributed to triggering public-sector debt crises. Once again, this illustrates the chain nature of finance. Default among private borrowers infects private lenders, and failure of private-sector financial markets can in turn imperil public-sector finances.

Ideas and Unintended Consequences

The functional role of finance in sustaining the neoliberal model is starkly clear. Yet, it would be a great mistake to think that this role was planned and intentional. Rather, it reflects the law of unintended consequences.

Neoliberal policy economists, like Alan Greenspan and Lawrence Summers, did not think the neoliberal economic model was unsustainable, nor did they think it needed finance to fill a persistent, growing demand shortfall. Instead, for reasons of true intellectual belief, self-serving ideology, or a combination of both, they believed the model would promote economic efficiency and freedom. That was the justification for both financial deregulation and the neoliberal policy mix of corporate globalization, flexible labor markets, small government, and abandonment of commitment to full employment.

Financial deregulation was justified in terms of the neoliberal theory of efficient markets. According to this theory, deregulated financial markets would increase saving and investment; improve the allocation of investment; lower transactions costs in financial markets; provide improved insurance that would stimulate productive risk taking; increase the stability of the system by increasing financial diversification and risk spreading; and improve investor portfolio opportunities, thereby making investors wealthier. This was the thinking that drove policy. However, the way it actually worked was completely different, reflecting the law of unintended consequences.

In reality, the neoliberal model of growth and global economic engagement hollowed out the economy, creating a growing demand gap. Yet, financial deregulation inadvertently created conditions in which financial markets filled the gap through debt expansion and repeated asset bubbles.

Neoliberal policy makers thus unintentionally created a mechanism that temporarily papered over the profound flaws in their growth model. This saved the model politically as it mitigated the effects of slower growth, wage stagnation, and widened income inequality. Moreover, the papering-over process lasted far longer than critics predicted because of the continuous nature and scale of deregulation and financial innovation. Every balance sheet in the country was increasingly levered with debt. That holds for households, government, the financial sector, and nonfinancial corporations. Total domestic debt to GDP had been roughly stable at 150 percent of GDP for approximately twenty-five years from 1952 to 1980. The next twenty-five years saw it rocket to 350 percent. No one could have predicted this or predicted when it would end. All that could be predicted is that when it did end, it would end badly (Palley, 1998a; Godley and Zeza, 2006).[13]

For neoliberals, the law of unintended consequences worked in both directions. At the beginning, it saved the model and preserved the economy from stagnation. At the end, it pushed the economy into the worst financial crisis and recession since the Great Depression, and now the economy confronts an even more profound and prolonged stagnation. The lesson is that ideas have consequences, and the application of false ideas is especially prone to unintended consequences.

The Paradox of Financial Reform

The financial crisis has revealed deep structural failings in the model of deregulated financial markets established over the past thirty years. Those structural failings expose the economy to grave risks of instability, and therefore need to be reformed. Given the mechanics of the crisis, the key elements of needed reform are easy to understand. The following ten-point plan (some of which has been implemented in the Dodd-Frank Wall Street Reform and Consumer Protection

---

[13] See Godley, W. and G. Zezza [2006], "Debt and Lending: A Cri de Coeur," Policy Note 2006/4, The Levy Economics Institute of Bard College; and Palley, T.I. [1998a], "Chapter 12, Recipe for a Depression" in *Plenty of Nothing: The Downsizing of the American Dream and the Case for Structural Keynesianism*, Princeton, NJ: Princeton University Press.

Act of 2010) would go a long way to remedying the problem of financial instability:

1. Financial market regulation should be comprehensive, covering all financial institutions on the basis of function (what they do) rather than form (what they call themselves). This would create a level playing field in which the shadow banking system, Wall Street investment banks, and the SIVs of commercial banks would all be subject to regulation. Regulatory avoidance should not be tolerated as a means of gaining competitive business advantage.

2. Lenders should be required to hold a "stub" ownership interest in all loans they originate. This would diminish the adverse "loan pushing" incentive that comes with MBS, CDOs, and the "originate to distribute" lending model.

3. A significant share of top management bonus pay should be in the form of long-dated stock options. This too would help remedy the adverse incentives of the "originate to distribute" model.

4. Financial firms should be subject to strict leverage limits based on higher equity capital requirements. This will help diminish insolvency risk by giving banks the capacity to withstand losses.

5. Lenders should be subject to reasonable liquidity requirements. This can diminish the risk of a run in the commercial paper market, and it is also relevant for monetary policy (about which more later).

6. The CDS market should be regulated and all CDS transactions should pass through market-clearing arrangements. This would help prevent a repeat of the AIG situation, in which the market was unaware of the extent of risk taken on by AIG, which eventually rendered AIG's insurance of no value.

7. It should be illegal for investors to purchase CDS insurance coverage on bonds they do not own. This would help prevent assassination of companies' credit standings by speculators hoping to profit from a bankruptcy.

8. As part of their capital structure, financial companies should be required to issue contingent convertible bonds (COCOs) that automatically convert into equity when existing equity is

eroded beyond a threshold by losses. This would help address the maturity mismatch problem that contributed to the run in the commercial paper market. The price of these bonds would also act as a "canary in the coal mine" by signaling in advance the riskiness of companies.

9. The Federal Reserve should abandon it exclusive reliance on interest rates for conducting monetary policy. Interest rate policy should be supplemented by a system of asset-based reserve requirements (ABRR), which consists of extending margin requirements to a wide array of assets held by financial institutions. ABRR require financial firms to hold reserves against different classes of assets, with the regulatory authority setting adjustable reserve requirements on the basis of its concerns with each asset class. That can help target specific asset bubbles and credit market malfunctions.[14]

10. There is a need for political reform that limits political contributions from financial firms. Those contributions buy political influence, and they helped drive the policies of flawed deregulation and light-touch regulation of the past thirty years. Unfortunately, this influence is also now blocking reregulation efforts of the sort described here.

Finally, consideration of reform brings up the paradox of reform. That paradox is financial reform that stabilizes the system also stands to deepen the tendency to stagnation. Recall that the neoliberal model is intrinsically prone to stagnation because of the demand shortfall it creates, which is why it needs financial exuberance to fill the gap. Effective financial reform would stabilize the system by limiting the possibilities for exuberance. However, because financial reform does nothing to remedy the underlying contradictions of the neoliberal model, this deepens the tendency to stagnation by removing the boost provided by financial exuberance. That is the financial reform paradox. Stabilizing the neoliberal model exacerbates the problem of stagnation.

---

[14] For more details about the benefits of a system of ABRR, see Palley, T.I. [2003a], "Asset Price Bubbles and the Case for Asset Based Reserve Requirements," *Challenge*, 46 (May–June), 53–72.

6

Myths and Fallacies about the Crisis

Stories about the Domestic Economy

In an unpublished draft preface to his *General Theory*, Keynes (1973, p. 470) wrote:

In economics you cannot convict your opponent of error – you can only convince him of it. And, even if you are right, you cannot convince him, if there is a defect in your powers of persuasion and exposition or if his head is already so filled with contrary notions that he cannot catch the clues to your thought which you are trying to throw at him.

For Keynes, the struggle was to persuade his contemporaries to abandon classical economics with its theory of automatic full employment that was so at odds with experience of the Great Depression. This book is about the financial crisis and the Great Recession, and the task is to expose the consequences of neoliberalism, which include the restoration of pre-Keynesian thinking.

Part of the act of persuasion is to articulate clearly and persuasively one's own interpretation of events, but part is also to show the limits of alternative hypotheses. Chapters 4 and 5 described the structural Keynesian explanation of the financial crisis and the Great Recession. The argument is that the crisis and recession were rooted in the neoliberal paradigm that spawned a flawed growth model, a flawed model of global economic engagement, and a flawed model of financial markets. Together, these three elements provide a comprehensive account of the economic history of the past thirty years. They explain developments in the real economy regarding wages and income distribution; developments in the global economy, including the emergence of global imbalances; and developments in the financial sector, including

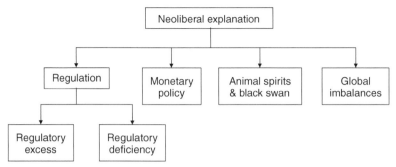

Figure 6.1. The neoliberal explanation of the financial crisis and the Great Recession.

the emergence of financial fragility. They also explain why the crisis took the form of a financial crisis, why the Great Recession has been so deep and intractable, and why the outlook is one of stagnation.

Now, it is time to address the competing explanations offered by neoliberal economists. Figure 6.1 provides a taxonomy that helps understand the orthodox approach to explaining the crisis. Whereas the structural Keynesian approach is a unified general account, the orthodox explanation is a collection of piecemeal hypotheses, some of which are mutually consistent and others of which are inconsistent.

The first hypothesis concerns regulatory failure. Hard-core Chicago School neoliberals view the failure as one of regulatory excess and excessive government intervention in financial markets. Soft-core MIT neoliberals view it as one of regulatory deficiency and failure of government to limit financial risk taking. The second hypothesis is failure of monetary policy, the argument being that the Federal Reserve pushed interest rates too low and held them there too long. The third hypothesis is animal spirits and black swans, whereby the crisis was due to a collapse of confidence combined with a surprise shock to the system that unleashed terrible unexpected consequences. The fourth explanation is that the crisis was due to global financial imbalances. This explanation, in turn, rests on several competing hypotheses about the cause of these imbalances.

Figure 6.1 highlights the difficulty of getting clean closure on debate about causes of the Great Recession. This is because many of factors identified in Figure 6.1 also play a role in structural Keynesian explanation discussed in Chapters 4 and 5. Thus, regulatory failure is an important ingredient in the process that allowed financial instability to develop. Similarly, low interest rates were critical in creating the housing price bubble that helped revive the economy after the last recession. Lastly, the U.S. trade deficit and global imbalances are part of the "triple hemorrhage" that hollowed out the U.S. economy's income- and demand-generating process.

In trying to understand the differences between the structural Keynesian and neoliberal explanations, it is worth distinguishing between "causes" and "cogs." Causes are fundamental drivers of the financial crisis and the Great Recession, whereas cogs are the mechanisms that transmitted the crisis. For instance, from a neoliberal perspective, monetary policy failure (i.e., excessively low interest rates) was a fundamental cause of the crisis. Contrastingly, from the structural Keynesian perspective, it was a cog, with the Federal Reserve being pushed to lower interest rates because the economy was unable to generate self-sustaining expansion after the recession of 2001.

This leads to a larger, more important point. From the orthodox perspective, the economic system is basically fine, and all that is needed is a patch. From the structural Keynesian perspective, the economic system is beset by fundamental failings, and it is those failings that drove policy in directions that postponed the crisis but also ultimately deepened it. A patch may stabilize the system but cannot rejuvenate it.

How should one choose between these competing perspectives? This book argues the test is that which offers the most coherent plausible explanation consistent with the historical record and the full range of developments over the past thirty years.

The Regulatory Excess Hypothesis

The regulatory excess hypothesis essentially blames government regulation and intervention in the housing market for the crisis.[1] There are a number of pieces to this argument, including tax deductibility of mortgage interest payments that encouraged a frenzied rush to home

---

[1] For a moderate statement of the regulatory failure hypothesis, see Makin, J.H. [2009], "A Government Failure, Not a Market Failure, *Commentarymagazine.com*, July/August 2009. For a more extreme statement, see Malanga, S. [2009], "Obsessive Housing Disorder," *City Journal*, 19(2), Spring, http://www.city-journal.org/2009/19_2_homeownership.html

ownership that drove up prices; the Community Reinvestment Act (CRA) that compelled banks to make unsound loans to low-income households, which both drove up home prices and caused mortgage defaults; and Fannie Mae and Freddie Mac that distorted the mortgage market through the implicit guarantee they received from the government. That guarantee supposedly created moral hazard in the wholesale credit market, as lenders to Fannie and Freddie felt they were guaranteed and therefore provided an ocean of credit that enabled Fannie and Freddie to fuel the bubble.

What's wrong with these stories? First, the mortgage interest deduction has been around for more than fifty years. It undoubtedly contributes to higher home prices and encourages U.S. households to hold more of their wealth in housing, but it is implausible to view it as the cause of the crisis because it has been around so long.

Second, the CRA was passed by Congress in 1977 and for much of the time has been viewed as largely ineffective, a feature that was sometimes touted as a reason for repeal. For instance, in 2000, the Cato Institute released a study titled "Should CRA stand for Community Redundancy Act?" The argument was that the CRA was being replaced by the subprime market.[2] Furthermore, only commercial banks and thrifts are obliged to follow CRA rules. This means nonbank lenders, who originated the bulk of subprime loans, were not subject to CRA, nor were the investment banks (Bear Stearns, Lehman Brothers, etc.) that bundled and resold these toxic mortgages as securitized loans. The CRA requires banks to lend to local communities, but it does not require they lend irresponsibly and make "No Doc NINJA" loans (no documents, no income, no job or assets).

Furthermore, huge loan losses and housing price declines have been recorded in prosperous cities such as Phoenix, Arizona; Las Vegas, Nevada; Miami, Florida; and San Diego, California. This is hard to square with the CRA being responsible for the bubble as these were not poor areas where CRA lending activity is focused. Finally, a study by the Minneapolis Federal Reserve reports that only 6 percent of higher-priced subprime loans were made by lenders covered by CRA, and these CRA loans performed similarly to other types of similar

[2] See Gunther, J.W. [2000], "Should CRA stand for Community Redundancy Act?" *Regulation* 23(3), 56–60, http://www.cato.org/pubs/regulation/regv23n3/gunther.pdfbee. My thanks to *Rortybomb* blog for this reference.

non-CRA-covered subprime loans.[3] Such facts make it impossible to believe that CRA caused the bubble.[4]

A third piece of the regulatory excess hypothesis concerns the government-sponsored enterprises (GSEs), Fannie Mae and Freddie Mac, who supposedly caused the bubble by financing it. Here is conservative economist Kevin Hasset (2008) of the American Enterprise Institute writing about this:

> The economic history books will describe this episode in simple and understandable terms: Fannie Mae and Freddie Mac exploded, and many bystanders were injured in the blast, some fatally. Fannie and Freddie did this by becoming a key enabler of the mortgage crisis. They fueled Wall Street's efforts to securitize subprime loans by becoming the primary customer of all AAA-rated subprime-mortgage pools. In addition, they held an enormous portfolio of mortgages themselves.[5]

As with the CRA story, there are significant inconsistency and overstatement problems with the Fannie Mae and Freddie Mac story. The GSEs participated in and facilitated the bubble but they did not cause it, and should instead be viewed as accessories.

First, Fannie Mae and Freddie Mac have been around more than forty years: The former was established in 1938 and the latter in 1968. Second, neither Fannie nor Freddie originated mortgages. Instead, both bought mortgages and securitized them, which means the original bad lending decisions were not theirs. Indeed, several mortgage lenders have been required to take back mortgages purchased by Fannie and Freddie on grounds that the mortgages were incorrectly originated and Fannie and Freddie were misled regarding their quality.

Third, Fannie and Freddie were late to the mortgage lending game and they were losing mortgage market share through most of the bubble. They jumped in late, after the bubble had actually peaked. That late arrival to the party explains their losses, but it also means they cannot have been the cause of the bubble.

---

[3] Bhutta, N. and G.B. Canner [2009], "Did the CRA cause the mortgage meltdown?" http://www.minneapolisfed.org/publications_papers/pub_display.cfm?id=4136, March.

[4] The impact of CRA on the bubble has been extensively analyzed by Barry Ritholz in his blog *The Big Picture*, http://www.ritholtz.com/blog/, and many of the preceding arguments are drawn from that source.

[5] Also see Calomiris, C.W. and P.J. Wallison [2008], "Blame Fannie Mae and Congress for the Credit Mess," *Wall Street Journal*, Tuesday, September 23, A.29.

Table 6.1. *Mortgage Originations, 2003–2009*

	2003	2004	2005	2006	2007	2008	2009
Conventional/ conforming share (%)	62	41	35	33	47	62	63
Total mortgage originations, $ billions	$3,945	$2,920	$3,120	$2,980	$2,430	$1,500	$1,815

Source: Conservator's report on the Enterprise' Financial Performance, Federal Housing Finance Agency, second quarter 2010.

Prior to 2005, the GSEs were not permitted to purchase nonconforming mortgages. Table 6.1 shows the rapidly declining share of nonconforming mortgages resulting from the flood of private-label mortgages, including subprime mortgages. The clear implication is that up until 2005, the housing bubble was not being funded by the GSEs, who were actually being squeezed out of the market. Indeed, that squeeze encouraged Fannie and Freddie to change their rules and buy nonconforming mortgages, which shows how Fannie and Freddie were followers of the bubble rather than causing it.

Moreover, even after they changed their rules and started buying private label nonconforming mortgages, Fannie and Freddie still lost mortgage market share. This is illustrated in Table 6.2, which shows the share of total mortgage-backed securities issued by the GSEs (Fannie and Freddie) and the Government National Mortgage Association (GNMA or Ginnie Mae). Their share collapses in 2004 under the onslaught of Wall Street private-label issues and keeps falling until 2007, when private label issuers withdrew with the end of the bubble. The implication is that the housing price bubble was fueled by Wall Street, and the GSEs played along. The subsequent recovery in Fannie and Freddie's mortgage shares after 2006 is not a case of fueling the bubble, but rather the only reason the housing market has stayed alive and avoided an even deeper and more terrible collapse.

Another piece of evidence about the non-role of Fannie Mae and Freddie Mac comes from their reported losses. The Conservator's report of August 2010 shows that 73 percent of their losses between January 1, 2008 and June 30, 2010 were attributable to their core business of guaranteeing single-family mortgages rather than their

Table 6.2. *Mortgage-Backed Security Issuance*

	2001 (%)	2002	2003	2004	2005	2006	2007	2008	2009
GSEs	67	68	70	47	41	40	58	73	72
GNMA	13	9	8	7	4	4	5	22	25
Total Agency	80	77	78	54	45	44	63	95	97

Source: Conservator's report on the Enterprise' Financial Performance, Federal Housing Finance Agency, second quarter 2010.

investment portfolios that contained their subprime holdings. Issuing these guarantees was what they were established to do and had been doing for decades, and their subprime activities are therefore not central.

Putting the pieces together, the evidence shows Fannie Mae and Freddie Mac were squeezed out of housing market finance when the bubble began. Throughout the bubble they had a declining share of the mortgage-backed security-issuance market and were significantly displaced by Wall Street. Lastly, the vast bulk of their losses were on their traditional business rather than reckless subprime purchases. Instead of causing the bubble, the evidence is consistent with a picture of Fannie Mae and Freddie Mac sitting on top of the bubble and rising with it as the bubble inflated their business. Only toward the end of the bubble in 2005 did they start departing from their mission, and that was in response to competitive pressure from Wall Street. Rather than driving housing market trends, they were following.

The final piece of evidence debunking the regulatory excess hypothesis comes from Paul Krugman who has pointed out that the real estate bubble extended far beyond the U.S. housing market and infected the entire U.S. commercial real estate market.[6] Table 6.3 shows the Case-Shiller private housing price index and the Moody's-MIT commercial real estate index from January 2000 to January 2009. The third row shows the ratio of these two indexes, which is normalized at unity in January 2000. The critical feature is that this ratio stays close to 1 throughout the period, showing how the two indexes essentially track each other. This shows that housing prices and commercial real estate prices both bubbled up together and have both fallen

[6] See Krugman, P. [2010a], "CRE-ative destruction," Conscience of a Liberal Blog, January 7, http://krugman.blogs.nytimes.com/2010/01/07/cre-ative-destruction/

Table 6.3. *U.S. Residential and Commercial Real Estate Prices*

	Jan. 2001	Jan. 2003	Jan. 2005	Jan. 2006	June 2006	Jan. 2007	Jan. 2009
Case-Shiller	100	121	157	180	184	180	130
Moody's/MIT	100	114	145	167	170	179	152
Ratio	1.00	1.06	1.08	1.08	1.08	1.01	0.86

Source: S&P/Case-Shiller national house price index and Moody's/MIT national commercial real estate price index. Normalized Jan. 2001 = 100.

together.[7] This is compelling evidence that the bubble involved much more than housing policy, the Community Reinvestment Act, and the activities of Fannie Mae and Freddie Mac because none of these were relevant for commercial real estate. Each argument of the regulatory excess hypothesis fails to stand up to scrutiny individually, and they all fail when it comes to explaining why the bubble extended into the commercial real estate market.

The reality is that the regulatory excess hypothesis is ideological and empirically unsupported. Its purpose is to blame the government. Given that it is largely invoked by Republicans, its purpose is also to blame Democrats. However, here too it fails, because Republicans controlled Congress from 1994 to 2006 and the presidency from 2000 to 2008. Consequently, Republicans had the opportunity to rein in Fannie Mae and Freddie Mac had they wanted to. In sum, there is neither economic nor political merit to the regulatory excess hypothesis, yet it has still been embraced by many economists and has become part of the political mythology about the crisis.

The Regulatory Deficiency Hypothesis

A second hypothesis is that the financial crisis was due to insufficient regulation. This is more difficult to assess because it is based on a counterfactual. Whereas the regulatory excess hypothesis involves assessment of the effects of actual regulations, the regulatory deficiency

---

[7] CRE prices have held up better than house prices during the bust. That is probably because the Federal Reserve and financial regulators have encouraged banks not to foreclose on commercial borrowers and instead engage in a process of "extend and pretend," whereby loans are extended under the pretence that the economy will eventually grow out of default.

hypothesis involves assessment of what would have happened had there been a particular set of alternative regulations.

With regard to regulatory deficiency, attention has focused on three key regulatory events – the repeal of the Glass-Steagall Act in 1999, the Commodities Futures Modernization Act of 2000, and the Securities and Exchange Commission's (SEC) 2004 net capital exemption rule. The 1999 repeal of Glass-Steagall allowed banks to become bigger by allowing them to undertake commercial and investment banking activities under one roof and by allowing commercial banks to engage in insurance activities. The Commodities Futures Modernization Act (CFMA) of 2000 exempted derivatives from regulatory oversight and allowed them to be traded off exchanges without central clearing requirements, capital requirements, or disclosure of counterparties. The Enron loophole (included in the Act at the behest of Republican Senator Phil Gramm) also exempted most over-the-counter energy and commodity trades from regulation. Lastly, the SEC's 2004 net capital exemption rule limited the amount of capital Wall Street's largest brokerage houses had to hold. This enabled the major investment banks' to double their leverage ratios (debt relative to equity), which jumped from approximately 15 to 1 in 2004 to more than 30 to 1 by 2008. Additionally, the SEC's rule allowed investment banks to adopt self-regulation in the sense that value-at-risk within banks was assessed using banks' own internal models of risk levels.

Did these regulatory measures cause the crisis? The repeal of Glass-Steagall allowed banks to bulk up in size so that their losses were ultimately larger. By combining commercial and investment bank activities, it also likely encouraged significantly more risk taking, as commercial banks increasingly adopted the practices and culture of investment banks. However, it was the shadow banks and the pure investment banks (Bear Stearns, Lehman Brothers, and Merrill Lynch) that proved the weaker links in the chain, thus it is unclear whether keeping Glass-Steagall would have made much of a difference to the events as they unfolded.

The exemptions in the CFMA allowed AIG to engage in reckless credit default swap transactions and also facilitated the oil and commodity price bubble of 2008. However, the commodity bubble came late in the game, after housing prices had peaked in mid-2006. As for AIG, its collapse came after Bear Stearns, Fannie Mae, Freddie Mac, and Lehman Brothers had already collapsed. Moreover, many of the insurance bets with AIG appear to have been side bets – that is, bets made by speculators on the sidelines, already anticipating the collapse of the housing market. This suggests that the CFMA was bad policy that amplified difficulties, but it was not the cause of the crisis.

Lastly, the April 2004 net capital rule exemption does seem to have played an important role in pulling down the investment banks by allowing them to take on vast debt-funded risks that wiped them out. However, the housing bubble was already underway by this time. Moreover, it is likely that the shadow banking system and unregulated affiliate structured investment vehicles (SIVs) of commercial banks would have been sufficient to finance the bubble without the investment banks taking on extra leverage.

The regulatory deficiency hypothesis argues that had these regulatory events not occurred, the financial crisis and the Great Recession would not have happened. The corollary proposition is that fixing financial regulation can restore prosperity, and that proposition points to the implausibility of the hypothesis.

Financial deregulation and resistance to updating financial regulation are integral elements of neoliberalism. At the philosophical level, they derive from the ideology of efficient markets. That makes it hard to imagine the three decades from 1980 to 2008 without financial deregulation and regulatory neglect.

More importantly, at the functional level, financial deregulation and regulatory neglect played a critical role in filling the gap in demand created by stagnation of wages. As shown in Chapter 4, rising debt and asset price inflation were essential for driving demand growth and sustaining the neoliberal model. Absent these engines of demand growth, the neoliberal model would have avoided a financial crash and instead stumbled into stagnation earlier. The implication is that had tough financial regulation blocked the emergence of financial fragility, it might have prevented an extreme financial crisis. However, it would have done nothing to correct the destructive effects of the neoliberal model on the income- and demand-generation process. Instead of a financial crisis plus the Great Recession, the economy would simply have hit the wall of stagnation a decade earlier.

Looking ahead, the implication is that after the fact, financial reform (of the sort implemented in the Dodd-Frank Wall Street Reform and Financial Protection Act of 2010) will not solve the problem of stagnation, and may even worsen it by removing the impulse of financial exuberance. Neoliberal policy makers are blind to this danger because their theoretical perspective denies the existence of a threat of stagnation. The thinking that got them into the problem of stagnation also obstructs them from fixing it.

That brings up the *13 Bankers* thesis of Johnson and Kwak (2010) who argue that the root cause of the crisis was the concentrated political power of finance. According to their argument, the Great Recession was purely the result of the financial crisis. The banks took on too much risk in a search for profits, and they were able to do so because of their political power, which gave them influence over regulators and politicians.

This power is now more concentrated because of bank consolidations caused by the crisis. Consequently, the banks pose an increased threat. They have become "too big to fail," which creates a moral hazard problem because banks can continue taking excessive risk, knowing they will be bailed out if things go wrong. And their political power means they are able to thwart legislation and regulation requiring them to put up more capital, which makes shareholders bear the risk of losses.

The Johnson and Kwak hypothesis is particularly attractive because of its explicit incorporation of politics and political power. However, a glass can be half-empty or half-full. Their hypothesis is half-right. Finance played a critical role in the neoliberal era, but the roots of the financial crisis and the Great Recession go deeper than excessive risk taking on Wall Street. That excess was part of a codependent relationship between financial markets and the neoliberal model of growth and global economic engagement.

The political power of finance mattered enormously, particularly with regard to financial regulation. However, that political power is part of a larger nexus of corporate power, and it was that larger nexus that drove the neoliberal policy agenda. Finance may have had the greatest influence regarding financial policy, but broader corporate power drove the overall model of growth and global engagement. Focusing only on the political power of finance misses that.

The Flawed Monetary Policy Hypothesis

A third widely presented hypothesis is that the Federal Reserve pushed interest rates too low and held them there too long, making the Fed responsible for the bubble. This argument is associated with Stanford economist John Taylor who argues had the Fed followed his so-called Taylor interest rate rule, the bubble would not have happened.[8]

According to the flawed monetary policy hypothesis, persistent low interest rates fueled the housing price bubble on both the demand and supply sides. Low interest rates attracted home buyers and also encouraged a chase for yield by lenders, which led to excessive mortgage lending. Thus, Taylor (2009) writes:

Monetary excesses were the main cause of the boom. The Fed held its target interest rate, especially in 2003–2005, well below known monetary guidelines that say what good policy should be based on historical experience. Keeping interest rates on the track that worked well in the past two decades, rather than keeping rates so low, would have prevented the boom and the bust.[9]

The Taylor rule is a policy rule for setting interest rates in response to inflation and economic growth. Figure 6.2 shows Taylor's counterfactual estimate of what interest rate should have been, and he argues that had his rule been followed, the bubble would not have happened.

Taylor's argument is riddled with problems. On one hand, it is absolutely right that had the Fed raised interest rates as Taylor suggests, the bubble probably would not have happened. Instead, the economy would likely have tumbled back into a second recession in 2003 and stagnation would have taken hold thereafter. Those who blame Federal Reserve interest rate policy want to claim that had the Fed raised interest rates, the economy would still have enjoyed the recovery it had, and it would also have avoided the bubble. That does not compute.

---

[8] Taylor, J.B. [2009], "How Government Created the Financial Crisis," *Wall Street Journal*, February 9. Taylor is an economist at Stanford University where the Economics Department is a center of neoliberal research. His argument extends beyond the Federal Reserve's interest rate policy and blames the government more generally for the crisis: "[O]ther government actions were at play: The government-sponsored enterprises Fannie Mae and Freddie Mac were encouraged to expand and buy mortgage-backed securities, including those formed with the risky subprime mortgages."

[9] Ibid.

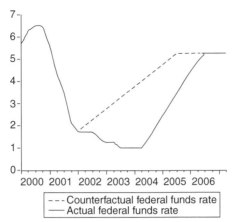

Figure 6.2. Actual versus Taylor's recommended federal funds interest rate. *Source*: Taylor (2007).

The reason the Fed pushed rates so low and held them there so long was that from 2001 to 2004, the economy was stuck in a second prolonged episode of "jobless recovery," and there were persistent fears of falling back into recession. Total employment peaked in February 2001 at 132.5 million and did not recover that level again until February 2005. Private-sector employment peaked in December 2000 at 111.7 million and did not recover that level again until May 2005. Table 6.4 shows the unemployment rate, capacity utilization rate, labor market participation rate, real GDP growth rate, and CPI inflation rate for the period between 2000 and 2005. Through to 2004, the data clearly show significant excess supply in the economy in the form of unused capacity, high unemployment, large numbers of discouraged workers who had left the labor market, and lowered the participation rate. Growth was also sluggish and had failed to rebound as usually happens after a recession. There was some modest inflation pressure, but the inflation rate was close to the Fed's target of 2 percent. Moreover, much of the inflation was attributable to the oil price spike caused by the Iraq war that began in late 2003, and oil prices received another jolt with Hurricane Katrina in 2005, which also triggered confidence fears about the U.S. economy. In sum, there is clear evidence of prolonged economic weakness that lasted until mid-2004 and warranted low interest rates to jump-start recovery and prevent a double-dip recession.

Table 6.4. *The Unemployment Rate, Capacity Utilization Rate,*
Labor Market Participation Rate, Real GDP Growth Rate,
and CPI Inflation Rate for the Period 2000–2005

	2000 (%)	2001	2002	2003	2004	2005
CPI inflation	3.4	2.8	1.6	2.3	2.7	3.4
Real GDP growth	3.7	0.8	1.6	2.5	3.6	2.9
Labor force participation rate	67.1	66.8	66.6	66.2	66.0	66.0
Unemployment rate	4.0	4.7	5.8	6.0	5.5	5.1
Capacity utilization	81.8	76.3	74.8	76.0	78.0	80.2

Source: Economic Report of the President (2009).

Taylor's (2007) counterfactual interest rate calculation is also fundamentally flawed. His estimate of what the interest rate should have been is based on actual economic data produced in part by the Federal Reserve's interest rate policy of which he is critical.

Moreover, his simulation methodology is doubtful because it uses past economic structure to simulate what an alternative economic policy might have looked like. However, the problem was that the economy was not acting as it had in the past, hence the jobless recovery despite easy monetary policy and massive fiscal stimulus.

Federal Reserve Chairman Ben Bernanke (2010b) has further rejected Taylor's claims by showing that if real-time forward-looking data (i.e., forecasts the Fed had available at the time it was setting interest rates) are used in the Taylor rule, the policy the Fed actually followed was the policy recommended by the Taylor rule.

Neither is Taylor's *ex-post* critique supported by the bond market. Table 6.5 shows the federal funds interest rate and the ten-year Treasury bond rate for the period between 2001 and 2005. The ten-year interest rate is virtually constant over this period, reflecting the fact that the market saw no danger of inflation or economic overheating. In a sense, the bond market was endorsing the Fed's policy (although some have argued that the market was distorted because of China's trade surplus – an issue that is discussed later).

This pattern of interest rates makes sense from a structural Keynesian perspective. The economy was being hollowed out by the flawed model of growth and global economic engagement, which together were creating growing demand weakness that lessened the

Table 6.5. *The Federal Funds and the Ten-Year Treasury Interest Rate, 2001–2005*

	2001	**2002**	**2003**	**2004**	**2005**
Federal funds rate	3.88%	1.67	1.13	1.35	3.22
Ten-year treasury bond rate	5.02%	4.61	4.01	4.27	4.29

Source: Economic Report of the President (2010), table B-73.

likelihood of inflation. This explains the behavior of long-term interest rates, and it also explains why conventional econometric models were unable to predict the crisis. The hollowing out of the economy meant the economic structure was changing. Consequently, econometric models could not predict events because they are estimated using historical data generated by the prior discontinued structure.

In sum, Taylor's critique amounts to playing Monday morning quarterback and his claims are not supported by the evidence. The Federal Reserve is not to blame for the bubble and it actually pursued reasonable interest rate policy given economic conditions. However, that does not mean that the explanations of Alan Greenspan and Ben Bernanke regarding the financial crisis are right. Nor does it exculpate Greenspan, Bernanke, and Federal Reserve policy makers and economists. They and other neoliberal policy makers are responsible for promoting the economic policies that created the conditions that undermined the economy and necessitated a bubble to keep it going. They pushed the neoliberal policies that undermined the economy and they blocked regulatory policy that would have helped contain financial instability.

The Yield Chasing, Animal Spirits, and Black Swan Hypotheses

Another hypothesis, which is part of the blame the Fed school, is that the Fed's low interest rate policy encouraged a chase for yield. This argument is also made by Taylor (2009):

The effects of the boom and bust were amplified by several complicating factors including the use of sub-prime and adjustable-rate mortgages, which led to excessive risk taking. There is also evidence the excessive risk taking was encouraged by the excessively low interest rates.

Low interest rates certainly explain why borrowers flocked to borrow but they do not explain why lenders failed to do due diligence. This is Alan Greenspan's conundrum, captured in his ruminations about having found a "flaw" in his theory.[10] The big insight from the chase-for-yield hypothesis is not that the Federal Reserve set interest rates too low, but rather that the neoliberal theory of efficiently functioning financial markets is a fiction.

The yield chasing story actually fits with Hyman Minsky's (1992, 1993) theory of financial markets, and not with the efficient markets theory of finance that has been used to justify financial deregulation in the United States and the global economy. According to efficient markets theory, the yield chasing argument is groundless because rational investors do not chase yield.

This leads to the ultimate neoliberal chutzpah, which is that yield chasing and market failure were the product of deregulation. Having pushed financial deregulation for forty years, neoliberals now want to argue the government is to blame for allowing deregulation. Here is Richard Posner (2009), neoconservative Chicago University law professor and federal circuit judge, writing in the *Wall Street Journal* opinion page:

The banking crash might not have occurred had banking not been progressively deregulated beginning in the 1970s.... Finally, let's place the blame where it belongs. Not on bankers, who are not responsible for assuring economic stability, but on the government who had that responsibility and failed to discharge it.

There is an old saying: All roads lead to Rome. For American conservative economists, all roads lead to government. Government is to blame if it regulates and it is to blame if it does not. That is a hard rap to beat: guilty if you did it and guilty if you did not.

The chase-for-yield hypothesis links with the animal spirits hypothesis developed by Akerlof and Shiller (2009). A surge of animal spirits caused the boom by promoting excessive optimism among both borrowers and lenders, creating a "Wile E. Coyote" economy that ran over the cliff. Once participants realized they were running in thin air, animal spirits went into reverse, creating the bust and the prospect of stagnation.

---

[10] Greenspan, A., in testimony to the House Committee on Oversight and Government Reform, October 23, 2008.

The term "animal spirits" was coined by Keynes (1936, p. 161) in his *General Theory*, and evolving animal spirits are an integral part of Minsky's theory of modern capitalism's inherent proclivity to financial instability. In principle, animal spirits can also be given an important role in neoliberal theoretical constructions of the economy – although doing so also undermines some of the claims regarding the optimality of laissez-faire markets and adds another reason for government intervention and regulation of markets. However, as an account of the crisis, the fluctuating animal spirits hypothesis is inadequate because it is like saying "gravity is responsible for plane crashes." Yes, that is true, but it is also uninteresting and unhelpful. Gravity is always present. The question is what part of the aircraft failed and why.

The animal spirits hypothesis lacks a structural account of the crisis. Animal spirits are an amplifying factor that is present at all times. However, the effect of fluctuations in animal spirits depends on the structure in which they are placed.

Viewed in that light, the animal spirits hypothesis is seductive but incomplete. Animal spirits fits with every theory, but every theory does not fit with the evidence. And the animal spirits hypothesis is of no help identifying which is the best theory because it fits with all.

A final hypothesis that resembles the animal spirits hypothesis in its abstract generality is Nassim Taleb's (2007) black swan hypothesis. Black swan events are defined as having three characteristics: they are outliers or rare events; have a large impact; and can be rationalized after the fact but are not predictable before. The crisis is described as a black swan event.

Taleb's black swan hypothesis is a paradox in that it is both extremely conservative and radically critical. As economics, it is shallow and conservative: as philosophical rumination, it is deep and radical. With regard to economics, it too easily becomes an apologetic that provides cover for existing theory and the failures of policy makers. As a philosophical rumination, it is profoundly critical of the attitudes and practices of economists and policy makers.

The economic shallowness of black swan theory stems from its framing of the world in terms of surprise rare events. This framing places it squarely within the orbit of mainstream economic theory, which also relies heavily on surprise shocks and random disturbances. These shocks are rationalized and described by mathematical probability theory, which has the additional benefit of conferring pseudoscientific legitimacy.

However, the appeal to probability theory suffers from two serious failings. First, it constitutes a form of social science mysticism in which explanation rests on a *deus ex machina*. Second, probability is not a good approach to history, which is a nonergodic process. People may talk about the probability of World War III but that is a linguistic and cultural convention. It has no basis in probability theory, which relies on an unchanging data (i.e., event) generating process. Probability theory makes good sense for analyzing games of chance like rolling of dice or picking playing cards; it makes good sense in chemistry analyzing molecular motion; but it makes little sense regarding political or economic history.

By adopting the language of probability theory black swan theory merges seamlessly with mainstream economic theory. In doing so it also provides economics with a cover that excludes the possibility the theoretical paradigm was straight plain wrong.

The reality is black swan theory is not a theory or explanation of the financial crisis and the Great Recession. Instead, it is a philosophical rumination about the limitations of knowledge, the importance of recognizing those limitations, and the implications that follow. These implications include guarding against intellectual hubris; keeping an open mind with regard to different theories; and maintaining awareness that group-think promotes conditions in which extreme events happen because people are unprepared and blind-sided.

This message about the limitations of knowledge connects black swan theory with a long tradition in the sociology of knowledge. It is also what gives black swan theory its critical dimension because mainstream economics and policy making have denied these limitations.

7

Myths and Fallacies about the Crisis

Stories about the International Economy

Another factor that is widely viewed as contributing to the financial crisis is the U.S. trade deficit and matching global financial imbalances. Chapters 4 and 5 have already shown how the trade deficit played a critical role in the structural Keynesian explanation by hollowing out of the U.S. economy, draining spending, and transmitting the crisis globally.

Mainstream accounts of the crisis also attribute an important role to global financial imbalances, but one that is very different from the structural Keynesian story. This chapter examines these accounts and shows how they are logically and empirically flawed. They survive because they serve political interests.

Changing Neoliberal Explanations of the Trade Deficit

As shown in Chapter 4, for the almost three decades between 1980 and 2007, the United States ran steadily increasing trade deficits. In 1980, the deficit was 0.9 percent of GDP; in 2007, it was 5.7 percent.

Figure 7.1 shows how the rising trade deficit has spawned three different stages of thinking among mainstream economists about the causes of the U.S. trade deficit. Stage 1 thinking (1980–2000) argued the trade deficit was due to a shortage of U.S. saving and it also argued that the deficit was cause for grave concern. Stage 2 thinking (2000–2005) argued the trade deficit was nothing to worry about and was even good for the economy. Stage 3 thinking (2005–present) argues that the U.S. trade deficit is due to excess saving among fast-growing emerging-market economies, combined with the desire to accumulate

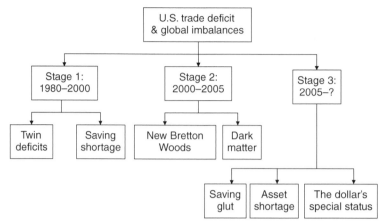

Figure 7.1. Changing explanations of the U.S. trade deficit and global financial imbalances.

dollar assets because of the dollar's special status. It too views deficits as essentially beneficial to the U.S. economy, providing U.S. financial markets are appropriately regulated. Each stage of thinking reflects the political preoccupations of the moment, which once again illustrates how economic theory is politically infused.

Stage 1: The Twin Deficits and Saving Shortage Hypotheses, 1980–2000

The first explanation of the trade deficit, which became popular in the early 1980s, is the twin deficits hypothesis that argues that the trade deficit is due to government's budget deficit. The twin deficits hypothesis is a form of saving shortage argument in which the budget deficit is the source of the shortage of saving. According to its logic, trade deficits result when government spends more than it takes in as taxes.

The twin deficit hypothesis emerged in the 1980s and is particularly associated with Harvard economist Martin Feldstein, who headed President Reagan's Council of Economic advisers. It is popular with conservatives as it provides yet another way of blaming the government, and it also makes the case for cutting government spending and shrinking government.

The twin deficit hypothesis has also been used to deflect criticism about China's mercantilist trade policies. Here is Stephen Roach (2004a), Morgan Stanley Asia's managing director, on the subject:

Yes, China accounted for the largest portion of America's $540 billion trade deficit in 2003. But this deficit was not made in Beijing – it was made in Washington. That's right – courtesy of a runaway federal budget deficit.

Moreover, despite being a pet theory of conservatives, it has become so woven into public discourse that even the liberal news media fall for it. Here is liberal columnist Nicholas Kristof (2006) writing in defense of China in the *New York Times*:

It's hypocritical of us to scream at President Hu Jintao, as we did during his visit last weekend about China's undervalued currency. Sure, that's a problem for the world economy – but not nearly as much as our own budget deficits, caused by tax cuts we could not afford.

The twin deficits hypothesis lacks plausibility and is woefully lacking in evidence. The reality is the trade deficit is the result of the international economic policies of the United States and its trading partners, combined with the state of the business cycle (spending on imports rises with income in booms and falls with income in slumps).

Despite this, the twin deficits hypothesis is difficult to refute in a cut-and-dried manner because there is a small fragment of truth in it, specifically that higher budget deficits tend to raise national income, and higher income generates some increase in imports. However, that induced effect is small and cannot begin to explain the scale of the trade deficit. At most, one could say the twin deficits are distant cousins, which is completely different from claims they are twin siblings.

As for evidence, both Germany and Japan have run persistent large trade surpluses while simultaneously running persistent large budget deficits. In the United States, the budget moved toward surplus in the late 1990s at the same time as the trade deficit was setting new record highs.

Despite its weak theoretical foundations and lack of supporting evidence, the twin deficits hypothesis refuses to die because it serves a clear political purpose. Thus, it was somewhat in abeyance at the outset of the Great Recession when fiscal stimulus was clearly needed.

However, it is now making a comeback and being enlisted to push fiscal austerity, including cutting Social Security. For instance, Martin Feldstein (2010), one of the hypothesis originators, is back to making twin deficit-styled arguments for fiscal austerity:

So, despite the rise in the household saving rate, unless federal government policies change to shrink future budget deficits, the U.S. will continue to be dependent on capital inflows from the rest of the world. If that happens, global imbalances will continue to add risk to the global economy.

He is joined in this by Fred Bergsten (2009) of the Peterson Institute for International economics, who writes:

Such massive budget deficits would almost certainly produce massive trade and current account deficits as well. The enormous government spending, along with private consumption and investment after recovery from the current crisis, would far exceed potential domestic production and drive up imports of goods and services. Financing the fiscal and external red ink would require huge capital inflows that would sharply expand our foreign debt.

The United States may or may not have a budget problem depending on the assessment of future economic growth, future tax policy, and future health care policy. However, the attempt to frame the trade deficit as a budget deficit problem is pure political polemic. The trade deficit is widely disliked by the American public for good reason as it is part of the nexus of channels that has undermined manufacturing and blue-collar prosperity. For conservatives, therefore, linking the trade deficit to the budget deficit does double duty. First, it distracts from the real cause of the trade deficit, which is corporate globalization and the United States' flawed international economic policies. Second, it promotes an antigovernment agenda. It is this politics that explains the longevity of the twin deficit hypothesis.

The Saving Shortage Hypothesis

The twin deficits hypothesis dominated the 1980s. In the mid-1990s, as the U.S. trade deficit continued growing and the budget deficit started falling, it was increasingly replaced by the saving shortage (or excess consumption) hypothesis. This latter explanation became especially popular during the stock market bubble of the late 1990s.

The leading proponent of the saving shortage hypothesis has been Wall Street economist Stephen Roach.[1] The basic claim is that the economy operates at full employment with finite capacity, and any demand in excess of this is satisfied through the trade deficit. Ergo, when Americans consume too much and save too little, it shows up through the trade deficit. The solution is simple: cut consumption and increase saving.

The saving shortage hypothesis has had much appeal. First, the rising trade deficit was accompanied by an increase in consumption as a share of GDP. Second, the saving shortage argument appeals to the puritanical streak in the American public as it blames the trade deficit on individual households and an excess of good times. Third, the argument is politically popular with conservatives as it justifies a plutocratic tax agenda aimed at increasing saving by privileging dividends, interest income, capital gains, and aimed at exempting from taxation income directed into saving accounts. Fourth, the saving shortage hypothesis has been popular with conservatives and corporations because it blames the trade deficit on households rather than U.S. policy makers' embrace of globalization.

The saving shortage hypothesis suffers from faulty logic and is inconsistent with the evidence. According to its logic, the United States has suffered from a combination of inadequate productive capacity combined with excess demand that together drove the trade deficit. That makes no sense. Over the past two decades, the United States has been systematically losing manufacturing as trade agreements such as NAFTA and China-PNTR have encouraged U.S. corporations to offshore production and investment. The problem has not been excess demand and inadequate capacity. Rather, the problem has been lack of incentives to produce in the United States. As capacity has been closed, the goods that were once produced in the United States had to be imported.

In the most recent business cycle (2000–2007), the economy was characterized for much of the time by jobless recovery, elevated unemployment, low capacity utilization, and demand shortage, all of which prompted the Federal Reserve to lower interest rates. These weak conditions are the opposite of those implied by the saving

[1] See, for example, Roach, S. [2004b], "Twin Deficits at the Flashpoint?' Morgan Stanley Global Economic Forum, August 16; and Roach, S. [2010], "Blaming China Will Not Solve America's Problem," *Financial Times*, March 29.

shortage hypothesis. Rather than being short of capacity, consuming too much and saving too little, the problem is the United States is not producing or exporting enough.

The saving shortage hypothesis also ignores the role of exchange rates in causing trade deficits. This disregard of exchange rates is equivalent to doing economics without regard to prices. The trade deficit begins with shoppers at Wal-Mart who decide to buy foreign goods rather than American-produced goods. They do so because foreign goods are cheaper than American goods, and that is where the exchange rate enters because it affects the relative price of foreign and American goods. Appreciation of the dollar makes foreign goods relatively cheaper, whereas depreciation of the dollar makes them relatively more expensive. The strong-dollar policy and China's under-valued exchange rate have together contributed to making American goods more expensive, which has increased imports, reduced exports, and also contributed to offshoring of production and investment. The saving shortage hypothesis makes no mention of this basic economics. Instead, it simply blames consumers for spending too much.

The United States could eventually find itself in a situation (and may even already be there) in which it lacks sufficient productive capacity to meet ordinary consumption needs. However, that would be due to closure of manufacturing capacity, not excess consumption and lack of saving.

In sum, the saving shortage hypothesis displays both the incoherence of mainstream economics and its trickiness. With regard to incoherence, on one hand, Americans have been repeatedly told there is a shortage of saving. On the other hand, they are repeatedly encouraged to go out and spend to avoid recession. Little surprise the public is confused. As for trickiness, sufficient downsizing of manufacturing will eventually create a situation in which the United States cannot support its normal consumption needs. This, however, has nothing to do with a saving shortage and is instead due to flawed international economic policy.

Stage 2: The New Bretton Woods and Dark Matter Hypotheses, 2000–2005

The economic triumphalism that marked the Clinton boom (1996–2000) spawned a second stage of thinking about the trade deficit. The

Clinton administration vigorously promoted corporate globalization through NAFTA, proliferation of free-trade agreements, the establishment of the WTO, the strong-dollar policy, and the establishment of permanent normal trading relations (PNTR) with China, which gave China the most-favored-nation (MFN) status regarding U.S. market access. These policies increased the trade deficit and undermined U.S. manufacturing, thereby creating the need for more benign explanations of the trade deficit that could rationalize policy makers' indifference to the deficit. This generated a second stage in thinking about the trade deficit.

The dominant stage 2 explanation was the New Bretton woods hypothesis, which argued the trade deficit posed no threat and was even to be welcomed (Dooley et al., 2003, 2004). According to the hypothesis, globalization had created a brave new world of opportunity in which emerging markets were industrializing. That industrialization was supposed to increase U.S. incomes via free trade organized around the principle of comparative advantage. However, as part of this process, emerging-market countries needed to acquire hard currency assets that supposedly provided collateral for U.S. foreign direct investment in those economies.

This situation supposedly created a parallel with the old Bretton Woods arrangement that ruled from 1945 to 1971. Back then, the United States was the dominant global economy and in the late 1950s, it started running trade deficits as the rest of the world accumulated dollar assets that were needed to finance growing global trade. Now, the United States was again running large systematic trade deficits, this time to provide collateral that could assist the industrialization of emerging-market economies. In this fashion, the new Bretton Woods hypothesis claimed to explain why the United States was running trade deficits and why the trade deficit was not bad. In effect, the United States was simply trading U.S.-produced financial assets for foreign-produced goods.

The new Bretton Woods hypothesis also purported to explain why emerging-market (EM) economies were running trade surpluses, contrary to conventional theory that predicted the reverse. According to conventional trade theory, capital should flow from capital-abundant rich countries (i.e., from the United States) to capital-scarce poor countries (i.e., to emerging markets), because rates of return are higher in capital-scarce economies. That was not happening. The new Bretton

Woods hypothesis explained this by claiming that developing countries needed to acquire collateral as surety for FDI; argued it was a good thing; and asserted it could go on for a long time.

The Dark Matter Hypothesis

A second new explanation of the trade deficit was the "dark matter" hypothesis of Hausmann and Sturzenegger (2005). Their claim was that the United States earned supernormal rates of return on its foreign investments (i.e., dark matter) and these supernormal returns meant it had nothing to worry about from running up large debts to the rest of the world via the trade deficit. As with the new Bretton Woods hypothesis, that meant the trade deficit was nothing to worry about; was of no consequence to the real economy; and could be safely ignored by policy makers.

A Partial Assessment

The twin deficits and saving shortage hypotheses represent stage 1 in mainstream thinking about the trade deficit, and became popular in the 1980s and 1990s. The new Bretton Woods and the dark matter hypotheses represent stage 2 in mainstream thinking, and became popular in the 2000s.

Both stage 1 and stage 2 thinking reflect the political economy of the period. Stage 1 corresponds to the inauguration of the neoliberal era characterized by an antigovernment tilt (hence the popularity of the twin deficits hypothesis) and the desire to shift the tax code in favor of the well-to-do (hence the popularity of the saving shortage hypothesis). Stage 2 corresponds to the era of the triumph of corporate globalization embodied in NAFTA, the WTO, and China-PNTR. Hence the popularity of the new Bretton Woods and dark matter hypotheses, which both brushed aside concerns with the trade deficit and even welcomed it.

A feature of both stage 1 and stage 2 thinking (and stage 3 too) is that neither criticize globalization, which is a touchstone of the neoliberal project. According to both stage 1 and stage 2, free trade and corporate globalization are beneficial and increase U.S. income by increasing global productive efficiency via application of the principle of comparative advantage. From a stage 1 perspective, the only problem is U.S. saving behavior. From a stage 2 perspective, there is no problem. In this fashion, both aim to inoculate corporate globalization against arguments that corporate globalization is the source of the trade deficit problem and that it is undermining the U.S. economy.

The problem with the new Bretton Woods and dark matter hypotheses is they represent the trade deficit as benign. However, now that the trade deficit and global financial imbalances are widely viewed as having contributed importantly to the crisis, the appeal of these theories has dimmed.

The problem with the saving shortage and twin deficits hypotheses is they do not fit the facts in any way, shape, or form. These are theories of excess demand, which means the U.S. economy should have seen full employment, high capacity utilization, inflationary pressures, and rising interest rates. But none of this was present. Instead, the period between 2001 and 2007 was characterized by extended jobless recovery, fear of slipping back into recession, and weak investment and employment growth – which is why the Fed kept the lid on interest rates.

Furthermore, the saving shortage and twin deficit hypotheses also argued that the trade deficit was ultimately a threat because of the danger of a dollar collapse. Their reasoning was that as foreign wealth holders accumulated ever more U.S. debt, their portfolios would eventually get saturated. At that stage, once foreigners became unwilling to acquire more U.S. debt, this was supposed to trigger a spike interest rates and the collapse of the dollar, which was how the crisis was supposed to happen. However, none of this happened.

These failings suggest that the saving shortage and twin deficit hypotheses must be discarded. Instead, they have been placed in abeyance, waiting for a political opportunity to resurface. Moreover, that opportunity is now at hand, with the conservative push for fiscal austerity.

This shows how such thinking about the trade deficit is never rejected because it supports neoliberal economic policy. Consequently, as long as the neoliberal project remains politically dominant, explanations of the trade deficit such as the twin deficits hypothesis, the saving shortage hypothesis, and the new Bretton Woods hypothesis are needed politically and will continue to resurface periodically.

Stage 3: The Saving Glut, Asset Shortage, and the Dollar's Special Status Hypotheses

Stage 2 thinking asserts that the trade deficit is of no concern. That is now viewed as wrong, necessitating another convolution of thought among mainstream economists about the U.S. trade deficit. This has produced a stage 3 thinking that centers on the saving glut hypothesis introduced by Federal Reserve Chairman Ben Bernanke (2005), which has now become doctrine and a critical part of neoliberal attempts to explain the crisis.

One country's trade deficit is, by definition, another country's trade surplus. Thus, instead of framing the global imbalance problem in terms of insufficient U.S. saving, the saving glut hypothesis reframes it as the product of excessive saving by EM economies.

With regard to the housing price bubble and the financial crisis, the argument is that EM economies (particularly China) increased their exports through export-led growth, ran large trade surpluses (saving), and then used those surpluses to buy U.S. bonds, thereby lowering U.S. interest rates and giving rise to the bubble.

The saving glut hypothesis is a brilliant piece of bait-and-switch political economy. It occupies the same space as the Keynesian critique by identifying the trade deficit as a problem, but it does so with an entirely different logic. However, close inspection reveals that its economic logic is faulty and it does not fit the facts.

Regarding its bait-and-switch aspect, to untrained eyes, framing the debate as a "saving glut" makes it looks as if the trade deficit problem is one of demand shortage, which causes unemployment. However, the saving glut hypothesis says nothing of the sort. Instead, it claims the trade deficit lowers interest rates, creating excess demand and asset bubbles. As regards globalization, the saving glut hypothesis sees it as good for efficiency (once again via the channel of trade), raising income, and causing no demand problem. As with stage 1 and stage 2 explanations of the trade deficit, the saving glut hypothesis therefore continues to defend corporate globalization against charges that it has undermined the U.S. economy and is a principal cause of the trade deficit.

The saving glut hypothesis is essentially a purely "financial" theory. Even though couched in the language of trade and export-led growth, its focus is on interest rates, not on offshoring and factory closures. In principle, the saving glut (i.e., foreign trade surplus and U.S. trade deficit) is even a good thing for the U.S. economy as foreigners are supplying saving on the cheap. Problems only arise if the U.S. uses those savings badly, so that according to the saving glut story, the real problem was U.S. financial markets and not the trade deficit.

Compare this with the Keynesian critique (see Chapter 4), which views globalization as hollowing out the productive structure of the economy, undermining income distribution, and creating a global shortage of demand. This is an entirely different logic that reveals how the saving glut hypothesis masquerades as Keynesian economics.

Analytically, the saving glut hypothesis is an updated global version of 1930s' pre-Keynesian loanable funds interest rate theory that Keynes discredited in his *General Theory*. Loanable funds theory claims interest rates are determined by demand and supply of saving. Because trade surpluses are accounted for as saving, they affect interest rates in an integrated global economy: hence, the claim that China's trade surplus significantly determines U.S. interest rates.

How does that happen? Whereas it is easy to see how a decision to export by a Chinese firm may lower goods prices and cause unemployment by displacing U.S. jobs (the Keynesian channel), it is difficult to see how the only effect of Chinese exports is to lower U.S. real interest rates and cause a boom (the saving glut channel). At its core, the saving glut hypothesis is based on the fiction that there is such a thing as a "loanable funds" market. According to this fiction, China hands its exports over to U.S. consumers in return for bonds, and because China wants to export a lot, it has to accept a low interest rate on the bonds.

The reality is the trade deficit involves a sequence of transactions beginning with an exchange of money for exports, followed by a second exchange of money for bonds. When one follows that sequence, it becomes clear that China is not the determining force behind U.S. interest rates. There is a very simple reason for this. China can only influence U.S. interest rates by first acquiring dollars to buy bonds. But China cannot create dollars. That is something which only happens within the U.S. economy with the cooperation of the Federal Reserve.

The first step is, therefore, the creation of dollar balances within the U.S. economy via the lending activities of U.S. banks to U.S. consumers.

The second step is the spending of those dollar balances by U.S. consumers on Chinese goods, which puts the dollars in China's hands. This is why the undervalued exchange rate is so important because it makes Chinese goods cheap compared to U.S. goods, thereby diverting spending to Chinese goods. The third step is, after the trade surplus has been created by the undervalued exchange rate, China enters the bond market and reinvests its trade surplus.

This is a very different story from the saving glut hypothesis. The initial lending by U.S. banks and the exchange rate are the critical factors, not Chinese saving. By conflating saving with the exchange rate, Chairman Bernanke sounds like Humpty Dumpty in Lewis Caroll's *Through the Looking Glass*: "When I use a word it means just what I choose it to mean."

One difficulty in overcoming the saving glut hypothesis is unwillingness of economists to carefully think through the process of trade deficit creation. A second difficulty is that China has affected U.S. interests, but not in the way the saving glut hypothesis claims. However, this creates a confusing similarity that provides the saving glut hypothesis with cover.

The main channel of influence on U.S. interest rates has been the flood of Chinese exports, which weakened U.S. manufacturing and the domestic economy. That caused the Federal Reserve to lower rates to ward off a double-dip recession in 2001–04. This is the Keynesian channel (the trade deficit caused economic weakness to which monetary policy responded) and it is completely different from Chairman Bernanke's saving glut story (China and other emerging-market economies pumped up the bond market).

A subsidiary channel is that China may have affected the structure of relative interest rates. This is because China predominantly bought safer government bonds. That shifted money toward these safer assets, lowering their interest rate relative to other rates. In this fashion, China has helped finance the U.S. budget deficit via its portfolio choices. However, balanced against this, China also helped cause the budget deficit by undermining jobs, wages, and tax receipts, so that the net effect is a wash.

Lastly, now that China has accumulated almost a trillion dollars of U.S. bonds, it can also affect U.S. interest rates by dumping those bonds. However, this power has been accumulated because U.S. policy

Table 7.1. *Decomposition by Firm Ownership
Structure of Chinese Exports in 2005*

	All Firms	**Foreign-Owned**	**Joint Ventures**	**Private Domestic**	**State-Owned**
Exports	100%	50.4	26.3	13.1	10.3

Source: Manova and Zhang (2008).

makers permitted China to run persistent large trade surpluses, and it has nothing to do with Bernanke's (2005) saving glut hypothesis.

The saving glut hypothesis misunderstands the macroeconomics of the trade deficit, emphasizing "after the fact" saving (China's trade surplus) rather than the undervalued exchange rate that causes the surplus in the first place. It also misunderstands the microeconomics by misrepresenting the nature of Chinese exports, which are misleadingly labeled "Chinese savings." Table 7.1 shows the vast bulk of Chinese exports are produced by foreign multinationals. Fifty percent of Chinese exports are produced by fully owned foreign subsidiaries, and another 26 percent of exports are produced by joint ventures involving foreign corporations. When viewed in this microeconomic light, it becomes clear that the issue is not about saving (as normally understood) but about globalization and international economic policy.

The U.S. trade deficit and China's trade surplus are joint products of neoliberal globalization. China's massive exports and trade surplus reflect the fact that multinational corporations have set up shop in China to create export production platforms that take advantage of China's cheap labor and lax standards. The true drivers of China's trade surplus and the U.S. trade deficit are a combination of forces consisting of U.S. international economic policy, offshoring by multinational corporations, and China's undervalued exchange rate policy.

Not only does the saving glut hypothesis neglect exchange rates and corporate globalization; it also suffers from a number of smaller inconsistencies. First, according to its logic, countries (like Germany and Japan) are saving because they have aging populations that are preparing for retirement. However, the United States also matches that demographic pattern, so it too should have run the surpluses. Furthermore, EM economies (including China) should have run deficits because of their younger demographic. Yet, the opposite occurred: the United States ran massive deficits and the EM economies ran massive surpluses.

Second, the saving glut hypothesis fails to explain why the United States was singled out. Just suppose for a moment that the hypothesis were true. In that case, all industrialized economies ought to have run huge trade deficits and had huge bubbles, yet that did not happen in the rest of the world (e.g., Germany and Japan).[2]

Third, the low interest rates supposedly induced by the saving glut should have spurred an investment boom in the United States, but that too did not happen, as shown in Chapter 4 (see Table 4.15). Instead, there was only a housing bubble.

Fourth and finally, not only has the saving glut hypothesis contributed to misunderstanding China's role in the crisis; it has also hampered dealing with China. By claiming that China sets U.S. interest rates, the saving glut hypothesis has encouraged the fiction that the United States needs China. That fiction has been very costly in the public policy debate over the past decade as it was used to justify inaction against China's exchange rate manipulation on grounds that the United States could not afford to antagonize China. Quantitative easing (the massive program of bond buying) by the Federal Reserve has now revealed the lie by showing the United States can finance its deficit by having the Fed by bonds, but a lot of damage has already been done because of this lie.

In terms of economics, proof is difficult, but the signature of events fits the Keynesian story. The saving glut hypothesis is built on incoherent macroeconomics, incoherent microeconomics, and does not fit the facts. Contrast it with the simple clear logic of the structural Keynesian argument. Export-led growth based on corporate globalization and undervalued exchange rates in EM economies poached demand from U.S. producers and contributed to massive trade deficits, factory closures, reduced investment spending, unemployment, and generally weak economic conditions. These conditions caused the Federal Reserve to lower its policy interest rate, thereby lowering market interest rates. These conditions also caused lower inflation

---

[2] Only Ireland and Spain had similar bubbles and that was due to the special circumstance of their joining the euro, which enormously lowered their interest rates to levels close to that of Germany.

expectations and expectations of future economic weakness, which further lowered long-term interest rates in bond markets.

The structural Keynesian hypothesis also explains why interest rates were low globally. Neoliberalism has been a global economic policy supported by a global consensus in the mainstream economics profession. Its policies have been adopted in the United States and Europe, while the World Bank and the IMF have pushed it on developing countries. This explains why income inequality widened globally (Milanovic, 2007). The combination of domestic application of neoliberal policies, corporate globalization, and export-led growth by EM economies created global demand shortage. That prompted central banks around the world to lower interest rates in various degrees in an attempt to head off depression conditions created by their own economic ideology.[3]

Why is the saving glut hypothesis so popular if it is so clearly wrong? There is a simple reason. The stage 1 saving shortage hypothesis is implausible at a time of massive unemployment, whereas stage 2 hypotheses, which claim the trade deficit and global imbalances are benign and inconsequential, are also implausible. That has created the need for another explanation, and the saving glut hypothesis fills the gap. It identifies the deficit as a problem and cleverly confuses debate by using the language of Keynesian economics, but avoids fingering the role of neoliberal globalization and multinational corporations in creating the deficit.

The use of the language of "saving gluts" is a case of bait and switch. It conjures up Keynesian arguments of demand shortage but in fact has nothing to with Keynesian arguments and policy recommendations. Indeed, rather than suffering from China's predatory exchange rate policies, the saving glut story would say that the U.S. economy benefitted from it. That is because when foreign countries subsidize their exports, via undervalued exchange rates or other means, those countries are effectively giving a gift (a "free lunch") by selling below cost.

---

[3] Former Federal Reserve Chairman Alan Greenspan has tried to use this global pattern of low interest rates to defend himself. The reality is that it is further evidence condemning the economic theory and policies he peddled as Federal Reserve chairman. See Greenspan, A. [2008], "Alan Greenspan: A Response to My Critics," ft.com/economists forum, April 6, http://blogs.ft.com/economistsforum/2008/04/alan-greenspan-a-response-to-my-critics/

The ability to confuse the debate makes the saving glut hypothesis brilliant political economy propaganda, but it is lousy economics. That it is so widely believed by economists is a statement about the state of modern economics.

The Asset Shortage Hypothesis

The saving glut theory has become the backbone of stage 3 accounts about the role of global imbalances in the crisis. The argument is that the housing price bubble and subsequent bust were caused by low U.S. interest rates, which were in turn caused by foreign countries' trade surpluses. In this fashion, the saving glut theory implicitly relieves the Federal Reserve and U.S. policy makers of any responsibility, which helps explain why former Federal Reserve Chairman Alan Greenspan has also endorsed the argument.

The saving glut hypothesis has now been further elaborated with an eye to explaining the asset price bubble. MIT economist Ricardo Caballero (2006, 2007) introduces the idea that the world economy has been suffering from a financial asset shortage. Consequently, the increase in demand for assets from EM economies, combined with a shortage of quality assets, has driven up asset prices and contributed to repeated asset bubbles.

To explain why the EM economies wanted to accumulate assets, Caballero's invokes the new Bretton Woods Hypothesis and argues that they wanted "hard currency" assets as collateral for their development. Additionally, to explain why the asset price bubble was largely restricted to the United States, he argues that EM economies are good at growing production and real saving but they lack high-quality financial institutions and financial markets that can supply financial assets. Consequently, their saving flowed disproportionately to the United States, driving up U.S. asset prices. Columbia University economist Guillermo Calvo (2009) has sought to further elaborate the asset shortage story by arguing that demand for assets combined with lax regulation led to the creation of poor-quality financial assets to satisfy this demand.

Putting the pieces together yields a compound hypothesis that is a mix of the regulatory deficiency, new Bretton Woods, saving glut, and asset shortage hypotheses. Not only does this compound hypothesis suffer from all the flaws and failings already identified; the asset shortage hypothesis introduces a host of additional problems.

Table 7.2. *Growth of Supply of U.S. Financial Assets*

	1980–1990	**1990–2000**	**2000–2007**	**1980–2007**
Nominal GDP (%)	108	72	41	405
NYSE composite index (%)	169	251	42	1,240
Nonfinancial sector debt (%)	174	68	75	702
Privately held Federal debt (%)	297	34	47	683

Source: Author's calculations using data from the Economic Report of the President (2010).

First, despite the claim that assets are accumulated as collateral, there is no evidence of countries like China pledging their billions of dollars as collateral. Second, the asset shortage hypothesis does not fit the evidence of the past thirty years. As shown in Table 7.2, a cursory look at the data shows there is no evidence of a financial asset shortage as the supply of financial assets has grown far faster than GDP. During this period, U.S. financial assets, measured by the Dow Jones index and nonfinancial sector debt, were growing far faster than GDP.

Moreover, Table 7.2 table shows the supply of financial assets was surging long before EM economies started running huge trade surpluses. The 1980s witnessed a stock market boom and leverage buyout bubble. The 1990s saw another stock market boom, the Internet bubble, and the beginning of the housing bubble. These were domestically driven events unconnected to the global financial imbalances that emerged later.

Indeed, during the 1990s, many EM countries were actually running trade deficits, which contributed to the raft of financial crises that hit EM economies between 1997 and 2001. During this period, EM economies were therefore suppliers of financial assets via their borrowing to finance their trade deficits, and through the wave of privatizations pushed by the IMF and World Bank.

Most importantly, there are far simpler explanations of the asset price bubble than the convoluted asset shortage story.[4] It is trivially obvious that asset prices went up because of changes in demand and

---

[4] See Palley, T.I. [2007b], "World Asset Prices: What's Really Going On?" January 1, http://www.thomaspalley.com/?p=61

supply, but the factors behind this change were not those identified in the asset shortage hypothesis. Here is a list of alternative factors:

1. Increased income inequality increased asset prices because the rich save more and buy more financial assets.
2. The increase in the profit share increased the fundamental value of assets.
3. Lower taxes on profits and the incomes of the rich increased both the fundamental value of assets and increased the asset-purchasing power of the rich.
4. Lower central bank interest rates to combat the weak state of global demand increased the discounted value of future profits, justifying higher asset prices.
5. Credit market innovations increased the supply of debt and allowable leverage, thereby increasing the supply of money chasing the existing pool of assets.
6. Aging baby boom populations in the industrialized countries increased retirement saving, thereby increasing demand for assets.
7. Finally, good old-fashioned investor mania contributed to higher asset prices, and nowhere is that more evident than the U.S. housing bubble.

These arguments provide a simple commonsense explanation of both credit and asset price developments over the past twenty years. If the principle of Occam's razor (simpler theories are better than complicated ones) applied, the asset shortage theory would never have seen the light of day.

Why the popularity of the outlandish asset shortage hypothesis? The answer is that it too defends neoliberalism. Like the saving glut hypothesis, it maintains that globalization is a good thing; the U.S. trade deficits are a natural outcome of asset shortages and is not troublesome; and asset bubbles are not only no cause for concern; they are a good thing that should be left alone because they increase the supply of assets and promote development.

The Dollar's Special Status Hypothesis

A final hypothesis is that the special status of the dollar caused the crisis. The argument begins with the observation that the dollar is the world's number one reserve currency. It then argues that the 1997 East Asian financial crisis showed countries the cost of being exposed to sudden capital flight and shortage of foreign currency reserves. Countries therefore embarked on a process of reserve acquisition by running large trade surpluses fueled by undervalued exchange rates. In effect, they built up large dollar holdings to provide insurance against future capital flight. The flip side of this dollar accumulation was large trade deficits with the United States.

This hypothesis has been advanced by Jorg Bibow (2008) of the Levy Institute, who writes:

The hypothesis put forward here is that systematic deficiencies in the international monetary and financial order have been the root cause behind today's situation. Furthermore, it is argued that the United States' position as issuer of the world's premiere reserve currency and supremacy in global finance explain the related conundrum of a positive income balance despite a negative international investment position.

It is also supported by IMF economists Lago, Duttagupta, and Goyal (2009):

The global crisis resurrected deep-rooted concerns about the functioning of the international monetary system. Despite its relative stability, the current "non-system" has the inherent weakness of a set-up with a dominant country-issued reserve currency, wherein the reserve issuer runs fiscal and external deficits to meet growing world demand for reserve assets and where there is no ready mechanism forcing surplus or reserve-issuing countries to adjust. The problem has amplified in recent years in line with a sharp rise in the demand for reserves, reflecting in part emerging markets' tendency to self-insure against costly capital account crises.

This line of argument ties back to the work of Robert Triffin (1961, 1968) who argued that the United States ran trade deficit in the 1960s for the same reason, namely to supply net dollar assets to the rest of the world.

The dollar reserve shortage hypothesis has a grain of truth but it is also very misleading. The East Asian economies were victimized by capital flight in 1997, which likely increased the demand among their central banks for international reserves to protect against future capital flight. However, over the last decade, they have accumulated foreign reserves far in excess of what can be justified in terms of financial precaution.

The sequence of developments is better understood as follows. The 1997 East Asian financial crisis produced massive exchange rate depreciations that were explicitly endorsed by the Clinton administration's strong-dollar policy. These depreciations spurred East Asian export growth, helping those economies recover from the crisis, and they occurred just as the United States was beginning its ten-year consumption spending boom fueled by domestic debt and the housing price bubble.

In effect, the East Asian economies stumbled onto a growth model that was highly effective given the U.S. consumption boom and U.S. international economic policy. They therefore stuck with the model because it worked so well, and not because they needed additional foreign reserves. In fact, for years their reserve holdings have far exceeded anything that can be economically rationalized.

It is also noteworthy that China, which has been the single largest contributor to the global imbalances, has also followed this growth strategy even though it was unaffected by the financial crisis of 1997 because of its capital controls.[5] This clearly shows that it is the desire for export-led growth via undervalued exchange rates that is the real cause of the imbalance problem rather than the dollar's special status and the need for international reserves.

Finally, the preference for dollar accumulation rather than accumulation of euro or yen also confirms that the intentional pursuit of export-led growth is the real issue. The reason the dollar is so special is because the United States is the world's largest consumer market and the U.S. consumer has played the role of "buyer of first and last resort." Countries have therefore acquired dollar assets because they want trade surpluses with the United States. That requires them to buy and hold dollars to maintain their undervalued exchange rates vis-à-vis the dollar.

This explanation of dollar reserve accumulation can be labeled the "buyer of last resort" theory of reserve currencies (Palley, 2006d). Put bluntly, the tribute other countries pay the United States through their trade surpluses is the result of their failure to generate adequate consumption spending in their own markets, be it due to poor income

---

[5] Moreover, China's undervalued exchange rate has amplified the imbalance problem by compelling other East Asian economies to undervalue their exchange rates so as to remain internationally competitive vis-à-vis China.

distribution or bad domestic economic policies. This forces them to rely on the American consumer.

Ironically, America's dispensation from trade deficit discipline stems from other countries' failure to develop an equivalent of the American consumer. Countries want to industrialize with full employment, but they lack adequate internal demand. Consequently, they must rely on the U.S. market. That is why Germany supplies BMWs and Mercedes-Benzes in return for paper dollar IOUs.

Seen in this light, it becomes clear that arguments about the dollar's special status are a fig leaf that gives countries cover for pursuing export-led growth. Arguments about reserve shortages and the dollar's special status are a major distraction. In today's world, there is no shortage of dollar reserves. The world is awash with dollars, and countries have easy access to dollar credits (both short and long term) via international capital markets.

Focusing on the dollar and precautionary reserve accumulation by EM economies (so-called self-insurance) misdirects attention away from the fundamental problem of intentional export-led growth strategies based on undervalued exchange rates that are the real source of global imbalances (Palley, 2006c). What is needed is global exchange rate management that prevents excessive trade imbalances, combined with sensible capital controls that protect against capital flight. That is a very different story from one that focuses on the special reserve status of the dollar as the source of the problem.

The New Neoliberal Consensus: Gato Pardo Economics

The collection of hypotheses described in Chapter 6 and this chapter are now being collated into a new neoliberal consensus about the crisis. This new consensus is described by Raghuram Rajan (2010), former IMF chief economist, in his book *Fault Lines*. The new consensus explanation of the crisis is illustrated in Figure 7.2 and involves three principal channels of causation.

The first channel is via global imbalances. These imbalances are attributed to East Asian governments looking to accumulate reserves after the crisis of 1997, which shifted their export-oriented economies into export overdrive. That created a global saving glut, which in turn impacted the United States by lowering interest rates.

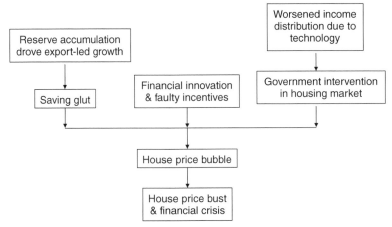

Figure 7.2. The new neoliberal consensus on the causes of the crisis.

The second channel of causation is via financial innovation and faulty incentives in financial markets. Financial innovation has increased the supply of risky financial assets that carry high returns. Faulty incentives then encouraged bankers, brokers, and dealers to take on massive amounts of risk as they were paid up front via commissions and bonuses that were unconnected to ultimate outcomes. The result was that they took on excessive risk, knowing they had nothing on the line as they would be paid before the true worth of their investment decisions was revealed.

The third channel of causation, which is the main innovation in Rajan's (2010) story, is to add income distribution. The story is that technological innovation caused a worsening of income distribution by increasing pay of higher-educated persons and lowering pay of less-educated blue-collar workers such as union members. The deterioration in income distribution prompted political intervention in the housing market aimed at making housing more affordable – a "let them eat credit" strategy. This argument has also been made earlier by Milanovic (2009).

The three channels together then produced the housing bubble, and the rest is history. The solution is threefold: (1) try and persuade China and other EM economies to desist from export-led growth and shift to more domestic demand-led growth; (2) discourage excessive risk taking in financial markets by removing government guarantees, reforming incentive arrangements that encourage excessive risk taking, and monitoring for excessive risk buildup and risk concentration; (3) invest in education to improve the quality of "human capital" and get rid of government intervention in the housing market.

What is wrong with the new neoliberal consensus? With regard to the reserve accumulation and the saving glut piece of the story, this chapter has already described the theoretical and empirical failings. The claim that the only effects of globalization and the trade deficit are to lower U.S. interest rates is bad theory, implausible, and inconsistent with the evidence. U.S. interest rates are not set in Beijing. Had the Federal Reserve imposed higher interest rates, it would only have avoided the housing price bubble at the cost of an earlier onset of stagnation that was the inevitable outcome of the neoliberal economic model (as described in Chapter 4).

Compare the reserve accumulation – saving glut hypothesis with the structural Keynesian hypothesis that argues that flawed U.S. international economic policy encouraged offshoring by U.S. corporations and export-led growth by foreign countries. Together, that created a triple hemorrhage of leakage of spending out of the economy via imports, offshoring of production and employment, and diversion of investment offshore. This lowered employment, undermined wages, and widened income inequality, thereby creating weak demand conditions that needed low interest rates as an offset.

With regard to the financial innovation–faulty incentives component, the story is broadly sensible, but it is also an inadequate description of the problem for several reasons. Neoliberal economists retain an "efficient markets" conception of the financial system, so that any problem must be due to a "market failure" (e.g., faulty incentives) or wrong-headed government intervention (e.g., guarantees or too-big-to-fail rules). The new neoliberal consensus aims to maintain this ideology, which has prevailed for thirty years. That is the fundamental difference from the Minskyian account of the financial dimension of the crisis described in Chapter 5.

According to Minsky's theory, financial markets are genetically prone to instability that accumulates gradually over time (Palley, 2009b, 2011). This Minskyian logic connects with Alan Greenspan's problem of having discovered a "flaw" in his theory. The fact that market discipline by lenders and shareholders failed so comprehensively is powerful evidence exposing the fiction of efficient markets. Addressing financial markets' inherent proclivity to instability requires systematic ongoing regulation, accompanied by permanent skepticism about finance. That is what the new consensus seeks to avoid, hence its continuous attempts to blame government for the crisis.

The third component of the new consensus is income distribution that spurred disastrous housing market intervention. According to the new consensus, there is nothing wrong with labor markets, which are working exactly as they should. It is just unfortunate that technological developments mean labor markets have produced inequality. As far as the new neoliberal consensus is concerned, there was no economic problem with labor markets and income distribution, only a political one. The economic problem only arose when government intervened in the housing market to try and ameliorate worsened income distribution.

This argument is totally unpersuasive. The claim that technology and lack of education caused worsened income distribution is a favorite neoliberal argument as it removes responsibility from policy makers and blames the victims. It says nothing about the changed bargaining power between workers and corporations; the decline of unions; globalization and the threat of job offshoring; and erosion of the minimum wage, the social safety net, and worker rights and protections.

Moreover, according to Rajan, the only effect of worsened income distribution was to provoke populist meddling. There were no effects regarding creating a shortage of demand, which is part of the Keynesian account of income distribution.

The claim that politicians' intervention in the housing market caused the crisis is also implausible. Chapter 6 showed the evidence does not support this argument. The Community Reinvestment Act was passed in 1977; Fannie Mae was established in 1938; Freddie Mac was established in 1968; and the mortgage interest deduction has been part of the tax code for more than fifty years. There may be good reasons to reform these features, but it is impossible to argue they caused the crisis.

Indeed, all the significant political interventions in financial markets in the decade preceding the crisis were on behalf of rich powerful financial interests – including the repeal of the Glass-Steagall Act in 1999, the obstruction of derivatives market reform in 1998, the Enron loophole in the Commodities Futures Modernization Act, which enabled commodity speculation, and the SEC's net capital rule of 2004, which permitted massively increased leverage for Wall Street's investment banks. That is the exact opposite of the political story told by Rajan in his new consensus fable.

The new neoliberal consensus story is brilliant political polemic that captures the language of Keynesianism while having zero Keynesian content. Thus, it talks of export-led growth and a saving glut, but this has nothing to do with globalization producing global demand shortage, wage erosion, and job loss. Instead, it is about globalization producing lower interest rates that should spur demand and investment.

It talks of financial excess, but this has nothing to do with financial markets' fundamental proclivity to speculation and instability. Instead, it is about technical incentive design failures and government interventions that supposedly promoted excessive risk taking.

Lastly, it talks about deteriorated income distribution, but this has nothing to do with the changed bargaining power and the creation of a demand gap that was filled by borrowing. Instead, it is about prompting political intervention in the housing market that causes the crisis.

Rajan's account of the crisis is "Gato Pardo" economics. *Il Gato Pardo* is a sweeping movie about social tumult in Sicily in the 1860s. The wily Prince of Salina and his nephew Tancredi are intent on preserving the existing class order, and as the crisis grows, Tancredi declares "Things must change if they are to remain the same." And they do, so that after the revolution, the old aristocracy remains in charge, allied by marriage to the new urban elite. The new neoliberal consensus aims to do exactly the same: offer the pretense of change while keeping things exactly as before.

Globalization remains unambiguously good, and policy should continue full steam ahead with the current model. Financial markets operate in accordance with the efficient markets hypothesis, and the challenge is to prevent government-induced distortions. Labor markets produce economically efficient distributions of income, and there are no concerns about bargaining power that need remedy. All that is needed is more education for the masses – but of course even that cannot be funded because of the adverse supply-side incentive effects of higher taxes, the threat of a government debt crisis, and the threat of trade deficits due to twin deficits.

Conclusion: Theory on the Fly

Chapters 6 and 7 have been long and difficult chapters that explore the plethora of hypotheses invented to explain the crisis. Crisis explanation has become a cottage industry among neoliberal economists because how the crisis is explained is of critical importance as it will influence what happens next. If neoliberalism is to remain the dominant frame for economic theory and policy, there is a need for an explanation that exculpates it.

Chapters 6 and 7 showed that neoliberal explanations do not add up in terms of theoretical coherence or consistency with the evidence. However, the sheer number of hypotheses makes the task of exposing this failing difficult.

The plethora of hypotheses also illustrates a feature of neoliberal economics that can be termed "theory on the fly." Every time there is a new observation requiring explanation, up pops a new theory that is accepted without regard to whether it fits the larger body of evidence.

This process of theory on the fly has parallels with Ptolemaic astronomy. Every time an observation appeared that was inconsistent with the Ptolemaic geocentric universe, another planetary epicycle was added to explain away the anomaly. Metaphorically speaking, neoliberal economists are now adding new epicycles to defend their Ptolemaic model of the economy. This process is reminiscent of Keynes's (1931) remarks about Hayek's book, *Prices and Production*, in which Hayek sought to explain the Great Depression:

This book, as it stands, seems to me to be one of the most frightful muddles I ever read.... And yet it remains a book of some interest, which is likely to leave its mark on the mind of the reader. It is an extraordinary example of how, starting with a mistake, a remorseless logician can end up in bedlam.

The same can be said of the new neoliberal consensus about the crisis.

The great challenge is how to get other theories on the table. The problem is not that there are no other theories; it is that they are excluded from the room. That leads to concerns about the sociology of the economics profession – a subject that is taken up in Chapter 11.

PART II

AVOIDING THE GREAT STAGNATION

8

The Coming Great Stagnation

The first half of this book has been backward looking, analyzing the causes of the financial crash of 2008 and the Great Recession. It is now time to look forward, and unfortunately the prognosis is not good.

The reason for this gloomy outlook is that the U.S. and global economies are beset by weakness and contradiction resulting from thirty years of neoliberal economic policy domination. However, the economy is not preordained, so that it is possible to change the outlook. The underlying problem is the neoliberal paradigm that has ruled policy making for the past three decades. The challenge is to replace that paradigm with a structural Keynesian paradigm that rebuilds a stable income- and demand-generating process that restores shared prosperity.

Economic policy is going to be absolutely critical. If policy makers get policy right, it will be possible to construct a prosperous future. If they get it wrong, there is a high likelihood the Great Recession will be followed by the Great Stagnation.

That leads to politics – the politics of policy and the politics of ideas. Getting it right will require change, but there are plenty of vested interests that will look to block change. That includes blocking policy change at the political level, and also blocking policy change by ignoring competing ideas regarding economics and economic policy.

The Danger of Stagnation

In the wake of the Great Recession, the global economy confronts a dangerous and challenging future. Immediately following the financial crisis of 2008, policy makers succeeded in stabilizing the economic system and checking a free fall. However, it has now become evident the global economy is beset by generalized demand shortage. In the industrialized countries, the demand shortage is explicit; in the EM economies, it is implicit in their reliance on exports to maintain employment. That makes for an outlook of global economic stagnation.

The core problem is that the forces that drove global growth over the past three decades are exhausted and existing policy is not up to producing shared prosperity. That means there is a need for a new approach to growth. However, so far there has been little progress in creating the political and intellectual space for a change of economic paradigm.

Given these conditions, in the industrialized North, two scenarios deserve special consideration. The first is labeled the "new normal." In this high-probability scenario, the existing orthodox economic paradigm remains policy dominant; policy makers accept a "new normal" marked by high unemployment that is justified on grounds it is structural. Wage stagnation and an attack on the welfare state are also justified on grounds of affordability.

The second scenario is labeled the "Weimar scenario." In this political scenario, extended stagnation and prolonged mass unemployment create conditions in which the forces of intolerance and hate are released. Both scenarios are profoundly disturbing.

Among EM economies, the outlook is more fractured. Some larger EM economies (China, India, Brazil) may be able to pursue "go it alone" development strategies owing to the size of their internal markets. However, smaller export-led economies are likely to be infected by the North's "new normal" economic malaise.

The Economic Outlook

It is now clear that the United States is experiencing a third episode of "jobless recovery" and slow growth that parallels the previous episodes in the business cycle recoveries of 1991–95 and 2001–04. Together, these three episodes provide firm evidence that today's U.S. business cycle is fundamentally different from that which held sway for thirty-five years after World War II. Moreover, the current episode of jobless recovery comes after an economic expansion that was the weakest since World War II.[1]

The difficulties confronting the U.S. economy have enormous negative implications for the global economy. That is because the global economy has relied on the U.S. economy to fuel global demand. Furthermore, Europe and Japan are both suffering on their own account from weak-demand conditions. Europe was hit hard by the U.S. financial crisis, whereas Japan languishes from problems related to its aging population and residual effects from its financial crisis of twenty years ago.

In the United States and Europe, all sectors of the economy (business, household, financial, and government) face strong head-winds, some of which are temporary and some of which are more permanent. A list of factors affecting most economies in varying degrees might include:

- The weakening of confidence and investor "animal spirits" in the wake of the financial crisis.
- The waning of inventory rebuilding that underpinned initial economic rebound after the financial crash.
- A weak investment spending outlook due to global excess capacity.
- In the United States, the construction sector remains depressed owing to overbuilding from the last boom and continued foreclosures.
- Waning fiscal stimulus and emerging fiscal austerity. In Europe, this is being driven by rolling public-sector financial crises. In the United States, it is being driven by politics at the federal level and budget balance requirements at the state and local government levels.
- In the international economy, there has been a fundamental failure to rebalance the U.S. trade deficit with China. Moreover, the U.S. trade deficit is increasing again – a problem that could be compounded by any weaknesses affecting the euro.
- The global trade imbalance problem is further exacerbated by the fact that almost all countries (including the United States) are looking to adopt export-led growth. This is impossible because of a fundamental fallacy of composition (some country has to import).

---

[1] See Bivens, J. and J. Irons [2008], "A Feeble Recovery: The Fundamental Economic Weaknesses of the 2001–07 Expansion," EPI Briefing Paper No. 214, Economic Policy Institute, Washington, DC, December.

Increased emphasis on exports also promises to aggravate exchange rate conflict and global deflationary tendencies.

- The global exchange rate problem remains unresolved and could get worse. There has been no resolution of the China currency problem, and to this has been added the problem of the euro. Exchange rate instability is bad for business confidence and complicates planning of investment spending.
- Global consumer spending stands to be weak owing to the destruction of housing and stock market wealth, destruction of jobs, wage stagnation, and reduced consumer confidence.
- U.S. consumption spending stands to be especially weak relative to historical patterns, because households are debt burdened and must restore their saving rate. Households will be additionally constrained by damage to credit histories that will limit access to credit.
- Banks everywhere are still grappling with commercial property losses, and U.S. banks face continuing difficulties related to their prior reckless residential mortgage lending.
- As banks remedy their past failings, they are likely to maintain tightened credit standards, and this will be exacerbated by financial reforms that raise capital standards and limit leverage ratios.
- In financial markets, there is the perennial problem of "bond market vigilantism" that could spike interest rates. Thus, interest rates could rise in response to phantom fears of inflation, and there is the persistent danger of speculative attacks on individual country bond markets that produce financial turmoil.
- Lastly, there is a danger of commodity market speculation that triggers temporary cost inflation, which lowers industrial-sector profits and real wages, thereby adversely impacting investment and consumer spending.

Why this Recession Really is Different

The fact that the economic outlook is so gloomy, despite extraordinary expansionary monetary and fiscal policy, speaks to the fact that the Great Recession is fundamentally different from the recessions of the past thirty years. Understanding the nature of this difference makes clear the danger of the Great Stagnation.

Table 8.1. *Brief History of the Federal Funds Interest Rate, June 1981–January 2010*

	High	**Low**
June 1981 (%)	19.10	
December 1992 (%)		2.92
November 2001	6.51	
May 2004		1.00
July 2007	5.26	
December 2008		0.16

Source: Board of Governors of the Federal Reserve.

As briefly discussed in Chapter 4, in past recessions and financial upheavals, U.S. economic policy makers were quickly able to restore growth by stepping on the financial accelerator and opening the spigot of credit. This pattern of monetary policy was captured in Table 4.10 (reproduced as Table 8.1 here), which showed the evolution of the Federal Reserve's federal funds interest rate over the three long cycles during the period between 1981 and 2010.

The federal funds rate is the overnight interest rate for loans between commercial banks, and it is the interest rate the Federal Reserve targets in its attempt to guide the macro economy. The federal funds rate peaked in June 1981 at 19.1 percent, almost two years after Federal Reserve Chairman Paul Volcker launched the Fed's war against inflation. Over the next eleven years, with modest ups and downs in between, it gradually fell to 2.92 percent in December 1992. The reduction to 2.92 percent helped the economy escape the recession of the early 1990s, and it also helped save the banking system, which was suffering from major loan losses. The mechanism was to lower the short-term cost of funds to banks (i.e., the federal funds rate) and thereby increase the spread between banks' cost of funds and banks' loan rate.

Over the 1990s, the federal funds rate again trended upward, hitting 6.51 percent in November 2000, which was shortly before the economy went into recession. Thereafter, the federal funds rate was progressively lowered, hitting 1 percent in May 2004. That helped restart the economy once again. It also accelerated the house price bubble that had begun in the late 1990s.

Following the May 2004 low, the federal funds rate reversed on an upward course, hitting 5.27 percent in July 2007. In August 2007, the subprime mortgage market detonator went off, and the Fed started reversing course again, pushing the federal funds to 0.16 percent in December 2008.

The important feature is that every time the economy got into trouble, the Federal Reserve was able to jump-start the economy by lowering interest rates. It did this not only for recessions as shown in Table 8.1, but also for major financial storms. Thus, when the stock market crashed in October 1987, the Federal Reserve lowered the federal funds rate from 7.22 percent in October 1987 to 6.58 percent in March 1988. Another episode was the Russian financial crisis of August 1998 that hit Wall Street and the U.S. financial system via the speculative activities of Long Term Capital Management. The Federal Reserve responded by lowering the federal funds rate from 5.55 percent in August 1998 to 4.74 percent in April 1999.

The twenty-five years from 1981 to 2006 marked a period during which the Federal Reserve was able to jump-start the economy in recessions and inoculate it against financial disturbances by adjusting the federal funds rate. Most economists labeled this period of apparent success the "Great Moderation," and the reputations of central bankers soared. The smoothing of the business cycle, the lengthening of expansions, the shortening of recessions, and the lowering of inflation were all attributed to improved central bank monetary policy, hence the boom in central banker reputations.

This explanation has been popular with economists because it implicitly applauds the economics profession. After all, improved policy was attributable to advances in economics and increased influence of economists within central banks. For instance, the Fed's current Chairman is a former academic economist, as are many of the Fed's board of governors and many presidents of the regional Federal Reserve banks.

However, there was always another, less celebratory explanation of what was going on, but it got little play time as the winners write history. That less celebratory account explains the Great Moderation as a transitional phenomenon, and one that has ultimately come at a high cost.[2] This alternative account emphasizes the changed economic

---

[2] See Palley, T.I. [2008c], "Demythologizing Central Bankers," *Asia Times Online*, April 8, http://www.atimes.com/atimes/Global_Economy/JD08Dj06.html

environment that followed with the retreat from policy commitment to full employment.

The great Polish economist Michal Kalecki observed that full employment would likely cause inflation because job security would prompt workers to demand higher wages. That is what happened in the 1960s and 1970s. The problem was exacerbated by the oil price shocks of the 1970s, which created further cause for conflict between capital and labor over whether wages or profits would bear the hit. However, rather than solving this political problem, economic policy retreated from full employment and assisted in the evisceration of unions. That lowered inflation, but it came at the high cost of rupturing of the link between wage and productivity growth and almost three decades of wage stagnation.

Persistent disinflation in turn lowered nominal interest rates, particularly during downturns, and provided the economy with a cushion of support. In particular, falling interest rates facilitated successive waves of mortgage refinancing that lowered interest burdens on borrowers and reduced cash outflows on new mortgages.[3] This improved household finances and supported consumer spending, thereby keeping recessions short and shallow.

With regard to lengthened economic expansions, the Great Moderation was driven by asset price inflation and financial innovation, which also financed consumer spending. Higher asset prices (especially house prices) provided collateral to borrow against, whereas financial innovation increased the volume and ease of access to credit. Together, that created a dynamic in which rising asset prices supported increased debt-financed spending, thereby making for longer expansions. This dynamic was exemplified by the housing bubble that began in 1996 and ran until mid-2006.

The important implication is that the Great Moderation was the result of a retreat from full employment combined with the transitional factors of disinflation, asset price inflation, and increased consumer

---

[3] Mortgage interest payments can be thought of as consisting of an interest payment plus a payment that compensates lenders for the effect of inflation that erodes the real value of their loan. When inflation is low, this second component falls and instead lenders are repaid at the end of the loan period. When inflation is high, this second component is high and instead lenders are repaid more upfront. When the loan period ends, the real repayment is small because inflation has reduced its value. Effectively, lenders are repaid earlier.

borrowing. An essential factor was the Federal Reserve's ability to lower interest rates in step-like fashion each recession.

All of these factors have now disappeared, which is why the system is in true crisis. The factors needed for the system to work are no longer there. The federal funds rate is near zero, so that there is no further room for reduction. Further disinflation will produce disruptive deflation that increases debt burdens. That will increase defaults and further weaken an already weak banking system.

Households are heavily indebted and no longer want or are able to take on debt. The decline in asset prices (especially housing prices) has destroyed financial wealth so that households lack collateral to back borrowing. Twenty years ago, households had relatively low debt burdens and therefore had unused borrowing capacity. That borrowing capacity was an unrecorded asset (a kind of off-balance-sheet asset) that could be called on to jump-start consumer spending, but now it is used up. Additionally, many households have seen their credit histories damaged by bankruptcy and default. Taken together, it means increased consumer credit cannot jump-start recovery as it did in the past.

Not only are many households not borrowing more, many are paying back debt – a process known as deleveraging. That process involves households increasing their saving rate and reducing consumption spending. Consequently, deleveraging further aggravates the underlying structural weaknesses in the demand-generating process.

Moreover, this time, lowering the federal funds rate to near-zero seems to have had a smaller positive effect on the economy. One reason is the stock of high-interest-rate loans has already been significantly refinanced in past recessions, leaving less benefit from another round of refinancing. Another reason is that many households who could have benefited from refinancing have not been able to. This is because housing prices have fallen so much that many owners are "under water" (i.e., have negative equity), and banks will not refinance loans. A corollary of this is that those who can refinance tend to be wealthier, higher-income households and these households tend to save most of the refinancing windfall rather than spend it. Consequently, the effect of lower interest rates on consumer spending has been far more modest than in the past.

Moreover, many households who have been able to refinance are choosing to refinance into shorter mortgages, such as fifteen-year mortgages instead of thirty-year mortgages. The saving on interest payments is therefore often outweighed by the increase in principal payments resulting from a shorter payback period. In the past, households used their interest saving from refinancing to increase consumption. This time, many are choosing to use interest payment reductions to increase their saving rate.

A third reason why the economic effect of lower interest rates has been muted is that asset prices were initially significantly overvalued. Thus, rather than increasing asset prices and generating a positive wealth effect on consumption as in the past, this time lower interest rates diminished the decline in asset prices that would otherwise have occurred. That mitigated the negative effect of falling wealth on consumer spending, but it did not increase spending.

These multiple factors and their effect on the economy can be understood through the metaphor of a car that symbolizes the economy. Demand (i.e., spending) is the gas that fuels the car (i.e., the economy). The problem is that the fuel line has been gradually getting clogged because of wage stagnation, rising income inequality, and the trade deficit that have together undermined the demand-generating process.

In prior recessions, these underlying structural effects could be overcome by increased household borrowing, which was like stepping on the gas, and that accelerated economic activity as consumers spent their borrowings. Every time there was economic trouble, the Federal Reserve took measures to encourage borrowing (i.e., stepped on the pedal), which got the car moving again.

This time, households have run out of borrowing capacity. Consequently, measures by the Federal Reserve to stimulate borrowing are not working. The mere stop in borrowing is like taking the foot off the pedal and causes the car to slow. However, now there are additional effects from the stock of debt accumulated from past borrowing, which is like a weight in the car's trunk that causes the car to slow even more. Furthermore, deleveraging means households are increasing their saving to repay debt, and that is like pressing on the brake, which further compounds the slowdown. Putting the pieces together, it is small wonder the car (i.e., the economy) is stuck.

Why U.S. Economic Policy is Failing

The car metaphor helps explain why U.S. economic policy is failing. Much attention is being devoted to the problems of deleveraging and the blockage of borrowing. However, that ignores the more fundamental problem, namely that the fuel line is clogged (i.e., the underlying demand-generating process is failing because of problems concerning wage stagnation, the trade deficit, and globalization). Even if the Fed could restart borrowing, it would be a short-term fix that does not remedy these deeper problems. Moreover, any short-term fix comes back to haunt the economy in the form of increased debt burdens and financial fragility. That is the lesson of the past thirty years and the financial crash of 2008.

U.S. policy makers have failed to come to grips with the fact that this recession is different and have not learned its lessons. Instead, they are still trying to resuscitate the old model. This is reflected in the current policy mix of conventional stimulus plus some financial reform. The hope is to revive a marginally less speculative version of the existing neoliberal model.

Current policy is not going to work because the existing paradigm is completely exhausted. It is futile to think it possible to revive the debt-fueled growth model of the past thirty years because U.S. households are debt saturated.

Following the Great Crash of 2008, policy makers confronted a threefold task:

1. Stop the economic free fall.
2. Jump-start the economy.
3. Ensure sustainable growth with shared prosperity.

In the United States, after much delay and indecision, policy makers succeeded in stopping the free fall. The U.S. Treasury's Troubled Asset Relief Program, combined with myriad of special lending and liquidity programs established by the Federal Reserve, stabilized financial markets and put an end to the liquidation trap that gripped financial markets in 2008 and early 2009. Although belated, the moves were effective.

However, with regard to jump-starting the economy and creating sustainable growth, policy has failed. At best, the economy confronts jobless recovery and subpar growth that will leave the unemployment rate high and wages stagnant for years to come.

The reason for this policy failure is refusal to confront the fundamentally flawed nature of the neoliberal paradigm, abandon it, and reconstruct economic policy along new lines. This failure is symbolized in President Obama's choice of economic policy team, headed by Larry Summers and filled with other personnel connected to the 1990s Clinton administration. Yet, as shown in Chapter 4, the Clinton administration was instrumental in putting in place so many of the policies that have proven so disastrous.

Instead of change, economic policy has opted for conventional measures of fiscal and monetary stimulus – albeit budget deficits have been larger and the Federal Reserve's interest rate is at record lows. Additionally, the Federal Reserve has pursued policies of quantitative easing whereby it has directly lent money to financial institutions, purchased private-sector mortgage-backed securities, and purchased U.S. Treasury bonds. The hope is that pumping extraordinary amounts of stimulus into the economy via budget deficits and monetary policy will jump-start private-sector demand and job creation.

The current policy mix fails to address the fundamental problem, which is that the existing paradigm has undermined the demand-generating process. The most immediate policy failure concerns the failure to plug the trade deficit, which undercuts the effectiveness of fiscal and monetary stimulus. The trade deficit's impact can be understood through the metaphor of a bathtub, with the tub representing the economy and the volume of water in the tub representing the level of total demand. Monetary and fiscal policy stimulus have opened the tap and poured demand into the bathtub, but it has then leaked out of the tub through the plug hole, which symbolizes the trade deficit.

Plugging the trade deficit leakage is therefore critical. But plugging the trade deficit alone is not enough. There is also a deeper need to rebuild a stable demand-generating process that does not rely on excessive debt and asset price bubbles. That requires improving income distribution and reconnecting wages to productivity growth. Plugging the trade deficit will give a boost to demand, creating breathing room to make further policy adjustments. But it does not remedy the deeper underlying problem in the U.S. economy, which is the reliance on debt and asset bubbles to fuel demand.

The failure of policy to jump-start growth has meant continuing job losses, continuing housing price weakness, and continuing home fore-closures. These developments create facts that make recovery even harder. For instance, when a factory closes and jobs are lost, the collection of skills and capital that comprise the business is disbanded, and it is difficult to reassemble them. Once a house enters the fore-closure process, it is hard to reverse, putting more pressure on housing prices and construction. And once a consumer or business files for bankruptcy, their credit record is tainted, making it harder to get future credit to finance consumption or investment. Such factors mean the longer it takes to jump-start recovery and growth, the more difficult it becomes for policy to succeed because stagnation sets in. In the current situation, delay is costly, which is why it is so urgent that policy change.

Even the Best Mainstream Economists do not Understand the Problem

The Obama administration has pursued an entirely mainstream policy, navigating between those economists calling for less economic stimulus and those calling for more. The problem is that stimulus is only part of the solution, and so far it has been impossible to get a hearing for the full solution.

The economy needs a policy cocktail. In terms of the car metaphor, it needs more gas (i.e., stimulus) but it also needs repairs that unclog the fuel line (i.e., policies that rebuild the demand-generating process). Calls for more economic stimulus are fully appropriate, but stimulus alone is insufficient and stimulus alone also poses dangers.

First, stimulus alone will likely fail, and at the end of the day that could leave the economy worse off by creating more debt without resolving the problem. Second, policy failure risks exhausting the public's appetite for real policy change. Third, exclusive focus on stimulus crowds out space for debate of other needed policies.

Large-scale stimulus is undoubtedly needed but it will only generate sustainable recovery if accompanied by other reforms. Absent those reforms, large budget deficits will ratchet up the debt without jump-starting sustainable growth. At some stage this risks creating a political demand for fiscal austerity, and it also burdens the federal government with massive debt obligations that create budget problems down the road.

A similar misunderstanding applies to monetary policy. The Federal Reserve has already lowered the federal funds rate to near-zero and it can effectively go no lower because of the zero lower bound. Liberal economist and Nobel Prize winner Paul Krugman (2010b) argues this is the fundamental problem:

Most of the world's large economies are stuck in a liquidity trap – deeply depressed, but unable to generate a recovery by cutting interest rates because the relevant rates are already near zero.

However, being stuck at the zero bound is merely a symptom. The real underlying problem is told in Table 8.1. Since 1981, the economic system has relied on ever-falling interest rates to escape the contradictions caused by hollowing out of the demand-generating process inflicted by the neoliberal paradigm. In past recessions, the Fed had room to lower rates, but this time it has hit the zero lower bound to nominal interest rates. The proximate cause of the problem is the zero bound, but the ultimate cause is the Federal Reserve needed to keep lowering interest rates to stave off stagnation.

Some economists (DeLong, 2009; Farmer, 2009) have argued that the Federal Reserve should start buying private-sector assets, including corporate bonds and equities. The claim is this would drive up asset prices, thereby implicitly reducing the cost of capital and stimulating business investment. It would also increase wealth and encourage consumption.

Harvard economist Gregory Mankiw (2009) argues the Fed can circumvent the zero nominal interest rate bound by simply charging a negative interest rate on loans and paying banks to borrow from the Fed. With a lower cost of funds, banks might lend more.

Undoubtedly, there is some truth in these claims. Buying assets and subsidizing lending would juice asset markets a bit and have some expansionary impact. Buying equities would surely also be welcomed by the country's richest segment that owns the bulk of privately held equities. Likewise, banks would rejoice at being paid to borrow from the Fed, which would be akin to giving them a printing press for profits.

The problem is that although these schemes might help ameliorate some of the problems caused by the zero lower bound to nominal interest rates, they would not resolve the underlying problem. The real story is that the neoliberal economic paradigm is exhausted and offers only stagnation: Hitting the zero bound on nominal interest rates is simply the manifestation of that fact.

Moreover, not only does the strategy not address the fundamental problem; it is also risky and embodies a contradiction. The risk is another asset bubble that imposes further collateral damage effects when it bursts. The contradiction is if the economy begins to revive, higher interest rates are likely to bring asset prices crashing back down and create fresh difficulties.

The Farmer-DeLong-Mankiw remedy is to blow harder when a bubble goes disastrously flat. From a political angle, it represents a fresh twist to the economics of plutonomy and trickle-down economics. The Republican approach to trickle-down economics has been to cut taxes on the rich. The claim is this will induce the rich to work harder and save more, some of which will trickle down to the rest. The New Democrat Wall Street version is to buy assets and subsidize capital, which will increase wealth and juice financial markets, and some of that will trickle down. Both are versions of the late John Kenneth Galbraith's "horse and sparrow" economics: Feed enough oats to the horse and some will pass through onto the road to feed the sparrow.

The Risk of Further Policy Failures

Not only is existing policy likely to fail, there also exist significant dangers that policy could actually worsen conditions. *Danger I*, which is the most immediate, is the revived push for fiscal austerity. Austerity has always been part of the neoliberal mental framework, being a complement to the small-government agenda. Now, Europe's sovereign debt woes (afflicting Greece, Italy, Spain, Portugal, Ireland and the United Kingdom) are adding strength to that push. Moreover, once one country implements fiscal austerity, there appears to be an austerity domino effect, as countries try to outdo each other in an attempt to appease bond markets.

Budget deficit reduction will eventually be required to avoid inflationary pressures once recovery is in place. However, premature deficit reduction and spending cuts will only deepen stagnation. That in turn will aggravate budget difficulties by reducing tax revenues, and it will also cause private-sector bankruptcies that further weaken an already weakened banking sector.

Danger II is that many central bankers are still obsessed with inflation and have itchy anti-inflation trigger fingers. That risks central banks mistakenly raising rates and truncating any recovery, which at best already promises to be anemic. In the United States, this threat has been on display in comments from the "inflation hawk" presidents of the Federal Reserve Banks of Kansas City, Philadelphia, and Richmond.

Danger III is that policy makers try to double down on the existing neoliberal policy mix that has already caused such damage. This danger is especially acute in Europe, but it is present everywhere. Moreover, it is likely to grow stronger if politics turns in a reactionary direction in response to extended high unemployment and economic stagnation.

The doubling-down tendency is evident in the continued push for new free-trade agreements modeled on an unchanged template. It is also evident in the widespread calls for more labor market flexibility and wage cuts in the wake of the Europe's sovereign debt crisis. Such policies stand to amplify the problem of wage stagnation and deteriorated income distribution and risk releasing the evil genie of deflation. Most worryingly, calls for such policies are coming from across the spectrum of mainstream opinion. For instance, conservative economist Laurence Kotlikoff (2010) writes:

Specifically, the Greek government would decree that all firms must lower their nominal wages and prices by 30 percent, effective immediately, and not change them for three months.

The slightly less conservative economist Barry Eichengreen (2010) writes:

Europe needs more flexible labor markets.... Europe will have to rely on wage flexibility to enhance the competitiveness of depressed regions. This is not something that it possesses in abundance. But recent cuts in public-sector pay in Spain and Greece are a reminder that Europe is, in fact, capable of wage flexibility. Where national wage-bargaining systems are the obstacle, the European Commission should say so, and the countries should be required to change them.

Perhaps the clearest statement comes from Jeffrey Miron (2010), director of undergraduate studies at Harvard University, who writes:

> To stimulate jobs growth, the U.S. needs a three-pronged approach ... the first prong should be scaling back of labor market policies that inflate wages and thereby reduce the demand for labor. This means lowering the federal minimum wage, ending the continual extension of unemployment benefits, and reducing protections for unions.

These recommendations come straight out of conventional economic theory that dominates the academy and is widely taught in undergraduate economics. That gives a clue to the source of the policy problem.

Danger IV is the loss of Keynesian policy credibility. Even if policy makers avoid the previously described pitfalls, existing policy is not going to revive shared prosperity. Because existing policy is being sold as "Keynesian," this creates a danger that when these policies fail to deliver, true structural Keynesian policies will be politically discredited without ever having been tried.

9

Avoiding the Great Stagnation

Rethinking the Paradigm

Crisis is a word that is widely bandied about, perhaps so much so that it may have lost some of its impact. However, in social science theory, crisis has a very particular meaning – a situation in which a system is unable to replicate itself. Viewed from that standpoint, the financial crash of 2008 and the Great Recession can be viewed as a real crisis, fundamentally different from the financial upheavals and recessions of the past twenty years. The important policy implication is that if the system can no longer reproduce itself, it must be refashioned. That creates a historic opportunity for change.

The Failure of Neoliberalism

Chapter 8 analyzed the economic forces making for the Great Stagnation and the failure of current policy to address the underlying problem. That problem is a broken demand-generating process that has resulted in global demand shortage and financial fragility.

This condition has been slowly brewing for twenty-five years. Increased financial fragility has been apparent in the lengthening string of financial crises that have hit both developed and developing economies. Examples include the European currency and banking crises of the early 1990s; the Mexican financial crisis of 1994; the East Asian financial crisis of 1997; the Russian debt and Long Term Capital Management crisis of 1998; the financial crises afflicting Brazil, Argentina, and Turkey between 1999 and 2001; the global stock market crash of 2001; and of course the financial crash of 2008.

The weakening of the demand-generating process has also been long detectable.[1] However, in developed economies, it was obscured by asset bubbles and increased indebtedness that kept the problem temporarily at bay – albeit at the cost of a larger ultimate financial crash and deeper recession. Simultaneously, developing economies appeared healthier because of their reliance on export-led growth, which had them piggy-backing on consumer demand in developed countries.

Behind these economic conditions lies the failed neoliberal economic paradigm widely referred to as the Washington Consensus, which undermined and destabilized the global demand-generating process. As described in Chapter 4, the main features of the Washington Consensus are

- retreat from commitment to full employment and a shift to obsessive concern with very low inflation;
- promotion of flexible labor markets in which unions are weakened and minimum wages and worker protections are eroded;
- support for a corporate version of globalization based on free-trade agreements and capital account liberalization that promotes industrial offshoring, limits possibilities for industrial policy, and limits macroeconomic policy options;
- attacking government via deregulation, privatization, and shrinking public investment.

Chapter 4 described this neoliberal paradigm in terms of a policy box that is shown again in Figure 9.1. Its effect is to put workers under siege from all sides, thereby contributing to income inequality and wage stagnation by severing the link between wages and productivity growth.

The neoliberal policy mix would have done great damage if implemented in just the U.S. economy. However, over the past thirty years, it was implemented in both the developed North and the emerging South, with the IMF and World Bank playing a crucial role in forcing implementation in the South. This global implementation multiplied its impact by creating an international "race to the bottom."

---

[1] See Palley, T.I. [2001a, 2002a], "Economic Contradictions Coming Home to Roost? Does the U.S. Face a Long Term Aggregate Demand Generation Problem?" Working Paper 332, Levy Economics institute of Bard College, June and *Journal of Post Keynesian Economics*, 25 (Fall), 9–32.

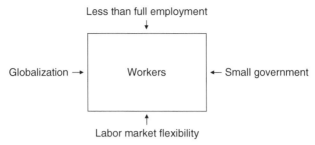

Figure 9.1. The neoliberal policy box.

The engine of this race to the bottom is international mobility of jobs and investment, global production sourcing, and unrestricted movement of financial capital. That cocktail has pressured workers and facilitated wage repression; pushed governments to shift tax burdens away from capital on to labor; and pressured governments to lower standards regarding corporate governance, labor markets, social protection, and the environment.

Initially, the main direction of competition was between North and South. However, South-South competition has become increasingly apparent, making the problem truly global. The entry of China into the global economy has been very important for this latest development, as exemplified by China's impact on Central America.[2] Chinese wage and employment conditions have exerted downward competitive pressures throughout the South via competition for exports, jobs, and foreign direct investment (FDI).[3]

The metaphor of a policy box captures the existing policy configuration and its effects. However, a real box has six sides and those extra sides give strength to the box. This logic also holds for the neoliberal box and this is where corporations and financial markets enter into the picture.

The enduring strength of the neoliberal policy box derives from a new relationship between corporations and financial markets that is

---

[2] See, for example, Gallagher, K. [2010a] "China Crashes CAFTA's Party," *Guardian. co.uk*, Saturday, June 5, http://www.guardian.co.uk/commentisfree/cifamerica/2010/may/31/china-cafta-central-america

[3] See Blecker, R.A. [2000], "The Diminishing Returns to Export-led Growth," paper prepared for the Council of Foreign Relations Working Group on Development, New York; and Palley, T.I. [2003b], "Export-led Growth: Evidence of Developing Country Crowding-out," in Arestis et al. (eds.), *Globalization, Regionalism, and Economic Activity*, Cheltenham: Edward Elgar.

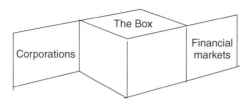

Figure 9.2. Side supports of the neoliberal policy box.

illustrated in Figure 9.2. This new relationship has been termed "financialization," and the box would collapse absent these side supports.[4]

The basic logic of financialization is that financial markets have captured control of corporations and economic policy, both of which now serve financial market interests along with the interests of top management. That capture has changed corporate behavior, while the political power of corporations and finance ensures political control that enforces the policies described by the economic policy box.

Six sides are more complicated than four. However, the extra complication is essential for providing a full understanding of the political economy of neoliberalism. The economic and political power of corporations is central in shaping policy. Financial markets also have a critical double role. One role, discussed in Chapters 4 and 5, is to fuel demand growth by financing borrowing and spurring asset price inflation. A second role is to change corporate behavior, forcing corporations to adopt a short-term focus on profit maximization and shareholder value extraction.

The financial crisis has focused attention on the problem of financial instability. However, the deeper problem of financial markets capturing and transforming the behavior of corporations has received no attention.

Viewed from this perspective, refashioning the system requires changing the four sides of the policy box shown in Figure 9.1, but it also requires a policy agenda addressing financial markets and

---

[4] See Epstein, G. [2001], "Financialization, Rentier Interests, and Central Bank Policy," manuscript, Department of Economics, University of Massachusetts, Amherst, MA, December 2001; and Palley, T.I. [2008b], "Financialization: What It Is and Why It Matters," in *Finance-led Capitalism: Macroeconomic Effects of Changes in the Financial Sector*, ed. Eckhard Hein, Torsten Niechoj, Peter Spahn, and Achim Truger, Marburg, Germany: Metroplis-Verlag, 2008 and Working Paper 04/2008, IMK Macroeconomic Policy Institute, Dusseldorf, Germany.

corporations. That agenda must change the behaviors of financial markets and corporations so that they serve better the public interest.

Structural Keynesianism versus Textbook Keynesianism
The flawed nature of the neoliberal paradigm points to the need for a new paradigm. This leads back to concept of structural Keynesianism, which was introduced in Chapter 2.

Traditional textbook Keynesianism views recessions as resulting from temporary interruptions in demand. It therefore recommends that economic policy step in and temporarily fill the demand gap until private-sector demand recovers.

Structural Keynesianism adds an additional concern with the strength and viability of the underlying demand-generating process. That process depends on the economy's institutions and structures, including economic policy. If the underlying structures that frame the demand-generating process are flawed, the economy will have a permanent tendency to demand shortage.

From a structural Keynesian perspective, the weakness of textbook Keynesianism is that it overlooks problems with the demand-generating process. Textbook Keynesianism works well when the demand-generating process is sound. That was the situation in the U.S. and European economies between 1945 and 1980, a period sometimes described as the "golden age" of capitalism. However, when the demand-generating process is faulty, as it is now, textbook Keynesian policy is not going to work – at least not on a sustained basis. Applying the patch of stimulus will provide temporary relief, but it does not fix the underlying problem regarding inadequate demand generation. That requires systemic adjustment, which in current context means economic paradigm change.

A structural Keynesian perspective spotlights the problem with current policy. The Obama administration, European leaders, the G-20, and the IMF have all followed traditional textbook Keynesian thinking. Given the depth of the Great Recession, policy makers have become "emergency" Keynesians, opening the spigots of fiscal and monetary stimulus and temporarily abandoning concerns with inflation targets and budget imbalances. Such policies bolster the level of demand and have ameliorated the recession. However, they have done nothing to address the failings in the demand-generating process.

The same criticism holds for liberal critics of the Obama administration, such as Princeton economist Paul Krugman and Berkley economist Brad DeLong. They have argued the administration has been too cautious and budget deficits have not been large enough.[5] However, they too rely on textbook Keynesian thinking so that their difference with the administration is one of degree rather than kind.

The U.S. and global economy are afflicted by demand shortage caused by thirty years of orthodox policy that has undermined the demand-generating process. In such conditions, massive stimulus is needed to fill the demand shortage, but it must also be accompanied by measures that repair the demand-generating process. Absent that, the economy will be prone to relapse if stimulus is withdrawn or even weakened, and sustainable recovery with shared prosperity will remain elusive. Moreover, there is a danger that persistent large deficits and money supply expansion will create new sources of financial fragility in the form excessive public debt, which could produce a public-sector financial crisis.

The Great Depression of the 1930s and the Golden Age of capitalism that followed World War II hold important lessons. Ultimately, escape from the Great Depression was driven by a combination of massive stimulus and reform of the demand-generating process. The stimulus was public works programs, rearmament that began in the late 1930s, and World War II spending that became the greatest public works program ever. The reform of the demand-generating process was the New Deal, which created a social safety net, promoted the rise of unions, and imposed financial reform that harnessed financial markets to the needs of consumers and industry. New Deal financial regulations, such as the Glass-Steagall Act of 1933 and the Securities Exchange Acts of 1934, were also critical because they tamed the financial system's proclivity to instability while still ensuring a steady flow of finance for enterprise.

These structural reforms meant that after World War II, contrary to widespread expectations, the U.S. economy did not fall back into depression. Instead, it enjoyed thirty years of spectacular prosperity,

[5] See Krugman, P. [2010c], "Now and Later," *New York Times*, June 20, http://www. nytimes.com/2010/06/21/opinion/21krugman.html. DeLong, J.B. [2010], "America's Employment Dilemma," *Project Syndicate*, January 27, http://www.project-syndicate. org/commentary/delong98/English

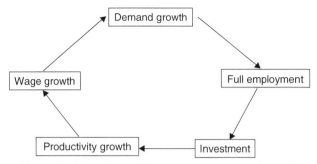

Figure 9.3. The 1945–1980 virtuous circle growth model.

initially triggered by accumulated pent-up wartime demand and accumulated household saving from financing the war, and then carried forward on the back of changed income distribution.

Repacking the Box: A Structural Keynesian Model

The blowup of the orthodox paradigm and the threat of the Great Stagnation create an opportunity for a new structural Keynesian policy paradigm that rebuilds the demand-generating process. The most critical need is to restore the link between wages and productivity growth that drove the 1945–80 virtuous circle model of growth. That model is illustrated in Figure 9.3. It rested on a simple logic whereby wage growth fueled demand growth, which created full employment. Full employment then spurred investment, which increased productivity and supported further wage growth.

The key to recreating this virtuous circle model is to repack the policy box along structural Keynesian lines. That involves taking workers out of the box and putting corporations and financial markets in the box, as shown in Figure 9.4.

A structural Keynesian box would reconfigure policy as follows:

1. Corporate globalization is replaced with "managed globalization" that embeds global labor and environmental standards that promote upward harmonization across countries instead of a race to the bottom.

Additionally, international economic governance arrangements must be strengthened, especially as regards exchange rates so as to unwind and then prevent a repeat of the huge trade imbalances of

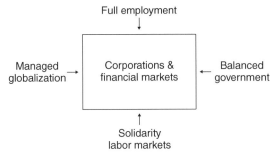

Figure 9.4. The structural Keynesian policy box.

recent years. That requires a system of managed exchange rates whereby countries set exchange rates on the basis of predetermined criteria and rules.

Capital controls must also be made a legitimate part of the policy tool kit to prevent boom-bust cycles driven by capital flows. Such controls can also help deter capital markets from striking against governments that want to improve income distribution and limit corporate power.

2. The antigovernment agenda is replaced with a balanced government agenda that balances the standing of markets and government. One part of this balanced government approach is ensuring that the government efficiently provides public goods (including law and order), health insurance, social insurance, education, and needed infrastructure.

Public investment has a critical role to play in creating jobs and helping restore full employment, enhancing private-sector productivity growth, and meeting the environmental challenges associated with global warming (Heintz et al. 2009; Pollin and Baker, 2010). There is an established economic literature (Aschauer, 1989a, 1989b; Munnell, 1990, 1992; Heintz, 2010) that documents how public infrastructure investment enhances the productivity of private capital. Over the last thirty years, such investment has fallen as a share of U.S. GDP, and reversing that decline can contribute to restoring growth with full employment.

A second part of a balanced government agenda is restoring the standing of regulation. This includes financial market regulation that limits speculation, increases transparency, and provides central banks with policy tools to address asset price bubbles and preserve financial stability. Those tools include adjustable balance sheet requirements such as liquidity requirements, capital requirements, reserve requirements, and leverage restrictions. Financial transactions taxes also have a place, both as a means of limiting destabilizing speculation and for raising revenue.[6]

Along with improved financial market regulation, there is a need for a new regulatory agenda for corporations. That agenda would restrict managerial power by enhancing shareholder control; use the tax system to discourage excessive managerial pay and short-term incentive pay that promotes speculation and myopic business management; limit unproductive corporate financial engineering (particularly stock buybacks); and provide representation for other stakeholders in corporations.

With regard to taxes, policy should restore tax progressivity, which has been eroded over the last three decades. A second reform theme should be to eliminate the preferential treatment given to capital income (dividends and capital gains) relative to labor income (wages and salaries). A third reform theme should be to abolish "job taxes" that link taxes to jobs. This means funding social security and unemployment insurance via general tax revenues rather than via payroll taxes. Health care financing also needs to be changed given that it is job cost, albeit privately paid for under the current system. A fourth reform should reduce the huge tax expenditures that give away tax revenue in the form of deductions. In particular, the mortgage interest deduction, which distorts property prices, should be phased out. A fifth reform could be abolition of corporate income taxes, but only as part of a package that increased tax progressivity and eliminated tax favoritism for capital income. Taxing corporations gives them an incentive to move: instead, governments should tax the owners who receive the profits.

3. A third pillar of the structural Keynesian box is the restoration of full employment as a policy priority. The past thirty years have seen central bankers elevate the significance of anti-inflation policy while

---

[6] See Baker et al. (2009) and Pollin et al. (2003) for estimates of the revenue that could be raised by a U.S. financial transactions tax. See Palley (2001b) for a discussion of the market-stabilizing properties of financial transaction taxes.

lowering their concern with full employment.[7] That tilt in priorities needs to be reversed, as weak employment conditions undermine the link between wages and productivity growth, and they may also lower productivity growth. Moreover, modest inflation lowers the rate of unemployment by greasing the wheels of labor market adjustment. Effectively, it lets wages in tight labor markets rise relative to wages in weaker labor markets, thereby encouraging job formation in markets where there is unemployment.

4. The fourth pillar of the structural Keynesian box is the promotion of "solidarity" labor markets that encourage creation of high-quality jobs that pay fair wages that grow with productivity.[8] This requires reviving unions so that workers can bargain effectively for a share of productivity gains; implementing a minimum wage that increases with market wages to provide a true wage floor; and increasing worker protections and unemployment insurance support so that workers have the confidence to press their wage claims and exercise their rights as workers.

Unions are especially important, and in hindsight it is clear that the spurt in union density between 1935 and 1945 was critical in bringing shared prosperity to the U.S. economy after World War II. Table 9.1 shows data on union density (defined as the percent of nonagricultural employees who are union members) and the share of income (including capital gains) going to the top 10 percent of income earners.[9] During the 1920s, union density declined and income inequality jumped. In the late 1930s and early 1940s, union density spurted and income inequality declined substantially to levels it was to hold until the early 1980s. Table 9.2 shows what happened after 1980 with the full

---

[7] For a detailed discussion of the importance of full employment and how to secure it, see Palley, T.I. [2007a], "Seeking Full Employment Again: Challenging the Wall Street Paradigm," *Challenge* 50 (November/Dec/ember), 14–50.

[8] For a discussion of the economics of solidaristic labor markets, see Palley, T.I. [1998], "Building Prosperity from the Bottom Up: The New Economics of the Minimum Wage," *Challenge*, 41 (July–August), 1–13. Also see Pollin, R. and S. Luce [2000], *The Living Wage: Building a Fair Economy*, New York: The New Press.

[9] Data are from Freeman, R.B. [1998], "Spurts in Union Growth: Defining Moments and Social Processes," in Bordo, Goldin, and White (eds.), *The Defining Moment: The Great Depression and the American Economy in the Twentieth Century*, Chicago: The University of Chicago Press; and Piketty, T. and E. Saez [2004], "Income Inequality in the United States, 1913–2002," manuscript, http://elsa.berkeley.edu/~saez/piketty-saezOUP04US.pdf

Table 9.1. *Union Density and Income Share of the Top 10 Percent,*
1925–1955

	1920	1925	1930	1935	1940	1945	1950	1955
Union density (% nonagricultural employment)	16.6%	10.8	11.2	12.8	26.0	34.2	30.5	32.0
Top 10 percent income share	39.1%	46.6	44.0	44.6	45.4	34.6	35.8	34.1

Sources: Freeman (1998) and Piketty and Saez (2004).

Table 9.2. *Union Density and Income Share of the Top 10 Percent,*
1973–2000

	1973	1975	1980	1985	1990	1995	2000
Union density	24.0%	22.2	23.0	18.0	16.1	14.9	13.5
Top 10 percent income share	33.7%	33.8	35.1	38.1	40.2	41.8	48.1

Sources: Hirsch and Macpherson (2003) and Piketty and Saez (2004).

implementation of the neoliberal program. Union density declined precipitously and income inequality spiked, reaching levels not seen since the end of the Roaring Twenties.[10]

The significance of unions for wages and income distribution is widely recognized. Although benefitting union members most immediately, unions also benefit nonmembers by setting wage norms and inducing employers to raise wages to avoid unionization.

Less recognized is the fact that unions have a deeper role to play in balancing the economy and society. One role is as political counterweight to the political influence of corporations and financial markets. A second role is to restrain excessive managerial pay that now resembles looting. Thus, there is empirical evidence that a union presence lowers total CEO pay and lowers the stock option component of pay (see Tzioumis and Gomez, 2007). From this standpoint, unions

[10] Union density data for this later period are drawn from Hirsch, B.T. and D.A. Macpherson [2003], "Union Membership and Coverage Database from the Current Population Survey: Note," *Industrial and Labor Relations Review*, 56 (January), 349–54.

are an important and valuable component of governance of modern capitalist economies.

In addition to conventional labor market interventions such as unions, minimum wages, unemployment insurance, and employee protections, there is also a need for social policies focusing on race and gender discrimination and family well-being (see Elson and Cagatay, 2000; Folbre, 2001). Such policies have a clear ethical justification, but more than that, they have a powerful economic justification.

Race and gender discrimination contribute to wage inequality and undermine wages, and thereby undermine the income- and demand-generating process. Policies reducing discrimination can therefore remedy that damage. Policies supportive of families and caregiving can yield similar benefits. First, channeling resources to households puts workers in a better bargaining position and may also reduce labor supply, both of which increase wages. Second, assisting households with the task of caring labor is a form of long-term human capital investment that increases adult productivity. All of these policies also have application in developing economies (see Seguino and Grown, 2006).

5. The fifth pillar of the structural Keynesian approach is that the whole is greater than the sum of the parts. The structural Keynesian policy box constitutes a system in which the parts are mutually reinforcing, which means policies must be implemented together to be fully effective. For instance, the benefits of unions and solidaristic labor market institutions will be undermined absent full employment or appropriately designed globalization and international economic engagement. Similarly, flawed international economic engagement will undermine policies aimed at full employment, while an antigovernment agenda will undermine the beneficial effects of good labor market arrangements.

The Great Recession signals the implosion of the neoliberal growth model that was implemented some thirty years ago. This makes the recession fundamentally different and it means there is a need for a new growth model.

In past recessions, policy makers merely had to jump-start the economy because the income- and demand-generating process remained sufficiently intact. The Great Recession has shown that this is no longer the case. Consequently, measures that stimulate demand, such as monetary and fiscal stimulus, cannot generate sustained growth with shared prosperity. That requires repairing the income- and demand-generating process.

Escaping the pull of stagnation requires that policy makers simultaneously jump-start the economy and rebuild the system. One without the other will fail. Stimulus without structural rebuilding will mean recovery is muted, whereas structural rebuilding without stimulus will leave the economy trapped in stagnation and unable to achieve recovery velocity.

U.S. policy makers have failed to recognize this imperative. Having successfully stabilized the economy after the financial crisis, policy makers implemented inadequate stimulus and failed to initiate structural rebuilding. Consequently, the recovery has been weak and risks stalling, while a return to full employment is not even on the horizon.

Escaping the Great Recession requires jump-starting the economy by increasing demand. Preventing the economy from getting stuck in stagnation requires a new growth model that rebuilds the income- and demand-generating process. Success requires the full policy package of stimulus and structural rebuilding. However, such policy holism is politically challenging. All the pieces should be implemented together and that is a more difficult political sell than simplistic silver-bullet policy.

Budget Deficits during the Transition to a New Paradigm

The structural Keynesian box provides a road map for repairing the demand-generating process. However, the global economy currently faces a severe demand shortage, and repairing the system will take time. That means traditional textbook Keynesian policies that stimulate demand will be vital during this interlude. Moreover, the period of need will be longer than usual, because the demand gap is not temporary. This poses a political problem because of widespread misunderstanding about budget deficits.[11]

One reason for large budget deficits is to fill the gap in demand caused by decline of business and consumer spending. A second

---

[11] For detailed discussions of the economics of budget deficits and fiscal austerity, see Pollin, R. [2010], "Austerity Is Not a Solution: Why the deficit Hawks Are Wrong," *Challenge*, 53 (6), 6–36; Palley, T.I. [2011b], "The Fiscal Austerity Trap: Budget Deficit Alarmism is Sabotaging Growth," *Challenge*, 54 (1), 6–31.

reason, related to the current recession, is private-sector deleveraging. The private sector is trying to save and pay back debts, but the laws of economics require that for every saver there must be a borrower. That means if the private sector wants to save more than it invests, someone must take that saving and spend it. Otherwise, income will fail to reduce saving and bring it into alignment with investment. That someone is government, which must borrow and spend the private sector's excess saving (i.e., run budget deficits) to prevent a further fall in demand and income. Because deleveraging can be a lengthy process, this means large budget deficits may be needed for an extended period.

A third reason for budget deficits is to finance public investment in infrastructure, education, and public goods. Such investment increases the productivity of private capital, and it is appropriate that it be financed with borrowing because it is long-lived. That way, future generations who will benefit from the investment also pay part of the cost.

Over the last thirty years, the share of U.S. national income devoted to public investment has fallen, creating a backlog of needs and opportunities. This combination of need for deficit spending and need for public investment creates a win-win policy opportunity. Large-scale deficit-financed public investment can spur economic activity during a period of rebuilding the demand-generating process.

Unfortunately, fiscal policy confronts a number of myths. One myth is that government spending crowds out private investment. The reality is that it crowds in private investment by increasing demand, which increases the need for productive capacity. The one time government spending can crowd out private-sector activity is when an economy is at full employment. In that special situation, resources are scarce, and government use of resources reduces the resources available to the private sector. However, the United States is far away from that situation.

Another related myth is that government absorbs saving, making less available to the private sector. In fact, in times of deep recession, government spending creates saving by preventing further declines in income that would reduce saving. The extra saving shows up in accumulation of government bonds that increase household wealth.

A final myth concerns claims that government is like a household and should therefore balance its budget like a household. The reality is that the household sector in aggregate has historically had rising debt. Today, the household sector owes more than it did 100 years ago, which is reasonable because it is larger and financial markets are more sophisticated. By that same logic, it is reasonable that government owe more, which means deficits can be legitimate.

Moreover, unlike individual households, government is an issuer of money via central banks. That means government can always repay its debt. The one danger is that paying debt by creating money may cause inflation, but that is an unlikely scenario in an economy with massive excess capacity and short of demand.

For all these reasons, large budget deficits are both feasible and needed to ward off stagnation. To minimize the interest burden of debt and to maximize the expansionary effect, the Federal Reserve should help finance the deficit by buying part of new Treasury bond issues. That way monetary policy and fiscal policy will be working in tandem.

The danger is that deficit myths, combined with animus to government, will prevail politically and prevent needed budget deficits. Worse yet, there is a risk that the politics of fiscal austerity will prevail, forcing a withdrawal of fiscal stimulus. That would worsen the problem of demand shortage and deepen the recession, thereby aggravating budget difficulties by lowering tax revenues. Such an out-come risks a repeat of the events of 1937 when, under pressure from fiscal conservatives, the Roosevelt administration cut back on public spending, thereby contributing to a second recession in the middle of the Great Depression.

Making the case for extraordinary large budget deficits now does not mean large deficits can continue forever. Over a longer time hori-zon, there is a need to implement fiscal consolidation as current bud-get deficits are likely unsustainable. However, the key to resolving this problem is the restoration of growth and not fiscal austerity that deepens stagnation. Much of the needed deficit reduction will come automatically with increased employment, but getting there requires abandoning the neoliberal paradigm and replacing it with structural Keynesianism.

Political Obstacles to Paradigm Change

The economic policies needed to avoid the Great Stagnation and restore shared prosperity are not difficult to understand. However, there are massive political obstacles to change.

The Third Way and the Split among Social Democrats
The greatest single obstacle is the capture of social democratic political parties by so-called Third Way thinking. In the United States, the Third Way is represented by the New Democrat wing of the Democratic Party. Its dominance is reflected in the ease with which former Clinton administration officials gained absolute control of the Obama administration's economic policy without significant debate.

Analytically, Third Way New Democrats accept the core beliefs of neoliberal economics. Thus, they reject the structural Keynesian view that organizing an adequate level of aggregate demand is a permanent part of the economic problem. Instead, they accept the view that laissez-faire economies largely solve the demand problem, except for occasional recessions where a temporary textbook Keynesian fix may be needed. Demand is therefore not a lasting problem, and the real problem is supply.

Consequently, Third Way Democrats focus on traditional microeconomic concerns about incentives and market failures such as monopoly, externalities, and provision of public goods. Unions and labor market protections are characterized as market failures rather than part of the structures needed for organizing demand and income distribution. As for macroeconomic policy, all that is needed is monetary policy that controls inflation and inflation expectations.

Third Way proponents are distinguished from hard-core neoliberals by their belief that market failures are more common, government can successfully address market failures, and government also has a role providing "helping hand" programs that soften the blows of the "invisible hand." In terms of the academia, hard-core neoliberals identify with the Chicago School of economics, whereas soft-core Third Way proponents identify with the MIT School.

The Third Way's capture of social democratic parties – New Democrats in the United States, New Labor in the United Kingdom, and New Social Democrats in Germany – creates a fundamental

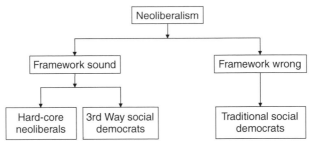

Figure 9.5. The political dilemma of neoliberalism.

political problem because it splits social democrats. This split is illustrated in Figure 9.5. At the most basic level, there is a divide between those who see the neoliberal economic paradigm as sound and those who see it as fundamentally flawed. Both hard-core neoliberals and Third Way social democrats see market fundamentalism as sound, while traditional social democrats see it as fundamentally flawed. The political problem is this splits social democrats, making it harder to dislodge the paradigm.

This division within social democrats creates a major political conundrum. On one hand, if traditional social democrats split from Third Way social democrats, they risk a full-blown triumph of market fundamentalism. On the other hand, sticking in fractious union with Third Way social democrats risks the gradual entrenchment of market fundamentalism.

Worse yet, this entrenchment is done with appeals to "bipartisanship." The Third Way therefore triangulates the economic policy debate, and in doing so it de facto legitimizes market fundamentalism and delegitimizes alternatives. This was the pattern in the United States during the Clinton presidency, and a similar pattern is discernible in Britain under Prime Minister Blair and in Germany under Chancellor Schroder.

A second political problem is the Third Way approach to economic policy risks discrediting structural Keynesian policy by association. Instead of offering a clear choice between neoliberalism and structural Keynesianism, the current political setup offers a choice between "neoliberalism" and "neoliberalism lite" – a choice between Coke and Pepsi. However, the Coke-versus-Pepsi choice is portrayed publicly as a choice between fundamentally different economic philosophies.

Should Third Way attempts (i.e., the Obama administration's policies) to deal with the crisis fail, there is a danger that failure will be interpreted as a failure of Keynesianism. In that event, structural Keynesianism will be labeled a failure and rejected without being given a chance.

Difficulties in Dislodging the Third Way

Dislodging the Third Way's hold over social democratic political parties is extremely difficult. First, there is the fundamental problem of money. Third Way social democrats attract huge amounts of money from business because the Third Way approach poses little threat to businesses, and it also allows business to control both sides of the political aisle.

A second difficulty to dislodging the Third Way is the capture of the economics profession by neoliberal ideas. The Chicago School of economics and the MIT School of economics are presented to the public as if they are worlds apart, when in reality they are siblings. For instance, writing in the *New York Times* magazine, Paul Krugman characterized the economics profession as being profoundly split between "freshwater" Chicago School and "saltwater" MIT school economists.[12] However, both schools actually share the same intellectual paradigm and their differences are of degree, not of kind. As in politics, the choice in the academia is really a choice between Coke and Pepsi, but it is presented as if it were a choice between radically different ideas. That representation serves to obstruct real alternatives.

A third obstacle is the state of public understanding of economics. After thirty years of atrophied political conversation, even though the public is aware that something is wrong, it may be unprepared for a real economic debate because of the neoliberal monopoly on economic discourse and education. This autism can be traced back to the Cold War, when the West was in geopolitical competition with the Soviet Union. That ideological competition fostered a rhetoric that idealized markets in terms of "natural" and "free," while demonizing collective economic action that was identified with authoritarian socialism.

---

[12] Krugman, P. [2009], "How Did Economists Get It So Wrong?" *New York Times*, September 6.

The Curse of Clintonomics

U.S. economic policy discourse also suffers from the curse of Clintonomics. The 1990s Clinton administration aggressively pushed the orthodox agenda. It was during this period that corporate globalization was cemented in place via NAFTA, the strong-dollar policy inaugurated after the 1997 East Asian financial crisis, and granting China full access to the U.S. market.

The Clinton administration also pushed the merits of fiscal austerity and budget surpluses; contemplated privatizing Social Security; rejected public investment-led growth; used rhetoric about the end of the "era of big government"; and eliminated the fundamental right to welfare established by the New Deal as part of its 1996 welfare reform.[13] Furthermore, the administration disregarded manufacturing, believing that the new IT economy had rendered manufacturing economically obsolescent and made the U.S. a postindustrial economy.

Finally, the Clinton administration pushed financial deregulation and blocked the modernization of financial regulation, allowing an explosion of risk taking on Wall Street. In particular, it was instrumental in the repeal of the Glass-Steagal Act (1933) that previously separated investment and commercial banking, and it also blocked regulation of the derivatives market. This neoliberal attitude was reflected in President Clinton's willingness to twice reappoint the guru of market fundamentalism, Alan Greenspan, as Chairman of the Federal Reserve.

The important point is that the economic policies of the Clinton administration were fundamentally neoliberal and were the same policies behind thirty years of wage stagnation and the financial crash. Yet, the Clinton Presidency coincided with the stock market and Internet booms, the beginning of the debt binge, and the beginning of the housing price bubble. This coincidence meant it was a period of significant job creation and economic prosperity. Even though that prosperity was built on foundations of sand, in the public's mind it was attributed to Clintonomics.

For ordinary people, who are not economic policy experts, this "coincidence" of prosperity and Clintonomics was interpreted as

---

[13] President Clinton referred to the era of big government being over in his January 1996 State of the Union address to Congress.

"causation." That belief makes it difficult to dislodge the Third Way wing of the Democratic Party as criticism of its policies and personnel are rebuffed by appeals to the Clinton era.

Europe's Economic Underperformance

A final political obstacle is Europe's economic underperformance. Europe is widely viewed as the standard-bearer of social democracy and Keynesianism. Thus, in public debate, the European economic model is often posited as the social democratic alternative to the neo-liberal U.S. economic model.

The great irony is that social democratic Europe has been more captured by neoliberal macroeconomic policy than the United States. The European Central Bank (ECB) and European finance ministries are dominated by economic policy makers trained in Chicago School economics, whereas the pragmatism of U.S. politicians has supported budget deficits and Keynesianism – albeit unstable asset bubble/ consumer debt Keynesianism.

In economics, macroeconomic policy trumps microeconomic policy. Consequently, Europe's adoption of hard-core macroeconomic policy has trumped its more social democratic microeconomic policy. As a result, the European economy has underperformed the U.S. economy, giving rise to perceived failure of the social democratic model when it has not been given a chance to succeed.

The period between 1950 and 1980 was an era when Europe pursued a combination of Keynesian macroeconomic policies and social democratic microeconomic policies. That era was a golden age for Europe, and the European model was shown to deliver. The past thirty years saw European policy makers abandon Keynesian inclinations. That undercut Europe's economic performance and undermined the appeal of the European model, making it harder to challenge the orthodox model.

Conclusion: Politics and Paradigms

In the late 1970s, British Prime Minister Margaret Thatcher coined the acronym TINA – "There Is No Alternative." By this she meant there is no alternative to neoliberal market fundamentalism. Mrs. Thatcher and Ronald Reagan succeeded in tainting the Keynesian social democratic approach to economics and economic policy. The result was a rejection of demand-management policies, a retreat from commitment to full employment policies, and abandonment of concern with the wage and income distribution generation process.

Mrs. Thatcher's TINA doctrine has ruled the roost politically and intellectually for thirty years. The financial crisis of 2008 and the Great Recession have tarnished market fundamentalism but they have not done away with the TINA myth. Instead, society has entered an intellectual vacuum in which market fundamentalism is tarnished but the taint on Keynesian social democracy remains.

The challenge is to persuade the public that there is an alternative. Neoliberals try to scare people by framing the debate as a choice between capitalism and authoritarian socialism, which is a tactic that has worked well for fifty years. The reality is that it is a debate about what type of capitalism we have.

The grave danger now is that market fundamentalism survives, policy dominant but unworkable. In that event, a "new normal" of permanent high unemployment and wage stagnation will become a near certainty in the United States and other Northern economies, and the Weimar political scenario of intolerance also becomes more likely. For emerging market economies, lack of adequate engines of demand growth of their own means they too will likely get caught up in the economic malaise caused by stagnation in the North.

10

The Challenge of Corporate Globalization

Globalization has been a central development of the past twenty-five years. Not only did it play a critical role in creating the conditions that led to the financial crisis; it is now a key factor driving the prospect of a long stagnation. Reforming globalization and reining in the existing model is therefore vital.

The Special Significance of Globalization

Chapter 4 showed how the flawed U.S. model of global economic engagement contributed to undermining the economy. This model can be termed corporate globalization as it was designed and sponsored by corporate interests.

Globalization represents one side of the neoliberal policy box discussed in Chapters 4 and 9. However, it has claims to be *primus inter pares* – the most important of the four sides. This special standing is because globalization negatively implicates all dimensions of the economy and economic policy.

There are two critical features to globalization. First, it has undermined the internal demand-generating process by fostering wage stagnation via international labor competition, expanding the leakage of spending via imports, and offshoring jobs and investment. Second, it provided a new architecture binding economies together.

One part of the new architecture involved reconfiguring global production by transferring manufacturing from the United States and (to a lesser degree) Europe to emerging market (EM) economies. This new global division of labor was then supported by having U.S. consumers

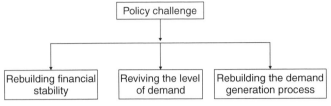

Figure 10.1. The Great Recession policy challenge.

serve as the global economy's buyer of first and last resort, which explains the U.S. trade deficit and the global imbalances problem.

The other part of the new architecture was financial and involved recycling of foreign country trade surpluses back to the United States, which had two effects. First, it abetted financial excess in the United States as foreign investors channeled funds into mortgage-backed securities. Second, the recycling process tied other economies to the U.S. property bubble so that when it burst, there was a massive spillover that damaged financial systems elsewhere, particularly in Europe.

The economic policy challenge of escaping the Great Recession and restoring shared prosperity is illustrated in Figure 10.1. Policy makers face a threefold challenge. First, policy must rebuild financial stability in light of the financial excess and fragility revealed by the financial crisis. Second, it must stimulate and revive demand so that the private sector increases output and employment. Third, it must rebuild the income-generating process so that the economy permanently generates a stable level of demand consistent with full employment and shared prosperity.

Globalization adversely implicates all three policy challenges. With regard to financial reform, attempts to regulate banks and financial markets risk triggering jurisdictional shopping whereby financial capital leaves countries that impose tough regulations and migrates to countries with lax regulation.

With regard to stimulating demand, globalization weakens policy because of increased trade openness. Thus, stimulus may leak out of the economy via spending on imports rather than domestically produced goods so that it creates jobs offshore rather than at home. Additionally, financial markets tend to dislike budget deficits, and they may try to punish governments that pursue stimulus policies. The classic example of this is France in 1983, where President Mitterand was forced to abandon his Keynesian policy aimed at restoring full employment under pressure from international markets.

Finally, globalization hampers rebuilding the demand-generating process. Chapter 9 framed the rebuilding challenge in terms of repacking the neoliberal policy box. In the pre-globalization era (1945–80), countries would have had more policy space to pursue a national strategy to repack the box. However, in the era of corporate globalization, "go it alone" national strategies are far more difficult because globalization imposes powerful constraints that restrict policy. Developing countries, including large EM economies like Brazil, have long complained about this aspect of globalization. Today, the United States is feeling some of the same policy space limits, albeit still on a much smaller scale.[1] For instance, attempts to change labor market institutions so as to raise wages and improve income distribution may be met by offshoring production and investment to countries with worker-unfriendly laws and institutions.

Figure 10.2 provides a heuristic map (think of it like a subway map) of the global economy, which consists of four parts. The global economic core consists of North America, Europe, and the export-oriented emerging economies. The resource-based economies and less-developed countries are placed outside of the core. That is because the less-developed economies are substantially disengaged from the core, whereas the resource-based economies conform to traditional periphery status in terms of center-periphery economic relations.[2]

The map helps understand how globalization complicates the policy problem. First, the countries and regions of the global economy are linked together by an international economic system, represented by the solid triangle in Figure 10.2. That system concerns arrangements governing trade, international financial markets, and global policy coordination. The system is part of the problem and has

---

[1] For a discussion of the policy space issue, see Grabel, I. [2000], "The Political Economy of 'Policy Credibility': The New-Classical Macroeconomics and the Remaking of Emerging Economies," *Cambridge Journal of Economics*, 24, 1–19; Bradford, C.I., Jr. [2005], "Prioritizing Economic Growth: Enhancing Macroeconomic Policy Choice," G-24 Discussion paper No. 37, April.

[2] Mexico as well as Japan, China, and other East Asian economies can be considered export-oriented economies. Brazil, Russia, Australia, and Latin American economies are part of the resource-based bloc. India is a little difficult to peg. Despite its size and recent economic growth success, it should probably be placed with the less-developed countries because of its still relatively low level of global engagement.

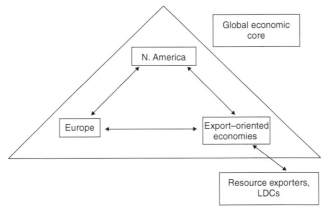

Figure 10.2. A map of the global economy.

contributed to the undermining of the demand-generating process, within both the U.S. economy and the rest of the global economy. Additionally, the system undermines policy effectiveness and limits space for "go it alone" national policy. That is why reform of globalization is so important.

Second, because countries are linked to each other, successful policy requires policy coordination. If country policies are working against each other, their effects will be correspondingly diminished.

Worse yet, countries may have an incentive to free-ride and take no action, hoping to be pulled along by the coattails of others while avoiding bearing any costs of action. Viewed from a global perspective, there is a need for policy coordination, yet viewed from the individual-country perspective, there can be incentives to evade and shirk such cooperation.

Third, the global economy consists of different regions with different conditions. There are many similarities across regions, but there are also differences. Regions vary in their stage of development, have different internal economics problems, and some are running trade surpluses whereas others are running deficits. That means there is no one-size-fits-all policy. Countries and regions need to take different actions, but those different actions must fit into a coordinated framework. In particular, all countries should work to increase demand because the global economy is short of demand, and all should also aim to build a stable sustainable demand-generating process within countries and in the global economy.

Fourth, reform of corporate globalization is critical. However, because globalization concerns the international system, reform requires international agreement, which makes the political process of reform even more difficult.

Fifth, one-third of humanity lives in resource-exporting countries and less-developed countries that are outside of the global core. Those countries have qualitatively different development problems that are not directly addressed in this book. However, it is ethically clear that their development needs to be a priority. Those needs should be promoted in ways that add to global demand (i.e., they should benefit by receiving resources) and support the underlying global demand-generating process in financially and environmentally sustainable fashion.

In sum, the global economic architecture is of profound importance. It shapes the dynamic of the global economy by shaping the way that countries and regions interact, and by determining what countries can do on their own and what they are willing to do together. The current architecture is flawed, which means there is a need to change the rules governing international trade, capital flows, and exchange rates. However, changing the architecture will require changing the architects, illustrating once again the importance of ideas and politics.

The Economics of Globalization

Globalization refers to the process of international integration of national goods, financial, and labor markets. It is a process that is being driven by technology, businesses' quest for profits, and policy.

Globalization changes the structure of economies and creates three forms of economic leaks. The first is *macroeconomic leakiness*, whereby there is a tendency for demand to leak out of the national economy owing to an increased propensity to import goods. The second is *microeconomic leakiness*, whereby there is a tendency for jobs to leak out of an economy if wages and other employment costs are not sufficiently low, labor markets are not sufficiently flexible, or taxes are relatively unfavorable compared to conditions elsewhere. The third is *financial leakiness*, whereby finance is free to flow across borders.[3]

---

[3] See Palley, T.I. [2000], "The Economics of Globalization: A Labor View," in Teich, Nelson, McEnaney, and Lita (eds.), *Science and Technology Policy Yearbook 2000*, American Association for the Advancement of Science, Washington, DC.

All three types of leakiness matter and they promote and amplify each other. Thus, increased trade increases macroeconomic leakiness, whereas increased financial leakiness promotes trade and foreign direct investment, which increases microeconomic leakiness.

All three types of leakiness also make national economic policy more difficult. Increased macroeconomic leakiness means more spending leaks out of the economy. That makes it harder to use traditional Keynesian stimulus measures to increase domestic demand as stimulus leaks out. Increased financial leakiness makes it hard to adopt policies that regulate finance as financiers will sell domestic financial assets, driving up interest rates. Increased microeconomic leakiness makes it harder to promote decent working conditions, promote a fair distribution of income, and protect the environment, because corporations will offshore jobs and investment.

The critical new feature of globalization is international mobility of the means of production (capital and technology). Trade has existed throughout human history and has yielded enormous economic benefits, as well as occasionally imposing costs on specific regions and industries. The game changer in globalization is the ability to move and coordinate production between countries at low cost. This has fundamentally changed the character of global competition, undermined the demand-generating process, and undermined governments' ability to conduct national economic policy.

Free trade created a "global marketplace." Globalization has created a "global production zone." The new reality was captured in the late 1990s by Jack Welch, then CEO of General Electric, who talked of ideally having "every plant you own on a barge." The economic logic was that factories should float between countries to take advantage of lowest costs, be they a result of undervalued exchange rates, low taxes, subsidies, or a surfeit of cheap labor.

Globalization has made Welch's barge a reality, giving rise to "barge economics" that has replaced the old economics of trade based on the theory of comparative advantage. In the old era of classical trade, countries competed regarding the most efficient production of goods. That competition lowered prices and also caused some dislocation as some industries closed. In the new era of globalization, the competition is for jobs. Before, companies wooed customers with cheaper goods: now, workers and governments kowtow to companies to retain jobs and attract investment.

From a Structural Keynesian perspective, the shift from free trade to globalization has numerous adverse consequences. First, it undermines the income- and demand-generating process by undermining worker bargaining power. The result is continuous downward pressure on wages and an increase in the profit share as workers settle for less to hold on to jobs. Globalization also pressures institutional arrangements (such as employment protections, minimum wages, and rights to unionize) supporting the income-generating process, again in the name of staying attractive to business. Furthermore, the income-generating process is also weakened at the after-tax level as governments are pressured to shift the tax burden from profits to wage income to increase their relative attractiveness to business.

Second, globalization undermines the effectiveness of standard Keynesian demand-management policy by increasing macroeconomic leakiness. Increased reliance on imports means fiscal and monetary stimulus tends to leak out of the economy as spending on imports rather than spending on domestically produced goods and services. Reduced policy effectiveness in turn discourages government from adopting such policies.

Not only is the effectiveness of Keynesian policy undermined; governments are also discouraged from pursuing either demand-management policies or structural policies that strengthen the demand-generating process. One reason is the free-rider problem. For instance, fiscal stimulus is costly as it increases the national debt. Governments may therefore prefer other countries stimulate demand so that they can piggyback for free on the induced economic expansion.

A second reason is the prisoner's dilemma, whereby globalization establishes a pattern of incentives that encourages noncooperative behavior. Every country believes it can do better going it alone, which results in all doing worse than if they cooperated. The prisoner's dilemma is illustrated in Figure 10.3, which shows the hypothetical payoffs to a policy game. There are two countries, A and B. Each country has two policy options: cooperate or cheat. The payoff to a country is highest (= 10) if it cheats and the other country cooperates, and lowest (= −10) if it cooperates and the other country cheats. For the system as a whole, the payoff is lowest if both countries cheat (−5, −5) and highest if both cooperate (5, 5).

		Country B	
		Cheat	Cooperate
Country A	Cheat	−5,−5	10,−10
	Cooperate	−10, 10	5, 5

Figure 10.3. The prisoner's dilemma and international economic cooperation.

The problem is each country has an incentive to cheat to try and get the highest payoff (10), but when both cheat, they actually get the lowest payoff (−5). What is needed is cooperative behavior, but the incentives are not there. The only way to get the cooperative outcome is some form of international coordination, perhaps backed up by sanctions disciplining countries that renege. That is why the design of the correct international architecture is so important.

Worse than that, corporate globalization aggravates these problems by design. A fundamental goal of neoliberalism is to weaken government restraints over markets and expand the power of capital. Putting governments in competition with one another accomplishes that. Corporate globalization does exactly that by increasing economic leakiness, which puts governments in competition, and that worsens the global economy's generic prisoner's dilemma problem.

One example concerns labor market protection, the minimum wage, and rights to join unions. Each country may feel it can do better by having weak labor market protections, thereby making itself more attractive to business. However, if all pursue that strategy, none is relatively more attractive to business. Instead, the net result is to weaken the global demand-generating process by lowering wages and the wage share, making all worse off.

A second example concerns fiscal stimulus, and it is exemplified by the situation in European economies like Portugal, Italy, Ireland, Greece, and Spain – the so-called PIIGS economies. Financial markets dislike budget deficits. Financial capital therefore tends to migrate to countries with lower deficits, increasing interest rates in large-deficit countries and lowering rates in small-deficit countries. Given this, governments have an incentive to pursue fiscal austerity to make themselves relatively more attractive to financial markets. However, none gain when all do this, and the only effect is to impose fiscal austerity that reduces demand and worsens recession.

A third example concerns exchange rates. Globalization and increased economic leakiness gives countries an incentive to depreciate their exchange rate to increase their competitiveness and also to make themselves more attractive to foreign investment. However, when all do this, exchange rates are unchanged, and the only effect is to create financial turmoil that may undermine business planning and investment.

In sum, corporate globalization is extremely problematic. The neoliberal policy box shows how corporate globalization contributes to undermining the demand-generating process. When the box is simultaneously implemented in other countries in the context of a neoliberal international architecture, its impact is multiplicative across countries. Thus, it undermines the effectiveness of structural Keynesian policies within each country, and it also undermines the willingness of governments to pursue such policies. The net result is a profound deflationary bias in the global economy.

Mending Globalization

Escaping the Great Recession and the pull of the Great Stagnation requires stimulating demand and rebuilding the income- and demand-generating process. Corporate globalization discourages both, which is why it must be radically reformed. The existing system imposes a global deflationary bias. The goal of reform should be to replace that bias with an expansionary bias.

Core Labor Standards

A first critical reform is implementation and enforcement of global core labor standards (CLS). Such standards are needed to build a sustainable demand-generating process and to address the ethical wrongs of globalization. CLS can improve income equality and create conditions in which wages rise with productivity. That will help remedy the current problem of global demand shortage and contribute to creating a new global demand-generating process consistent with full employment. It will also promote shared prosperity by having workers share in rising productivity.

CLS refer to five core articles of the International Labor Organization (ILO) concerning freedom of association and protection of the right to organize, the right to organize and bargain collectively, the prohibition of all forms of forced or compulsory labor, the abolition of exploitative child labor, and the elimination of discrimination in respect of employment and occupation. These standards are very much in the spirit of "rights" and are intended to hold independently of a country's stage of development. This links CLS with the discourse of human rights.

Two of the standards are affirmative in character, giving workers the right to organize and bargain collectively, while three of the standards are prohibitive in character, banning forced labor, exploitative child labor, and discrimination. The standards are all "qualitative" in nature, not "quantitative." That means they do not involve labor market interventions contingent on an economy's stage of development. Contrary to the claims of opponents, CLS do not impose on developing countries quantitative regulation befitting mature economies. No one is asking developing countries to adopt the U.S. minimum wage.

Lastly, the freedom of association and right-to-organize standard is particularly important. This standard covers labor unions, but it also covers civil society and religious organizations. As such, it promotes democracy and civil liberty, which constitute essential goals of development along with higher living standards.

Opponents of labor standards assert they are a form of "hidden protection" for developed-country workers and claim standards would retard growth and development. However, there are strong theoretical and empirical grounds for believing labor standards would raise global growth, and that developing countries stand to gain the most.

One source of economic benefit is static efficiency gains, whereby CLS correct distortions in labor markets, resulting in better resource allocations that raise output and economic well-being. Raising wages via labor standards can increase productivity because higher wages elicit greater worker effort and reduce malnutrition. Giving workers the right to join unions can neutralize excessive bargaining power of employers, thereby increasing both employment and wages. Eliminating discrimination can raise employment, output, and wages by ensuring efficient matching of jobs and skills. Lastly, eliminating inappropriate child labor can contribute to higher wages for adult workers, which can promote economic development by contributing to better child nutrition and helping human capital formation by supporting lengthened years of schooling. Far from reducing employment in developing countries, these static efficiency effects will raise employment and higher wages will increase employment by increasing consumption spending and countering demand shortage.

Dynamic economic efficiency gains refer to gains that come from changing the path and pattern of economic development. With regard to such gains, CLS can encourage firms to pursue business plans focused on increasing productivity rather than plans that aim to increase profits by squeezing workers and redistributing existing productivity.

At the global level, CLS can help block the problem of race-to-the-bottom competition between countries, which results from situations of prisoner's dilemma. Market incentives often lead agents to pursue actions that seemingly benefit individuals but actually turn out to be harmful when all choose such actions. A classic example is bribery that appears to benefit the individual but ends up harming all when all choose to bribe. The same holds for labor exploitation, which promotes "low road" competition between countries marked by a degraded environment, lack of public goods, and lack of investment in skills.

The hallmark of globalization is increased mobility of production and capital between countries. This has allowed business to pit countries in adverse competition that erodes environmental and workplace regulations and undercuts wages of all workers – both in the North and South. Multinational corporations may actually exploit South-South divisions even more than they exploit North-South divisions, pitting developing countries in destructive competition to secure foreign investment. CLS can help rein in this adverse competition by establishing standards applying in all countries.

Another feature of corporate globalization has been the adoption of export-led growth strategies. Countries that were early to adopt this strategy have benefitted, but with so many countries adopting this strategy, its underlying destructive prisoner's dilemma character is being revealed. Export-led growth is deflationary, promotes financial instability, and is unsustainable.

One flaw with export-led growth is that it encourages countries to engage in race-to-the-bottom competition as each tries to gain competitive advantage over its rival. A second flaw is that it creates global excess capacity and problems of export displacement, whereby one country's export sales displace another's. Both of these flaws create deflationary pressures. A third flaw is that it promotes financial instability by encouraging countries to seek competitive advantage through undervalued exchange rates – a strategy that China has been particularly adept at exploiting. However, since everyone cannot have an undervalued exchange rate (some must be overvalued), one country's gain comes at the expense of others. Moreover, in the case of China, its gain has come at the expense of both developing and developed countries. Thus, China has sucked industries out of the United States and has also sucked foreign direct investment away from other developing economies.

In sum, global application of the strategy of export-led growth increases global supply while simultaneously undermining the global demand-generating process. Production is shipped from poorer Southern countries to richer Northern countries, but at the same time the incomes and buying power of Northern consumers is undermined. That makes export-led growth globally unsustainable.

Instead, countries need to shift to a new strategy that relies more on domestic demand-led growth, which would allow the benefits of development to be consumed at home. CLS are critical to a new domestic demand-led growth strategy as they can help tie wages to productivity growth, thereby building the necessary domestic demand-generating process.[4]

A final benefit of CLS concerns politics and governance.[5] There is now growing awareness that transparency, accountability, and democratic political competition enhance growth and development. They do so by limiting corruption and cronyism, promoting institutions and policy processes responsive to economic conditions, and promoting fairer income distribution. By protecting freedom of association and the right to organize, CLS contribute positively to both the overall

---

[4] See Palley, T.I. [2002b], "Domestic Demand-Led Growth: A New Paradigm for Development," in Jacobs, Weaver and Baker (eds.), *After Neo-liberalism: Economic Policies That Work for the Poor*, Washington, DC: New Rules for Global Finance. Also published as "A New Development Paradigm: Domestic Demand-Led Growth," *Foreign Policy in Focus*, September, http://www.fpif.org/

[5] See Palley, T.I. [2005b], "Labor Standards, Democracy and Wages: Some Cross-country Evidence," *Journal of International Development*, 17, 1–16.

development of civil society and the specific development of labor markets and worker-based organizations.

A Global Minimum-Wage System

A second critical reform is the establishment of a global minimum-wage system. This does not mean imposing U.S. or European minimum wages in developing countries. It does mean establishing a global set of rules for setting country's minimum wages.

The minimum wage is a vital policy tool that provides a floor to wages and reduces downward pressure on wages. The barrier created by the floor also creates a rebound ripple effect that raises wages in the bottom two deciles of the wage spectrum.[6] Furthermore, it compresses wages at the bottom of the wage spectrum, thereby helping reduce inequality. Lastly, an appropriately designed minimum wage helps connect wages and productivity growth, which is critical for building a sustainable demand-generating process.[7]

Traditionally, minimum-wage systems have operated by setting a fixed wage that is periodically adjusted to take account of inflation and other changing circumstances. Such an approach is fundamentally flawed and inappropriate for the global economy. It is flawed because the minimum wage is always playing catch-up, and it is inappropriate because the system is difficult to generalize across countries.

Instead, countries should set a minimum wage that is a fixed percent (say 50 percent) of their median wage – which is the wage at which half of workers are paid more and half are paid less. This design has several advantages. First, the minimum wage will automatically rise with the median wage, creating a true floor that moves with the economy. If the median wage rises with productivity growth, the minimum wage will also rise with productivity growth.

Second, because the minimum wage is set by reference to the local median wage, it is set by reference to local economic conditions and

---

[6] Using U.S. data to estimate wage curves, Palley (1998c) reports that the minimum wage has a ripple effect that reaches through the bottom two deciles of the wage distribution. Using U.S. micro data, Wicks-Lim (2006) reports the minimum wage has a ripple effect that reaches the bottom 15 percent of the workforce.

[7] For a more extensive discussion of the economics of minimum wages, see Palley, T.I. [1998b] "Building Prosperity from the Bottom Up: The New Economics of the Minimum Wage," *Challenge*, 41 (July–August), 1–13.

reflects what a country can bear. Moreover, because all countries are bound by the same rule, all are treated equally.

Third, if countries want a higher minimum wage, they are free to set one. The global minimum-wage system would only set a floor: it would not set a ceiling.

Fourth, countries would also be free to set regional minimum wages within each country. Thus, a country like Germany that has higher unemployment in the former East Germany and lower unemployment in the former West Germany could set two minimum wages: one for former East Germany, and one for former West Germany. The only requirement would be that the regional minimum wage be greater than or equal to 50 percent of the regional median wage. Such a system of regional minimum wages would introduce additional flexibility that recognizes that wages and living costs vary within countries as well as across countries. This enables the minimum-wage system to avoid the danger of overpricing labor while still retaining the demand-side benefits a minimum wage confers by improving income distribution and helping tie wages to productivity growth.

Finally, a global minimum-wage system would confer significant political benefits by cementing understanding of the need for global labor market rules and showing they are feasible. Just as globalization demands global trade rules for goods and services and global financial rules for financial markets, so too labor markets need global rules.

Managed Exchange Rates

A third critical reform concerns the global system of exchange rates. Exchange rates matter more than ever because of globalization. However, the current system of exchange rates is dysfunctional. It contributed to the emergence of massive global financial imbalances that are a critical part of the crisis, and the system now contributes to political tensions between countries, as none wants to bear costs of correcting these imbalances.

With regard to the U.S. economy, the overvalued dollar contributed to the trade deficit and offshoring of jobs and investment, all of which were important factors in undermining the income- and demand-generating process. The overvalued dollar has also weakened the effects of stimulus by increasing imports rather than domestic production, thereby hindering recovery from taking hold. With regard to other economies, undervalued exchange rates have been an important factor driving export-led growth based on attracting foreign direct investment.

The existing system is justified by appeal to orthodox arguments that flexible exchange rates generate stable sustainable outcomes. In fact, they are neither stable nor sustainable. The 1990s witnessed a series of exchange rate crises, as speculative capital flows whipsawed exchange rates, first appreciating them and then crashing them. This was exemplified by the East Asian financial crash of 1997. That turbulent experience prompted many governments to intervene, creating the current problem of undervalued exchange rates.

The situation is exemplified by China's currency market interventions aimed at keeping the Chinese yuan undervalued. China's actions in turn force other East Asian countries to intervene to keep their exchange rates undervalued so as not to lose competitiveness versus China. The result has been a generalized overvalued dollar that has contributed to the massive U.S. trade deficit, devastation of the U.S. industrial base, and undermining of the income- and demand-generating process.

The problem of misaligned exchange rates is persistent and long-standing. The current problem is dollar overvaluation. In the 1990s, the problem of overvalued exchange rates afflicted Latin America and, to a lesser degree, East Asia. This problem of rolling exchange rate misalignments is bad for the global economy and often results in costly crises. Even when there is no ultimate crisis, such misalignments cause inefficiency by misallocating production across countries and distorting trade. Rather than competing on the basis of productivity, too often countries compete through undervalued currencies that confer an exchange rate subsidy.

For much of the past fifteen years, the costs to the U.S economy were obscured by the debt-financed boom, while other countries were happy to go along because U.S. trade deficits created matching trade surpluses that spurred export-led growth. Now, the system has imploded and the costs have become evident.

The current global exchange rate system is a suboptimal arrangement. There are many theoretical reasons for believing that foreign exchange markets are prone to mispricing, and there is also strong empirical evidence that exchange rates persistently depart from their theoretically warranted levels. The existing system also permits strategic manipulation so that some countries (particularly in East Asia) actively intervene to undervalue their currencies. That has made for a lopsided world in which half reject intervention and half are neomercantilist – a configuration that has created economic and political tensions.

It is possible to do better than the current system. The immediate need is for a coordinated global realignment of exchange rates that begins to smoothly unwind existing imbalances. The 1985 Plaza currency accord provides a model of how this can be done. China's participation is critical as it has the largest trade surplus with both the United States and Europe. Moreover, other East Asian countries with trade surpluses will resist revaluing unless China revalues for fear they will become uncompetitive. Finally, this realignment must be credible, and markets must believe it will hold. Absent that, business will not make the changes to production and investment patterns needed to restore equilibrium.

Beyond such realignment, there is a need for systemic reform to avoid recurring misalignments. The solution is a target zone system of managed exchange rates for major currencies. Such systems rely on a number of parameters that would need to be negotiated by participants. These choices include the target exchange rate, the size of the band in which exchange rates can fluctuate, and the rate of crawl, which determines the periodicity and size of adjustments of the target exchange rate.

The rules for intervening to protect the target exchange rate must also be agreed on. Historically, the onus of defense has fallen on the country whose exchange rate is weakening, which requires it to sell foreign exchange reserves. That is a fundamentally flawed arrangement, because countries have limited foreign currency reserves, and the market knows it. Consequently, speculators have an incentive to try and "break the bank" by shorting the weak currency (i.e., forcing the central bank to buy its own currency and sell its reserves until they are used up, at which point it must capitulate) and they have a good shot at success given the scale of low-cost leverage financial markets can muster.

Instead, the onus of intervention must be placed on the strong-currency country. Its central bank has unlimited amounts of its own currency for sale so it can never be beaten by the market. Consequently, if this intervention rule is credibly adopted, speculators will back off, making the target exchange rate viable.

Intervening in this way will also give an expansionary tilt to the global economy. When weak countries defend exchange rates, they often use high interest rates to make their currency attractive, which imparts a deflationary global bias. If strong-surplus countries do the intervening, they may lower their interest rates and impart an expansionary bias.

In sum, a sensible managed exchange rate system can increase the benefits from trade, diminish exchange-rate-induced distortions, and reduce country conflict over trade deficits. The means are at hand, but the political domination of neoliberal ideology has blocked change.

In the United States, discussion of exchange rate policy is still blocked by simplistic free-market nostrums. It is also blocked by mistaken fears that a managed system would surrender sovereignty and control. Yet, that is implicitly what has been happening. By absenting itself from the market, the United States has de facto allowed other countries to set the exchange rate, and that means the United States has been letting itself be strategically outgamed.

Other countries have had no incentive to change because they have benefited from the overvalued dollar. The net result is that the global economy is locked in a suboptimal system that promises stagnation and conflict. Escaping that system requires political leadership, as the system of exchange rates is a system that is agreed between nations.

Legitimize Capital Controls

Undervalued and misaligned exchange rates are one major problem afflicting global economy. A second problem is unrestricted international flows of capital, which was the dominant problem of the 1990s. Capital inflows followed by outflows created rolling boom-bust cycles. Massive inflows distorted asset prices, promoted credit booms, encouraged foreign borrowing, and appreciated exchange rates. This was the pattern behind the string of financial crises that included Mexico in 1994, East Asia in 1997, Russia in 1998, Brazil in 1999, and Argentina in 2000–02.

The 1990s problem of unstable capital flows prompted governments to switch to manipulating exchange rates. Thus, the unstable international hot money flows of 1990s sowed the seed of the current problem of undervalued and manipulated exchange rates. That speaks to the need for capital controls that give policy makers the power to limit inflows and outflows.

One control is to tax currency transactions – the Tobin tax.[8] A second control is to require part of capital inflows be deposited interest free with central banks for a period of time before being released. This penalizes inflows, and the penalty can be adjusted according to economic conditions. Thus, the proportion deposited and the holding period can both be adjusted at the discretion of the central bank, depending on whether it wants to discourage or encourage inflows.[9]

Once again, the problem is that neoliberal ideology discourages such policies. In the 1990s, the IMF explicitly fought to prohibit such controls by making prohibition of capital controls part of its articles of association. That would have obliged IMF member countries to repudiate capital controls. U.S. economic policy still requires that trade agreements outlaw such controls.[10] Although the current crisis has spawned some musings at the IMF about changing policy attitudes to capital controls, there is no evidence of deep-seated acceptance of such controls, and economic orthodoxy is still robustly against them.[11]

Rewrite Trade Rules

Another area of reform is trade rules, which need to be significantly rewritten. Market access must be contingent on adherence to core labor standards, a global minimum-wage system, and participation in a system of managed exchange rates.

---

[8] For a discussion of the economics of capital controls, see Palley, T.I. [2009c], "Rethinking the Economics of Capital Mobility and Capital Controls," *Brazilian Journal of Political Economy*, 29 (July–September), 15–34. For a discussion of the Tobin tax, see Palley, T.I. [2001a], "Destabilizing Speculation and the Case for an International Currency Transactions Tax," *Challenge*, (May–June), 70–89.

[9] For a discussion of the economics of controlling capital inflows by requiring deposits with central banks, see Palley, T.I. [2005c], "Chilean Unremunerated Reserve Requirement Capital Controls as a Screening Mechanism," *Investigacion Economica*, 64 (January–March), 33–52.

[10] See Gallagher, K. [2010b], "Obama Must Ditch Bush-era Trade Deals," *Comment Is Free*, Thursday, July 1, http://www.guardian.co.uk/commentisfree/cifamerica/2010/jun/30/obama-bush-us-trade

[11] See Ostry, J.D. et al. [2010], "Capital Inflows: The Role of Controls," Research Department, International Monetary Fund, February 19, http://www.imf.org/external/pubs/ft/spn/2010/spn1004.pdf

Another important change is the treatment of value added tax (VAT). VAT is a form of sales tax, and under existing WTO trade rules, it is refunded on exports. That gives countries using VAT systems an unjustifiable international competitive advantage over those (like the United States) that raise tax revenues differently. Moreover, it encourages countries to adopt VAT systems, which are regressive. That is because they tax consumption, and poorer households spend proportionately more on consumption and therefore pay a higher effective tax rate.

This favorable trade treatment of VAT is the result of a historical policy blunder. In the late 1940s, when the global economy was being reconstituted after World War II, VAT schemes were almost non-existent. At that time, the United States was the undisputed global economic superpower, keen to promote global economic recovery, and trade was a relatively small part of economic activity. The United States therefore mistakenly agreed to refundability of VAT payments under the General Agreement on Tariffs and Trade (GATT). That rule was then grandfathered into the World Trade Organization (WTO), which was established in the 1990s and replaced the GATT.

The rule should have been abolished when the WTO was created, but U.S. corporations and neoliberal policy makers were keen to push corporate globalization. The Clinton administration therefore let it pass rather than trigger a trade confrontation that could have derailed the corporate globalization process.

The current treatment of VAT is wrong on two counts. First, it discriminates in favor of countries using VAT systems, giving them a competitive advantage. Second, it encourages countries to shift to VAT systems even though they are regressive in that they disproportionately tax lower-income households. The solution is to abolish VAT refunds on exports. The global trade system should not discriminate in favor of one tax regime over another. That is a matter of domestic political choice.

Two other areas needing a fundamental rewrite are trade rules governing intellectual property rights concerning patents and copyrights, and rules that give international investors the right to sue governments under binding international arbitration. Neither is of macroeconomic significance but both reveal starkly the audacious nature of the corporate globalization project.

That project aimed to impose, in the name of free trade, a set of global rules that operated for the benefit of large corporations. The project was audacious in its arrogance of imposing a one-size-fits-all approach and in choosing a size that benefited corporations. Even ardent neoliberal free-trader Jagdish Bhagwati (2002) of Columbia University has been critical of these rules.

With regard to intellectual property rights, the essence of the new rules is that countries have to effectively adopt U.S. laws regarding copyright and patents to participate fully in the global trading system. This constitutes a form of corporate economic imperialism that breaks with the past. Historically, trade rules were exclusively concerned with governing international competition, and copyright and patent law were therefore excluded as matters of domestic commerce.

Corporate globalization aims to take away the power of countries to chart their own economic course, hence the imposition of global patent and copyright rules. The same holds for new trade rules giving foreign investors the right to sue countries under binding international arbitration. This grants foreign investors rights that domestic citizens do not have and undermines national sovereignty. Such developments are fundamentally undemocratic and should be rolled back.

Lessons from History

The global economy is beset by recession and contradiction. Escape from recession is blocked by shortage of demand. The contradiction is that neoliberal corporate globalization promotes a pattern of development that increases global supply while simultaneously undermining global demand. This problem was hidden for twenty years by asset price inflation and borrowing that filled the demand gap, but the economic crisis has exposed it. The implication is that the global economy needs a new model of development that attends to domestic demand, and U.S. economic history offers powerful salient lessons.

Globalization represents the international integration of goods, labor, and financial markets. In the late nineteenth and early twentieth centuries, the U.S. economy underwent a similar process of integration. The U.S. economy was continental in scope, and the creation of a successful national economy required new laws and institutions governing labor markets, financial markets, and business. This is the history of the antitrust movement of the Progressive era and the history of the New Deal that created Social Security, the Securities and Exchange Commission, and labor laws protecting workers.

These institutional innovations solved the structural problems that caused the Great Depression and they generated America's famed blue-collar middle class. Today, the challenge is global institutional innovation that will create shared global prosperity. Meeting that challenge means profoundly reforming corporate globalization.

The Problem of Lock-in

Reason and evidence point to the need to reform corporate globalization, but that is easier said than done because of the problem of "lock-in." Lock-in is a concept developed by economic historians to describe how economies get stuck using inefficient technologies. It also applies to institutions because economies and societies can get locked into suboptimal institutional arrangements. This has relevance for globalization where the arrangements governing the global economy are suboptimal, which poses problems of how to change them. The economics of lock-in helps understand the problem and suggests how to solve it.

Lock-in arises because a technology adopted first may gain a competitive advantage that encourages others to adopt it, even though other technologies are superior and would be chosen if all were at the same starting point. An example of lock-in is a narrow-gauge railroad that is less efficient than broad gauge on which railcars are more stable and can carry greater loads. However, once a stretch of narrow gauge has been laid, there is an incentive for additions to be narrow gauge to fit the existing track. Moreover, the incentive increases as the size of the rail network grows.

Lock-in has enormous relevance for globalization, which has seen the creation of new institutions and patterns of economic activity. Trade agreements and financial market opening have created new rules, fostering new patterns of global production and setting the basis for future trade and investment negotiations.

Globalization lock-in matters because today's global economy has been designed with little attention to income distribution and labor, social, and environmental issues. This is because the system was largely stitched together in the last quarter of the twentieth century, a period of neoliberal laissez-faire intellectual dominance. This design was locked in through a steady flow of corporate-sponsored trade agreements, both multilateral and bilateral.

The economics of lock-in helps understand what is going on and it also suggests an escape from the problem. Recalling the example of narrow-gauge railroads, the market can produce a gradual escape by cherry-picking the most profitable parts of the existing network, causing it to gradually implode. Thus, a parallel wide-gauge track may be built on the most profitable segments of the existing narrow-gauge network, draining the latter's profitability while promoting the gradual buildup of a wide-gauge network.

This provides a metaphor for globalization. The modern global economy has been built on a narrow-gauge rail, and countries now need to find a way to build a broad-gauge replacement. That points to several policy measures. First, countries should stop building more narrow-gauge track, which means no more trade agreements without high-quality labor and environmental standard; commitment to a global minimum-wage system; exchange rate provisions guarding against currency manipulation and unfair competition based on undervalued exchange rates; acceptance of capital controls; and changed intellectual property and investor rights.

Second, developed democratic economies should start cherry-picking the existing "narrow-gauge" trade system and promote "broad-gauge" trade agreements. For instance, the United States and Europe could negotiate a Trans-Atlantic Free Trade Agreement (TAFTA) that includes proper labor and environmental standards, commitment to a common minimum-wage system, and a managed exchange rate agreement. Similar agreements could be negotiated with Canada, Japan, and South Korea. All of these countries would have little difficulty complying with standards, and together they comprise approximately 75 percent of the global economy. Such a trading bloc would quickly become a "broad-gauge" magnet for other countries.

Third, multilateral institutions, such as the IMF and World Bank, must be thoroughly house-cleaned. These institutions must be made to promote labor and environmental standards, legitimacy of capital controls, and legitimacy of managed exchange rates. Under pressure of events, there has been some movement in this direction, but that movement is half-hearted and easily reversible given the deep neo-liberal convictions of the staff appointed over the past thirty years. A thorough remake will require not just policy change, but also personnel change. Absent that, policy change will not stick.

The bottom line is it is still possible to escape corporate globalization lock-in. The key is creating a new dynamic in which forces of competition promote progressive upward harmonization in place of the existing dynamic that promotes a race to the bottom.

Conclusion: Mend it or End it

The phenomenon of lock-in means there will be costs to escaping the current mode of corporate globalization. If all goes well and a cooperative spirit prevails, those costs can be small. However, that is unlikely. Corporations that have benefitted from corporate globalization will fight tooth and nail against change. Likewise, countries that are exploiting the system will also fight to keep it. This explains the political alliance between autocratic China and large U.S. multinationals like Caterpillar and Boeing.

The tragedy of the current era is that the acceleration of global economic integration triggered by changing technologies occurred at a time of dominance by neoliberal economics. That resulted in the creation of a form of globalization that blocks shared prosperity.

It could have been done differently by expanding a social democratic globalization built on the post–World War II model of social and economic inclusion. In that alternative world, NAFTA would have stood for North Atlantic Free Trade Agreement. However, the opportunity was missed.

At this stage, there are two possible responses to corporate globalization: mend it or end it. Mend it means putting in place the policy recommendations discussed previously, which will shift globalization onto a path that promotes shared prosperity rather than a race to the bottom. This corresponds to a structural Keynesian model of globalization that bolsters the global demand-generating process by shifting countries away from export-led growth and attending to the deficiencies of global governance and repeated instances of prisoner's dilemma.

End it means rolling back many of the agreements put in place over the past two decades and restarting the process. Under this latter scenario, the global economy will revert to a regionalist system organized around economic blocs that share common goals and a common state of development, with tariffs and capital controls between blocs. Thereafter, the gradual process of integrating blocs can begin again, this time getting it right.

There will be significant costs to an "end it" strategy. Many corporations will face significant losses as they have invested in global production networks, or even abandoned production and transformed themselves into marketing agencies (like Nike or Gap) that source globally from low-cost, exploited workers. This will produce temporary price increases, but it will also produce large numbers of jobs as production is brought back.

Most importantly, the costs are worth it if the system defies reform. Staying the current course entails a future of wage stagnation, massive inequality, and continuous economic insecurity. It is better to pay the up-front costs of change, even if large, to rescue a prosperous future, rather than bear the costs of a flawed globalization that permanently renders shared prosperity a thing of the past.

11

Economists and the Crisis

The Tragedy of Bad Ideas Revisited

Chapter 2 addressed the tragedy of bad ideas and noted how bad ideas are often behind the most destructive of man-made disasters. That connects with the central thesis of this book, which is that the financial crisis and the Great Recession can ultimately be traced to bad ideas in economics which have driven bad policy.

In the social sciences, history is the data-generating process that tests grand ideas and theories. The second half of the twentieth century tested the ideas of authoritarian communism and showed them to be horribly flawed. Now, history is exposing the flawed reasoning behind market fundamentalism that dominates current economic thinking.

However, being proved wrong by history does not mean ideas fade away. In the former Soviet Union, authoritarian communism was proved odious and flawed fifty years before it finally passed away. This slow demise reflects the fact that the process of historical proof is messy and controversial in unfolding. It also reflects the existence of powerful political and sociological obstacles to change.

Political and sociological obstacles resisted the abandonment of authoritarian communism, and political and sociological obstacles (albeit very different ones) now resist turning away from neoliberalism. Chapter 9 identified and discussed political obstacles to change. Another obstacle to change is the economics profession which is intellectually dominated by neoliberal market fundamentalism.

In the 1930s and 1940s, there was similar academic resistance to Keynesian economics, and the history of that resistance recently surfaced at a memorial service for the late Paul Samuelson, held on April

10, 2010 in Cambridge, Massachusetts. At that service, Professor Jim Poterba, a colleague of Samuelson's at MIT, recounted how the MIT economics visiting committee tried to force Samuelson to call off the publication of his path-breaking 1948 economics textbook on grounds that Keynesian economics was too left-wing.[1] Similar resistance exists today and it may be worse in that it is more camouflaged and more sophisticated.

Whereas the connection between politics and policy is linear and direct, it is less easy to see the connection between academic econ-omists and economic policy. The metaphor of a restaurant can help. There are two waiters (Republicans and New Democrats) but only one chef (mainstream economists) who is trained exclusively in the neoliberal school of cooking. The challenge is to get one of the waiters (New Democrats) to carry the cooking of another chef (a structural Keynesian economist).

Naturally enough, the existing chef is opposed to introducing a rival. That opposition fits with a basic principle of economics, subscribed to by right and left, that people are self-interested. Ironically, whereas mainstream economists are willing to apply that principle to under-stand the behavior of others, they are reluctant to apply it to under-stand their own behavior as economists.

The Crisis, the Destruction of Shared Prosperity and the Role of Economists

In many ways, economists can be viewed as the high priests of neoliberalism. Scratch any side of the neoliberal policy box, and you find a justification that comes straight from mainstream economics.

1. Corporate globalization has been justified by an appeal to the the-ory of free trade based on comparative advantage, and by an appeal to neoclassical arguments for deregulating financial markets and allow-ing uncontrolled international capital flows. The party line on global-ization was succinctly summarized by Stanley Fischer (1997), a liberal

---

[1] This story is reported by Paul Krugman [2010d], "Samuelson Memorial," *Conscience of a Liberal Blog*, April 20, http://krugman.blogs.nytimes.com/2010/04/11/samuelson-memorial/Cited

former professor of macroeconomics at MIT and former managing director of the IMF:

Put abstractly, free capital movements facilitate a more efficient allocation of global savings, and help channel resources into their most productive uses, thus increasing growth and welfare. From the individual country's perspective, the benefits take the form of increases in both the potential pool of investible funds, and the access of domestic residents to foreign capital markets. From the viewpoint of the international economy, open capital accounts support the multilateral trading system by broadening the channels through which developed and developing countries alike can finance trade and investment and attain higher levels of income. International capital flows have expanded the opportunities for portfolio diversification, and thereby provided investors with the potential to achieve higher risk-adjusted rates of return. And just as current account (trade) liberalization promotes growth by increasing access to sophisticated technology, and export competition has improved domestic technology, so too capital account liberalization can increase the efficiency of the domestic financial system.

2. The small-government agenda comes straight from Milton Friedman's (1962) arguments for a minimalist or "night watchman" state. Friedman's support for a minimalist government was driven by political concerns about freedom and concerns that government was doing things for which there was no economic justification. However, he accepted a role for government to remedy market failure.

Subsequent adherents of Chicago School economics have recommended that even market failures be ignored because government interventions to fix them can give rise to more costly government failures via regulatory capture, bureaucratic incompetence, and political self-dealing.[2] That argument has been used to justify the rollback of antitrust regulation even in situations where markets are failing, and to justify cutbacks in the provision of public goods and public investment. It is epitomized by the paradigm of self-regulation that argued (with such disastrous consequences) the financial sector could be charged to regulate itself with regard to risk taking.[3]

---

[2] See Chapter 2, footnote 9 for a discussion of this evolution of thinking among neoliberal economists.

[3] British economist Willem Buiter (2008) caustically sums up the relation between regulation and self-regulation: "Unfortunately, self-regulation stands in relation to regulation the way self-importance stands in relation to importance and self-righteousness to righteousness. It just isn't the same thing." See Buiter, W.H. [2008],

3. The influence of Milton Friedman is also present in the retreat from full-employment policy. Friedman (1968) proposed the theory of a "natural" rate of unemployment that was adopted and endorsed by almost the entire economics profession. The theory maintains that monetary policy cannot affect the long-run rate of unemployment, and it abandons the earlier Keynesian notion of a trade-off between inflation and unemployment, whereby a society can have lower unemployment if it is prepared to accept slightly higher inflation.

The important policy consequence of the natural rate theory was that it provided justification for the Federal Reserve's abandonment of concern with unemployment and shift to a focus on inflation. According to natural rate theory, monetary policy can have no lasting impact on employment, so policy should instead minimize inflation as inflation is undesirable and it is the only thing monetary policy can permanently affect. The determination of employment should be left to market forces and the claim is that the economy will gravitate quickly to full employment.

4. The "flexible" labor markets agenda has also been driven by neoclassical economics and its view of labor markets. The argument is that competitive markets ensure workers are paid their contribution to value of production – a corollary of which is that managers and CEOs are paid their contribution. This theory, which is found in all conventional textbooks, has fueled an attack on unions, minimum wages, and employment protections, all of which are characterized as unnecessary labor market "distortions" that lower employment.

Friedman's (1968) theory of the natural rate of unemployment also endorsed this thinking, maintaining that such institutions raised the natural rate of unemployment:

In the United States, for example, legal minimum wage rates, the Walsh-Healy and Davis-Bacon Acts, and the strength of labor unions all make the natural rate of unemployment higher than it would be. (p. 9)

Mainstream micro economists have always pushed the labor market flexibility agenda as they deny income distribution affects employment. Friedman's natural rate approach joined macro economists with micro economists in support of the labor market flexibility

"Self-Regulation Means No Regulation," *FT.com/maverecon*, April 10, http://blogs.ft.com/maverecon/2008/04/self-regulation-means-no-regulation/

agenda. The result was the entire mainstream economics profession supported the agenda.

5. Increased corporate power has been justified by the shareholder value model of corporations, which claims wealth and income is maximized if corporations maximize shareholder value without regard to interests of other stakeholders. To the extent that there is a principal-agent problem that causes managers not to maximize shareholder value, this can be solved by using bonus payments and stock options to align managers' interests with shareholder interests.

6. Lastly, expansion of financial markets has been promoted by appeal to the theory of efficient markets and claims that speculation is stabilizing.[4] Additionally, the theory of a market for corporate control asserts that corporations are disciplined by shareholders and act in a way that promotes shareholder interests, which in turn is good for broader economic interest.[5]

Arrow-Debreu competitive general equilibrium theory and Markowitz-Tobin portfolio theory have been invoked to justify exotic financial innovation in the name of risk spreading and portfolio diversification.[6] The argument was that slicing and dicing of assets into different income tranches created new assets (e.g., collateralized debt obligations) with different risk – return properties that expanded the portfolio opportunity space by covering more states of world. Those newly created assets could then be recombined to enhance investor returns with lower risk. Bundling mortgages as mortgage-backed securities (MBS) also increased liquidity by increasing saleability. The claim was that such financial engineering effectively created additional wealth and made everyone better off. Meanwhile, portfolio diversification would render a collapse near impossible.

The combination of the efficient market hypothesis and the theory that stock markets drive real investment was used to justify the claim

---

[4] See Fama, E. [1970], "Efficient Capital markets: A Review of Theory and Empirical work," *Journal of Finance*, 25 (May), 383–416; Friedman, M. [1953], "The Case for Flexible Exchange Rates," *Essays in Positive Economics*, Chicago: Chicago University Press.

[5] See Jensen, M.J. and W.H. Meckling [1976], "Theory of the Firm: Managerial Behavior, Agency Costs and Ownership Structure," *Journal of Financial Economics*, 3, 305–60.

[6] See Arrow, K.J. and G. Debreu [1954], "Existence of an Equilibrium for a Competitive Economy," *Econometrica*, 22, 265–90; Markowitz, H. [1959], *Portfolio Selection*, New York: Wiley; and Tobin, J. [1958], "Liquidity Preference as Behavior towards Risk," *Review of Economic Studies*, 25 (February), 65–86.

that "wild west" financial markets do a good job directing investment and the accumulation of real capital.[7] Lastly, the Sharpe-Merton-Black-Scholes models of risky asset pricing gave mathematically precise ways of pricing risky assets.[8] This gave confidence to take massive risks that were supposedly immune from meltdown because the pricing formulas and assumptions about probability distributions said so.

Putting the pieces together, modern economics played a critical role in the making of the financial crisis and Great Recession. The fingerprints of economists and modern economic theory are all over the neoliberal policy box, which undermined the demand-generating process and now threatens the Great Stagnation. Modern finance theory drove attitudes about shareholder value maximization and corporate governance. It also justified the piling up of leverage and risk in the financial sector, which produced the financial crash of 2008. In the media, charlatan quants are widely blamed for the excesses of financial risk taking. Those quants were let loose and guided by the ideas contained in neoliberal economic theory.

The Vulnerability of Orthodox Economics

The ideas of economists have played a critical role in creating the conditions that gave rise to the financial crisis and the Great Recession, and the economics profession has played a double role in propagating those ideas. First, it provided justification for the policies adopted. Second, it has blocked alternative ideas from making it to the policy table. In effect, the economics profession acts a screen through which ideas must pass. Some are labeled as true and given the seal of approval. Others are labeled as wrong and are consigned to exclusion.

The economics profession and the dominant ideas are part of an intellectual establishment that serves particular interests. That establishment

---

[7] The theory that stock markets drive real investment is known as q theory of investment. It was proposed by Tobin and Brainard (1968) and is based on observations contained in Keynes's *General Theory*. The basic claim is that firms invest more when their stock prices are high because that signals a high demand for capital by the investing public.

[8] See Sharpe, W. [1964], "Capital Asset Prices: A Theory of Market Equilibrium under Conditions of Risk," *Journal of Finance*, 19, 425–42; Black, F. and M. Scholes [1973], "The Pricing of Options and Corporate Liabilities," *Journal of Political Economy*, 81, 637–54; and Merton, R.C. [1973], "Theory of Rational Option Pricing," *Bell Journal of Economics and Management Service*, 4, 141–83.

is clad in a powerful armor that damps criticism and blocks change. Just as there are political obstacles to policy change, so too there are obstacles to change in economic thinking. The challenge is to find chinks in the armor through which an opening for change can be forged.

One such opening is crisis, the importance of which was recognized by Milton Friedman (2002): "Only a crisis – actual or perceived – produces real change" (p. xiv). Crisis opens the public to change, and this is a real crisis and therefore a real opportunity for change.

A second opening is the abject failure of the economics profession to anticipate the crisis, a failure that has left the profession vulnerable. Economics may not be able to predict daily events but it should at least anticipate seismic shifts.

This vulnerability of the profession was inadvertently exposed by Queen Elizabeth II. On a visit to the London School of Economics in November 2008, the queen politely asked why no one had predicted the crisis. Her question stumped her distinguished hosts. In fact, not only did economists miss the crisis, but large numbers of them predicted a continuing boom.[9]

In a strange way, history has repeated itself with the profession's re-embrace of pre-Keynesian economics. In 1929, Irving Fisher, then the greatest of all American economists, confidently predicted the stock market would soon reach new record highs and there was no end in sight to the Roaring Twenties expansion of economic prosperity. Two months later, Wall Street experienced the Great Crash and the economy entered what was to become the Great Depression.

The scale of economists' miss is easily illustrated. In testimony to the Joint Economic Committee of the U.S. Congress on March 28, 2007, Ben Bernanke, Chairman of the Federal Reserve declared: "At this juncture, however, the impact on the broader economy and financial markets of the problems in the subprime market seems likely to be contained." Adam Posen (2007a), who currently serves on the Bank

---

[9] It is not strictly true that no one predicted the crisis. Rather, none from the mainstream economics profession predicted it. Economists Dean Baker (2002) and Robert Shiller (2005) both identified the housing price bubble. However, neither framed the bubble in terms of a larger financial crash and the Great Recession. Godley and Zezza (2006) clearly foresaw the serious macroeconomic dangers inherent in rising U.S. household indebtedness and the trade deficit but did not predict the financial crash. Australian economist Steve Keen (1995, 2006) developed a theoretical framework that explains the crisis and started warning of its imminence in 2006. Modesty permitting, this author (Palley 2001a, 2006b, 2006c) also predicted a serious downturn of depression proportions – although I did not foresee the path involving the financial crash.

of England's Monetary Policy committee, declared in an April 2007 op-ed titled "Don't Worry About U.S. Mortgages":

In summary, there will be no large negative impact on growth from the current real estate bust in the United States, though some individual homeowners and communities are suffering.

Five months later he (Posen, 2007b) doubled down in a September op-ed titled "A Drag, Not a Crisis":

This non-crisis will put a small drag on the US economy into spring of 2008, but not more than that, especially with the Federal Reserve ready to act. When this financial shock turns into a non-event, it will only serve to demonstrate that securitization and financial innovation did what it was supposed to do: disperse the risk and protect bank capital such that the real economic impact of financial fluctuations is limited.

As the crisis was gaining strength, the International Monetary Fund (IMF), which is charged with monitoring the world economy and serving as early warning system, declared in its *World Economic Outlook Update* of July 2007:

The strong global expansion is continuing, and projections for global growth in both 2007 and 2008 have been revised up to 5.2 percent from 4.9 percent at the time of the April 2007 *World Economic Outlook*.... With sustained strong growth, supply constraints are tightening and inflation risks have edged up since the April 2007 *World Economic Outlook*, increasing the likelihood that central banks will need to further tighten monetary policy.

The IMF's misreading of economic conditions was then trumped by Ken Rogoff, Harvard professor and former IMF Chief Economist. In an op-ed published in July 2008, Rogoff (2008a) advocated raising interest rates just as the crisis was accelerating:

The global economy is a runaway train that is slowing, but not quickly enough. That is what the extraordinary run-up in prices for oil, metals, and food is screaming at us.... The world as a whole needs tighter monetary and fiscal policy. It is time to put the brakes on the runaway train before it is too late.

Two months later, Rogoff (2008b) trumped himself with a *Washington Post* op-ed celebrating the Federal Reserve's decision to let Lehman Brothers fail, a decision now widely recognized as having catastrophic consequences:

This past weekend, the U.S. Treasury and the Federal Reserve finally made it abundantly clear they won't bail out every significant financial firm in America. Certainly this came as a rude shock to many financiers. In allowing the nation's fourth largest investment bank, Lehman Brothers, to file for bankruptcy, and by forcefully indicating that they are prepared to see even more bankruptcies, our financial regulators showed Wall Street that they are not such creampuffs after all.

The general state of unawareness in the economic profession is captured by Olivier Blanchard (2008), MIT professor and IMF Chief Economist, in an August 2008 paper celebrating the state of macroeconomics:

For a long while after the explosion of macroeconomics in the 1970s, the field looked like a battlefield. Over time however, largely because facts do not go away, a largely shared vision both of fluctuations and methodology has emerged. Not everything is fine. Like all revolutions, this one has come with the destruction of some knowledge and suffers from extremism and herding. None of this is deadly however. The state of macro is good.

This celebratory attitude was shared by Marvin Goodfriend (2007), Carnegie-Mellon Professor of economics and former chief monetary policy advisor at the Richmond Federal Reserve, in a 2007 article titled "How the World Achieved Consensus on Monetary Policy":

The worldwide progress in monetary policy is a great achievement and, especially considering the situation 30 years ago, a remarkable success story.

The blindness to realities is spread throughout the branches of mainstream macroeconomics. With regard to the international economy, Michael Dooley, David Folkerts-Landau, and Peter Garber, of the University of California, Deutsche Bank, and Brown University, respectively, wrote a widely cited paper, titled "An Essay on the Revised Bretton Woods System," that predicted an era of stability:

The economic emergence of a fixed exchange periphery in Asia has reestablished the United States as the center country in the Bretton Woods international monetary system ... there is a line of countries waiting to follow the Europe of the 1950s/60s and Asia today sufficient to keep the system intact for the foreseeable future.[10]

A similarly complacent view of the state of the international economy was expressed by Ricardo Hausmann, Harvard University professor

[10] Dooley, M., D. Folkerts-Landau, and P. Garber [2003], "An Essay on the Revised Bretton Woods System," National Bureau of Economic Research working paper 9971, September, http://www.nber.org/papers/w9971

and former Chief Economist of the Inter-American Development Bank, in a December 2005 *Financial Times* op-ed "Dark Matter Makes the US Deficit Disappear," coauthored with Federico Sturzenegger:

In 2005 the US current account deficit is expected to top $700bn. It comes after 27 years of unbroken deficits that have totaled more than $5,000bn, leading to concerns of an impending global crisis.... But wait a minute. If this is such an open and shut case, why have markets not precipitated the crisis already? Maybe it is because there is something wrong with the diagnosis.... In a nutshell our story is simple. Once assets are valued according to the income they generate, there has not been a big US external imbalance and there are no serious global imbalances.[11]

The idea of the "Great Moderation" that had tamed the business cycle, which is now so decisively discredited, was openly endorsed in 2004 by Federal Reserve Chairman Bernanke (2004):

One of the most striking features of the economic landscape over the past twenty years or so has been a substantial decline in macroeconomic volatility.... Several writers on the topic have dubbed this remarkable decline in the volatility of output and inflation "the great moderation." ... My view is that improvements in monetary policy, though certainly not the only factor, have probably been an important source of the Great Moderation.

Endorsement of the conduct of monetary policy and the broad macroeconomic policy regime also came from Alan Blinder, Princeton University professor, former Vice-Chairman of the Board of Governors of the Federal Reserve System, and a leading economic policy advisor to the Democratic Party. In a 2005 paper coauthored with Ricardo Reis, Blinder eulogized Greenspan at his retirement as Federal Reserve Chairman as the greatest central banker ever:

This paper seeks to summarize and, more important, to evaluate the significance of Greenspan's impressive reign as Fed chairman – a period that can rightly be called the Greenspan era.... Rather than keep the reader in suspense, we might as well reveal our overall evaluation right up front. While there are some negatives in the record, when the score is toted up, we think he has a legitimate claim to being the greatest central banker who ever lived. His performance as chairman of the Fed has been impressive, encompassing, and

---

[11] Hausmann, R. and F. Sturzenegger [2005], "Dark Matter Makes the US Deficit Disappear," *Financial Times*, December 7, http://minerva.union.edu/dvorakt/383/ps/deficit/hausmann%20sturzenegger%20FT.pdf

overwhelmingly beneficial – to the nation, the institution, and to the practice of monetary policy.[12]

The one mainstream economist who predicted accurately the financial crash and its aftermath is Nouriel Roubini, former assistant secretary in the Treasury Department under Larry Summers in the late 1990s. For that Roubini deserves credit, but it is also noteworthy that Roubini got the economics completely wrong. Thus, his explanation of how a crash would develop ran as follows:

The basic outlines of a hard landing are easy to envision: a sharp fall in the value of the US dollar, a rapid increase in US long-term interest rates and a sharp fall in the price of a range of risk assets including equities and housing.[13]

In fact this "dollar collapse" view about how a possible financial crisis might develop was widely held by many mainstream economists, including Fred Bergsten (2005) of the Peterson Institute, Barry Eichengreen (2004) of Berkley, and Maurice Obstfeld of Berkley and Ken Rogoff of Harvard (2007). All were wrong, but only Roubini made the astutely accurate and well-timed call of a catastrophe.[14]

In sum, this record is a damning indictment. It is not an isolated failure, but a widespread and comprehensive failure of understanding at the top of the profession by economists holding the highest policy positions and teaching at the most elite universities.

Obstacles to Change

The link between economics and the economic policies that created the crisis, combined with the scale and scope of failure within the

---

[12] Blinder, A. and R. Reis [2005], "Understanding the Greenspan Standard," Working Papers 88, Princeton University department of Economics, Center for Economic Studies, August.

[13] Roubini, N. and B. Setser [2005], "Will the Bretton Woods 2 Regime Unravel Soon? The Risk of a Hard Landing in 2005–2006," paper prepared for a conference organized by the Federal Reserve Bank of San Francisco, February, p. 5, http://www.frbsf.org/economics/conferences/0502/Roubini.pdf

[14] See Bergsten, C.F. [2005], "A New Foreign Economic Policy for the United States," in *The United States and the World Economy: Foreign Economic Policy for the Next Decade*, Institute for International Economics, Washington DC; Eichengreen, B. [2004], "The Dollar and the New Bretton Woods System," manuscript, University of California at Berkeley, December; Obstfeld, M. and K. Rogoff [2007], "The Unsustainable U.S. Current Account Position Revisited," in Richard Clarida (ed.) *G7 Current Account Imbalances: Sustainability and Adjustment*, Chicago: University of Chicago Press.

economics profession, makes a case for major change in economics. Yet, that does not appear to be happening.

The balance of this chapter explains why this is so. Just as there are political obstacles to policy change (discussed in Chapter 9), so too there are obstacles to intellectual change. The myth is that ideas compete on a level playing field. The reality is much more complex.

The Neoclassical Monopoly: Coke versus Pepsi

One major obstacle to change is the absolute dominance of neoclassical economics that claims to be the only true economics and, in the name of truth, blocks other points of views. However, a major difficulty exposing this narrowness is that it is obscured by a family split among neoclassical economists that makes it look as if economics is far more pluralistic than it is.

The split is between hard-core neoliberals who believe that real-world market economies approximate perfect competition and soft-core neoliberals who do not. Hard-core believers are identified with the Chicago School, whose leading exponents include Milton Friedman and George Stigler. Soft-core believers are identified with the MIT School associated with Paul Samuelson. The soft-core MIT School includes well-known liberals such as Paul Krugman, Brad DeLong, Dani Rodrik, and Larry Summers. It also includes Joseph Stiglitz who, although more radical at the policy level, shares the same overarching economic theory.

This hard-core versus soft-core split obscures the underlying uniformity of thought. Hard-core and soft-core economists go after each other tooth and nail, creating an illusion of deep intellectual difference, but the reality is that they share a common analytical perspective. In effect, the debate in mainstream economics resembles competition between Coke and Pepsi. They too go after each other tooth and nail, claiming huge differences in taste, but the reality is that they are both colas.

Figure 11.1 provides a description of modern economics. The discipline is divided into neoclassical economists (probably more than 95 percent) and heterodox economists, which includes Keynesians, Marxists, and institutionalists. Hard-core Chicago School economists claim real-world market economies produce roughly efficient (so-called Pareto optimal) outcomes on which public policy cannot improve. Thus, any state intervention in the economy must make someone worse off.

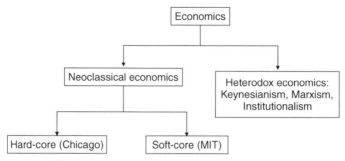

Figure 11.1. The makeup of modern economics.

The soft-core MIT School, by contrast, argues that real-world economies are afflicted by pervasive market failures, including imperfect
competition and monopoly, externalities associated with problems
like pollution, and an inability to supply public goods such as street
lighting or national defense. Market failures also include information
failures, which is why economists like Joe Stiglitz and George Akerlof
are part of the MIT School. For MIT economists, policy interventions that address market failures – including widespread information
imperfections and the nonexistence of many needed markets – can
make everyone better off.

None of this debate between Chicago and MIT is about fairness,
which is a separate issue. Indeed, neither the Chicago School nor
the MIT School say market outcomes are always fair, because actual
market outcomes depend on the initial distribution of resources. If
that distribution was unfair, current and future outcomes will be
unfair, too.

That said, Chicago economists seem to believe real-world outcomes
are acceptably unfair and, more importantly, that attempts to remedy
unfairness are too costly because tampering with markets causes economic inefficiency. Moreover, they believe that government intervention tends to generate its own costly failures because of bureaucratic
incompetence and rent seeking, whereby private interests try to steer
policy to their own advantage. MIT economists tend to espouse the
opposite: fairness is important, the real world is unacceptably unfair,
and government failure can be prevented by good institutional design,
including democracy.

These differences between Chicago and MIT reflect the intellectual
richness of neoclassical economics. However, that richness provides

no justification for a neoclassical monopoly that asserts and permits only one economics. That is the essential point.

This reality of economics is difficult to convey and therefore difficult to challenge. One reason is that soft-core MIT economists like Paul Krugman and Joseph Stiglitz share values with heterodox economists, and shared values are easily conflated with shared analysis. A second reason is that heterodox and soft-core MIT School economists also often agree on policy, even if their reasoning is different. A third reason is the tendency of the profession to hype the scope of its internal divisions in terms of a battle between "freshwater" (Chicago School) and "saltwater" (MIT School) economics, thereby making the profession look more pluralistic. A fourth reason is that most people are incredulous that economists could be so audacious as to enforce one view of economics.

However, the evidence is there. For instance, Notre Dame University recently closed it economics department, which was heterodox, and replaced it with a neoclassical department. The claim was that the heterodox department lacked standing and publication success, but that was inevitable given the neoclassical monopoly that made that type of success impossible.[15]

Another example is provided by Professor Dani Rodrik of Harvard University who recently published a book titled *One Economics, Many Recipes: Globalization, Institutions, and Economic Growth*. Rodrik is one of the most enlightened neoclassical economists, yet the title of his book inadvertently spotlights all the obstructions to creating an open-minded economics. At one and the same time, he criticizes the hard-core neoliberal Washington Consensus while also arguing there is only "one economics." Thus, Rodrik criticizes the hard-core neoliberal policies that heterodox economists have long criticized, yet implicitly denies the legitimacy of heterodox analysis.

To lay readers this may seem like a storm in a teacup, but it is not. Heterodox economics includes core theoretical concepts that are

---

[15] The dissolution of the Notre Dame Economics department took place in two steps. In 2003, a new neoclassical department of economics and econometrics was established and the old department was stripped of new positions and barred from teaching graduate students. In 2009, the old department was permanently closed and its remaining faculty relocated to other departments and institutes. See Glenn, D. [2009], "Notre Dame Plans to Dissolve the Heterodox Side of Its Split Economics Department," *Chronicle of Higher Education*, September 16, http://chronicle.com/article/Notre-Dame-to-Dissolve/48460/

fundamentally incompatible with neoclassical economics in either of its two contemporary forms. These concepts result in significantly different explanations of the real world, including income distribution and the determinants of economic activity and growth. Moreover, they often result in different policy prescriptions.

Those theoretical differences explain why neoliberal policy rooted in neoliberal economics has proved so disastrous, and the different policy prescriptions are critical for escaping the looming great stagnation and creating shared prosperity. They are especially critical for understanding the phenomenon of globalization. Absent an opening of economics that makes space for heterodox thinking, it is going to be difficult to get policies for shared prosperity on the political table and keep them there.

The Cuckoo Tactic

The neoclassical monopoly and the suppression of alternative views are supported by tactics that can be labeled the "cuckoo tactic." The cuckoo takes over the nests of other birds by surreptitiously placing its young in their nests and having others raise them. In many regards, neoclassical economics does the same to Keynesian economics. This serves to create confusion, blur distinctions, and promote the claim that Keynesian ideas are already fully incorporated in mainstream economics.

One example of this strategy is "emergency Keynesianism." Thus, in times of crisis, many mainstream economists turn to recommending Keynesian policies based on expansionary discretionary fiscal policy and robust interest rate reductions, even though their theoretical reasoning is hard-pressed to justify such actions.

A second example is so-called New Keynesian economics, which is how MIT economists describe their version of macroeconomics. New Keynesians claim that employment fluctuates because of imperfect competition in goods markets and "menu" adjustment costs that prevent firms from adjusting prices. In other words, price rigidity is the problem. Yet, it is impossible to read Keynes's (1936) *General Theory* honestly and interpret Keynes in this way. However, that is what New Keynesians do, and their adoption of the Keynesian label serves to confuse debate and dismiss authentic Keynesian claims about the exclusion of Keynesianism.

The reality is that New Keynesian economics should really be called "New Pigovian" economics as it is firmly rooted in the intellectual tradition of Arthur Pigou, who emphasized market imperfections. That is cruelly ironic, as Pigou was Keynes's great intellectual rival at Cambridge University in the 1930s.

The Paradigm of Perfection

A second, deeper obstruction is the paradigm of perfect markets. Neoclassical economists, both soft-core and hard-core, believe in the paradigm of perfect markets. Although such markets do not exist and have never been seen to exist, the ideal underlies neoclassical theory.

The perfect markets argument is that if such markets existed, there would always be full employment. The logic is that perfect markets allow realization of all the benefits from mutually beneficial commercial exchange, and rational agents will always want to reap those benefits. Why would anyone let them go to waste? Given this ideal, if rational agents are not realizing these full benefits (e.g., there is mass unemployment), there must be some market impediment.

This "perfect markets" reasoning helps understand orthodox explanations of the crisis. The crisis has produced a huge economic contraction involving massive costs, and it is therefore inconsistent with perfect markets. Hard-core Chicago School economists explain the crisis as the product of imperfect markets caused by excessive government intervention and policy failure. Soft-core MIT School economists explain it as the result of failure to appropriately regulate markets (i.e., failure to correct preexisting market failure such as proclivities to excessive risk taking).

These responses also explain how orthodox economics will answer the queen's question why no one saw the crisis coming. Hard-core neoclassicals already have an answer: government failure. For soft-core neoclassicals, the theoretical challenge is to identify a new market failure they previously failed to incorporate in their theoretical models. That work is already underway. Every time something goes wrong, either blame an unanticipated shock (a black swan) or add a new market imperfection.

Two important points follow from this response. First, the paradigm of perfection remains unchanged, and a new imperfection will be found. Second, that means orthodox economists still see no reason to open economics to other paradigms.

The Science Myth in Economics

Another obstacle to change is the science myth in economics. That myth supports the neoclassical monopoly by supporting the claim that neoclassical economics is the only true economics.

The science myth in economics is not that economics is a science. Rather, the myth in economics is that science produces the truth.

The essence of the scientific method is that theories and hypotheses are tested against empirical evidence to see whether they are consistent with the evidence. If a hypothesis is consistent (i.e., not falsified), it can be accepted. If it is inconsistent, it should be rejected. This is the way natural science works and it can also be applied in economics. That means economics can be a science.

However, as argued long ago by the famous philosopher of science Sir Karl Popper (1959), the critical feature of the scientific method is that it does not prove hypotheses as true: It only shows which hypotheses are false. This means there can, in principle, be many hypotheses that are accepted because more than one can be consistent with the evidence.

Moreover, even if only one hypothesis is accepted, that does not mean science has discovered the truth. Future evidence may show up that is inconsistent with the hypothesis. Alternatively, a new hypothesis may be developed that explains more and fits with other facts with which the existing hypothesis does not. The bottom line is that it is impossible philosophically to know the truth, because we can never know the future with certainty.

This has enormous relevance for economics, because the data about the economy are so rich, so complex, and so inconclusive that many theories pass muster. Thus, there are many competing theories about income distribution, economic growth, development, inflation, and trade and globalization, all of which are consistent with the empirical data. On top of this fundamental methodological problem there are also tremendous difficulties operationalizing the scientific method in economics. One difficulty is the inability to set up laboratory conditions and run controlled experiments with the economy. Moreover, even when economists can create lab conditions, the conditions are so artificial that there is doubt about the real-world relevance and plausibility of the experimental results.

A second difficulty is that of reflexivity. People are learning beings and therefore are always changing because of experience. For instance, having experienced the financial crisis, if it were possible to rerun events, they would turn out slightly different because of changed reactions. Reflexivity means economics itself changes the world by changing understandings, which in turn feeds back to affect actions and further changes the world and understanding.[16]

These difficulties operationalizing the scientific method in economics compound the fundamental problem already inherent in the scientific method. Science cannot prove truth; it can only falsify. In economics (and social science generally), the problems of operationalizing the scientific method mean the screen for falsifying hypotheses is much coarser than it is in natural science. Consequently, many hypotheses pass the test. It is this that makes economics much closer to sociology and history than to physics.

Given this, according to the scientific method, space should be made for all theories and hypotheses that satisfy the data. Yet, this is exactly what neoclassical economics refuses to do. Instead, it uses the science myth, of science producing the true answer, to claim that neoclassical economics is the single true economics. That then justifies suppressing all other economic theories. In the academia, this translates into economics departments blocking the teaching of competing theories – although the pretense of open-mindedness is maintained by high-minded claims that those ideas are free to be taught elsewhere.

Why does the science myth survive in economics? One reason is that it is also widely held by the public. Not only is the science myth of one truth simple; people also like the comfort of certainty and just one answer. That gives psychological support to the science myth.

Professional economists also buy into the science myth. They too are members of the public and also like the comfort of one theory.

---

[16] The problem of reflexivity and knowledge has long concerned philosophers of science and sociologists of knowledge. George Soros has been a leading advocate of its relevance for economics. See Soros, G. [1987], *The Alchemy of Finance*, New York: Simon and Schuster. Atomic physics has a somewhat analogous problem known as the Heisenberg uncertainty principle. The mere fact of observing a subatomic particle changes that particle by casting light on it.

With methodology no longer part of the economics curriculum, many know little about the limits of the scientific method. And of course, the neoclassical monopoly also benefits mainstream economists financially and professionally by limiting professional competition.

Lastly, the science myth in economics is a useful tool of social control because it gives monopoly power to those who control economic knowledge. Given that economic knowledge has real-world consequences via economic policy, the economically powerful have little interest in discrediting a myth that bolsters their power.

The limits of the scientific method in economics have profound implications for how economics should be viewed. The late Robert Heilbronner described economics as "worldly philosophy." That makes sense. Just as philosophers are divided on the nature of truth and understanding, economics is divided on the workings of the real world. Paradigms should coexist in economics, just as in other social sciences. Yet, in practice, the dominance of the belief in "one economics," particularly in North America and Europe, has led increasingly to a narrow and exclusionary view of the discipline. That narrowness contributed to the making of the crisis and it stands in the way of reforms needed to restore shared prosperity and avoid stagnation.

Sociological Obstructions

The fact that economics produces multiple competing theories requires choosing between theories. This raises questions about what determines the choice, which leads to issues of economic and political sociology.

At the level of the individual economist, there is a clear economic interest both in signing on to the dominant paradigm and limiting competition. Signing on to the paradigm is professionally rewarded, and limiting competition also increases individual rewards. The economic logic of self-interest applies as much to the behavior of neoclassical economists as it does to the behaviors of others.

At the level of the academia, economics is a club in which existing members elect new members. This club arrangement poses an intractable sociological obstruction to opening economics to alternative points of view. That is because club members only elect those who subscribe to the current dominant paradigm. This process is another place where the science myth plays such an important role because the myth can be invoked to blackball all who subscribe to a different point of view.

Finally, business and other vested economic interests have an incentive in supporting the continued dominance of neoclassical economics. That is because of its friendly attitude to existing patterns of wealth and income distribution, and its friendly attitude to the current neoliberal policy configuration, which supports those patterns.

In sum, neither individual economists, nor economics departments, nor business have an incentive to admit that neoclassical economics is just one among several competing perspectives. That would undermine the authority, influence, and economic value of the neoclassical monopoly, and each part of the system has an interest in maintaining the monopoly.

Follow the money is often a useful principle for understanding something. With regard to climate change or drug research, follow the money is a trusted first test. Climate change research funded by Exxon Mobil is rightly viewed with skepticism, and so too is pharmaceutical research funded by drug companies. But when it comes to economics, there is denial. Corporate funding of business schools and corporate-endowed chairs in economics are deemed inconsequential and assumed to have no impact on research outcomes. Likewise, there is lack of skepticism toward research produced by elite business-funded think tanks.

Neoliberal economists emphasize the capture theory of regulation, and their arguments have much merit. Business will seek to capture regulators by paying off regulators and politicians so that regulation is toothless and even turned to business's advantage. The same logic supports a capture theory of economics, and here too the science myth plays an important functional and psychological role. With regard to function, the belief in one true answer increases the payoff from capture of economics. With regard to psychology, the science myth wards off cognitive dissonance among individual economists who would otherwise have to reflect on the role of power in influencing ideas.

Power and Ideas

Ironically, the notion of a capture theory of economics, in which self-interest drives the capture of economics by business interests, links neoclassical economic logic with Marxist analysis. Control of ideas is valuable because it bolsters power and wealth, and power and wealth are therefore directed to controlling ideas. Keynes recognized the power of ideas, writing in his *General Theory* (1936):

[T]he ideas of economists and political philosophers, both when they are right and when they are wrong, are more powerful than is commonly understood. Indeed, the world is ruled by little else. Practical men, who believe themselves to be quite exempt from any intellectual influences, are usually the slave of some defunct economist.

But Keynes's analysis is thin on why particular ideas triumph. For that, we must look to the ideas of Karl Marx in *The German Ideology* (1845):

The ideas of the ruling class are in every epoch the ruling ideas, i.e. the class which is the ruling material force of society, is at the same time its ruling intellectual force. The class which has the means of material production at its disposal, has control at the same time over the mental means of production, so that thereby, generally speaking, those who lack the means of mental production are subject to it.

This logic makes much sense with regard to economics. In the Marxian schema, shown in Figure 11.2, power and wealth are applied to influence (+) ideas, and ideas then support (+) the existing structure of power and distribution of wealth.

That power and wealth influence ideas should come as no surprise. Americans would have no problem with that claim applied to the former Soviet Union. However, the psychological longing for truth makes it hard to admit the claim also holds in every society, including democratic societies such as the United States. This conflict of reality and psychological longing generates cognitive dissonance, and that dissonance is contained by denial.

A society in which the distribution of power is at odds with ideas will be marked by social discord. Over time, one or other must give until some reconciliation is achieved. If that does not happen, discord can be profound and extended.

The question now is: Has the financial crisis and the Great Recession changed the distribution power, which includes awakening political awareness? If not at all, economics will likely remain essentially unchanged.

One place where change may have occurred is U.S. domestic politics, where free-market rhetoric may have worn thin. This creates political space, which could usher in a new politics that drives change in

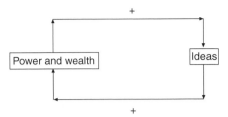

Figure 11.2. The Marxian construction of the relation between power, wealth, and ideas.

economics. However, judging by the Obama administration's agenda, initial indications of change are not strong, and the politics of "Coke versus Pepsi" look set to continue.

A second place is the redistribution of power from the United States to China, which could also drive change in economics. How that works out depends on the evolution of the U.S.-China relationship and the evolution of internal Chinese politics. If the relationship turns more contentious, that could drive a rewriting of international economics – particularly the theory of trade. If China continues to be successful with its market-state Keynesianism, that too could drive change. However, if Chinese elites join the existing global ruling class, that would reinforce the existing paradigm.

Expert Opinion and Open Society

Democracies and autocracies tend over long periods to grow at roughly the same rate. The big difference is that democracies tend to grow smoothly whereas autocracies are characterized by growth spurts followed by long periods of stagnation and even calamity. This pattern of feast and famine is costly.

One explanation for the superior growth pattern of democracies is that they are societies open to criticism and alternative ideas. When something goes wrong, the democratic process enables them to change policies and make course corrections. Autocracies have no equivalent mechanism. Consequently, when things go wrong, they cannot change course and thus hit the wall of stagnation.[17]

---

[17] See Siegle, J.T., M.M. Weinstein, and M.H. Halperin [2004], "Why Democracies Excel," *Foreign Affairs*, September–October, 57–71.

The critical feature of open societies is that they are open to alternative ideas. Above all, that requires being open to the fact that one can never be certain of having the truth. The scientific methodology only allows disproof of hypotheses. It is impossible to prove something as true because tomorrow it might be falsified and we cannot know the future with certainty.

The U.S. economy is now paying the price of closed-mindedness in economic policy. It has been through a financial crisis and now faces an era of stagnation. This outcome is the product of thirty years of policy dominated by one set of ideas and closed to alternatives and warnings of looming problems.

In a sense, the United States has fallen into an analogue of the closed-society trap of autocracies. For autocracies, the trap is rooted in a monopoly of the political process. The economic crisis has revealed that democracies face an analogue trap rooted in a monopoly on expert opinion. Expert opinion often guides political policy makers. When expert opinion becomes monopolized and closed-minded, as has happened in economics, it can create a policy trap.

Democracies still have the great advantage over autocracies in that they have the freedom to change policy course when they hit stagnation. But how soon they do so and how extensively they do it depends on the extent that monopoly expert opinion can be overcome and new ideas introduced.

Vested interests ensure that expert opinion will not simply roll over, no matter how catastrophic the situation. Indeed, catastrophe can invite "staying the course" on grounds that "rocking boat" with change is dangerous and risky.

Finally, even if today's neoclassical monopoly in economics were dismantled, the crisis holds a valuable long-term lesson for democratic societies. That lesson is that political openness is insufficient. Society must also have openness of expert opinion and openness of thought in the academia. That requires full representation of thought, not lip service to representation, as is currently the case.

12

Markets and the Common Good

Time for a Great Rebalancing

The central theme of this book has been the role of neoliberal economic policy in creating an economy that was destined to hit the wall of stagnation. However, as discussed in Chapter 2, neoliberalism is more than just an economic theory. It is also a philosophy of how society should be organized based on beliefs about the relation between economic organization and freedom.

Beginning with Hayek, and carried forward in more extreme form by Milton Friedman and his Chicago School colleagues, neoliberals argued for a radical reshaping of society that elevated markets and diminished government and other collective institutions. The ethical justification for this reshaping was the advancement and protection of freedom, and the case was further bolstered by claims about the benefits of economic efficiency that would follow.

This logic was most clearly captured by British Prime Minister Margaret Thatcher. With regard to the economy, it was captured in the Thatcherite slogan, "There is no alternative (TINA)," to market fundamentalism. With regard to society it was captured in Mrs. Thatcher's comment that "[t]here is no such thing" as society. Instead, "[t]here are individual men and woman and families, and no government can do anything except through people and people look to themselves first."[1]

Neoliberalism has ruled the intellectual and policy roost for the past thirty years, but the financial crash of 2008 and the Great Recession have opened the door to reversing that dominance. At

---

[1] Interview for *Woman's Own*, September 23, 1987, http://www.margaretthatcher.org/speeches/displaydocument.asp?docid=106689

the economic level, the crisis overtly challenges orthodox economic theory, its description of the workings of market economies, and its claims about the efficiency of market outcomes. Less overtly, but no less importantly, the crisis also challenges the neoliberal view of social relations. That view emphasizes extreme individualism, which in practical terms translates into shifting the balance of power in favor of markets and against government and collective institutions such as trade unions.

Thirty years of widening income inequality, followed by the deepest economic crisis since the Great Depression of the 1930s, now speak to need for rebalancing the relation between markets and other elements of society. That rebalancing is warranted on both economic efficiency grounds and larger societal concerns about the common good.

The Fallacy of the Philosophy of Greed is Good

The neoliberal case for tilting society so heavily in favor of markets rests on views about individuals and their relation to each other. In one sense, Mrs. Thatcher was right: Individuals and the choices they make are the raw input into the process determining outcomes.

Neoliberalism takes individuals as formed and works from there. Given well-formed individuals, it argues that the pursuit of self-interest leads to good social and economic outcomes. This view of society finds its rawest expression in Gordon Gecko, the hero of the 1987 movie *Wall Street*, whose philosophy was that greed is good.

Orthodox economists, wanting a more academic justification of the philosophy of greed-is-good, appeal to the famous passage from Adam Smith's *Wealth of Nations*: "It is not from the benevolence of the butcher, the brewer, or the baker that we expect our dinner, but from their regard to their own interest. We address ourselves not to their humanity but to their self-love, and never talk to them of our own necessities but of their advantages" (1976a [1784], p. 27). In Smith, the concepts of self-interest and greed are described as self-love.

The unseen sleight of hand in modern economics is the assumption of well-formed moral individuals. That assumption is critical to the neoliberal argument. However, Adam Smith, the misappropriated patron of neoliberal economics, made no such assumption.

For Smith, individuals were socially formed in particular ways and absent that formation, the pursuit of self-love could be disastrous. These thoughts are developed in his *Theory of Moral Sentiments*, published in 1759, twenty-five years before the *Wealth of Nations*. Smith's *Theory of Moral Sentiments* is overlooked and ignored by orthodox economists who appeal exclusively to his *Wealth of Nations*. The reality is that it is the foundation-stone on which rest the conclusions of *The Wealth of Nations*. Without that foundation-stone concerning the moral development of individuals, the conclusions about the benefits of exchange based on the pursuit of self-love implode.

For Smith, justice is the pillar that makes the system work: "Justice, on the contrary, is the main pillar that upholds the whole edifice" (1976b [1790], p. 86). Justice and social order in turn derive from a sense of duty and good conduct that is both natural and socially developed:

Nature, however, has not left this weakness, which is of so much importance, altogether without a remedy; nor has she abandoned us entirely to the delusions of self-love. Our continual observations upon the conduct of others, insensibly lead us to form to ourselves certain general rules concerning what is fit and proper either to be done or to be avoided. (1976b [1790], p. 157)

Social conditioning and education then reinforce this process:

There is scarce any man, however, who by discipline, education, and example, may not be so impressed with regard to general rules, as to act upon almost every occasion with tolerable decency.... Upon the tolerable observance of these duties, depends the very existence of human society, which would crumble into nothing if mankind were not generally impressed with a reverence for those important rules of conduct. (1976b [1790], pp. 162–163)

Smith's *Theory of Moral Sentiments* rounds out the critique that neoliberalism rests on a collection of fallacies. Earlier, Chapter 2 described the Keynesian critique of the claim that laissez-faire market economies generate economically efficient outcomes. Keynes explained why monetary credit-based market economies can generate persistent large-scale unemployment that the market mechanism is unable to solve.

Chapter 2 also explained why market economies do not unambiguously advance freedom. That is because they create "unfreedoms" for some persons at the same time that they advance the freedoms of others. Put bluntly, the freedom to starve is not freedom. Furthermore, income and wealth inequality also create political inequality, which undermines political freedom, and that political inequality can then undermine market efficiency by enabling the wealthy to politically rig market rules in their favor. Indeed, this political rigging of markets was an important factor in the financial crisis of 2008, explaining the excessive deregulation of financial markets and the refusal to implement new regulations that addressed financial innovation.

Smith's analysis of the necessity of moral sentiments completes the critique. Well-formed individuals are essential to the working of the market system, but well-formed individuals are socially produced. Therein is the fallacy of worship of self-interest and animus to government. This combination is toxic for liberal society because worship of self-interest destroys the moral sentiments needed by liberal society, whereas animus to government blocks the reproduction of those moral sentiments.

Chicago School economists advocate a minimalist "night watchman" state in which the role of government is restricted to policeman, judge, and jailer – provider of national defense, protector of person and property, and enforcer of contracts. Their MIT siblings see an additional role for the state to remedy microeconomic problems of commercial monopoly, natural monopoly, public goods, externalities, and information failures. But from Adam Smith's perspective, the night-watchman state needs essential ingredients to be successful. In particular, Smith believed it needs a sense of justice among the citizenry toward each other:

> Society, however, cannot subsist among those who are at all times ready to hurt and injure one another. The moment that injury begins, the moment that mutual resentment and animosity take place, all the bands of it are broke asunder, and the different members of which it consisted are, as it were, dissipated and scattered abroad by the violence and opposition of their discordant affections. If there is any society among robbers and murderers, they must at least, according to the trite observation, abstain from robbing and murdering one another. Beneficence, therefore, is less essential to the existence of society than justice. Society may subsist, though not in the most comfortable state, without beneficence; but the prevalence of injustice must utterly destroy it. (1976b [1790], p. 86)

Society can exist without goodwill among citizens (which Smith terms beneficence), but it cannot exist without a sense of justice among its

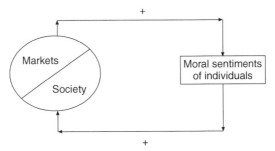

Figure 12.1. The virtuous circle of moral sentiments.

citizenry. That sense of justice ensures laws are obeyed so that property rights and contracts are essentially self-enforced.[2] That is a fundamentally different perspective from the orthodox position that holds that individuals, in the name of self-interest, should try and get away with whatever they can.

Without self-enforcement, the system becomes prohibitively expensive and inefficient. First, there are formal enforcement costs associated with increased policing and litigation, private expenses to secure person and property, and costs of an expanded judiciary and correctional system. Second, and even more costly, are the tremendous losses of potential economic gain that follow from withdrawal from commercial contracting because of fear that contracts will be unenforced or prove hugely costly to enforce.

The critical feature about Smith's moral sentiments is that they are not automatically reproduced. Reproduction needs the right conditions. This includes a sense of identity with society that comes with sharing in the benefits and limited inequality. If people do not feel the system values them, they will not value the system. Reproduction of moral sentiments also requires appropriate socialization and investment via activities like education, which is why education is a fundamental obligation of the state.

When these conditions are present, there exists a virtuous circle between individuals' moral sentiments, markets, and society, as shown in Figure 12.1. Market outcomes produce benefits that strengthen (+)

---

[2] This argument was made by Manfred Bienefeld in ad hoc comments at a workshop on globalization and labor held at the University of Northern British Columbia, September 19–20, 2008.

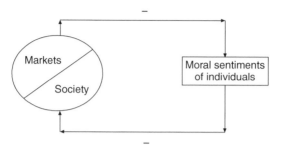

Figure 12.2. The neoliberal vicious circle of moral sentiments.

individual's moral sentiments, which strengthens social bonds and increases (+) the benefits from market activity.

Appropriate moral sentiments for liberal society have existed because of what was done in the past. The neoliberal fallacy is to assume that existence is natural and permanent. This assumption leads to policy recommendations that end up deconstructing the citizenry that the night-watchman state needs for its own success. This deconstruction is illustrated in Figure 12.2, which shows the neoliberal vicious circle of moral sentiments. Now, socially sanctioned exclusive pursuit of self-interest results in market outcomes that erode (−) individuals' moral sentiments, contributing to erosion of social bonds and a worsening (−) of market outcomes, which further erodes moral sentiments. In effect, the creed of greed is good results in behaviors that deconstruct the foundations the night-watchman state needs to function. That, in a nutshell, is the Smithian critique of Milton Friedman, Ayn Rand, Margaret Thatcher, and Gordon Gecko.

Smith's analytical insights about the formation of moral sentiments are supported by experimental evidence that confirms the socially corrosive properties of the neoliberal creed. Thus, Frank et al. (1993) report that studying neoclassical economics, with its belief that greed is good, can create bad citizens. In controlled surveys of U.S. college students, they found that exposure to neoclassical economics inhibits cooperative behavior and reduces honesty.

These findings have direct and profound economic implications. To the extent that neoliberalism has made pursuit of narrow self-interest the cultural and behavioral norm, it has likely impacted individuals' behavior. For instance, if managers take self-interest as their guiding principle, that will worsen principal-agent problems by diminishing managers' sense of responsibility to shareholders and their sense of the obligations of stewardship. This can explain the explosion of managerial pay and pay practices that can degenerate into corporate looting.

Another example concerns the U.S. mortgage crisis where massive lending fraud has become evident. The pursuit of self-interest likely encouraged some explicit borrower fraud, but more importantly it encouraged fraud-like behaviors all down the transaction chain, beginning with realtors and moving on through valuation assessors, mortgage brokers, mortgage insurers, mortgage lenders, mortgage securitizers, and rating agencies. Everyone had a self-interest to get the deal done to earn commissions and profit bonuses, which encouraged loan pushing rather than responsible lending. This role of fraud repeats the findings of William Black (2005) in his analysis of the late 1980s financial crisis in the Savings and Loan industry.

The lesson is solid ethics among individuals is an important ingredient of efficient financial systems, and undermining those ethics produces major efficiency losses. As recognized long ago by Adam Smith, healthy moral sentiments are indeed critical for market economies.

The Liberal Ethical Critique

Adam Smith's moral sentiments critique, John Maynard Keynes's economic efficiency critique, and Amartya Sen's unfreedom critique constitute a pragmatic realist critique of neoliberalism. Together they show that neoliberal claims about markets, economic efficiency, and freedom do not stack up.

To this realist critique can then be added the liberal ethical critique espoused by John Rawls (1971) in his *Theory of Justice*. Rawls asks that you imagine a veil of ignorance is placed over you so that you do not know your identity, your economic and social status, your intelligence and abilities. In that case, given you might be anyone – a homeless person or a multimillionaire – would you support current economic and social arrangements? Or would you choose an alternative, more egalitarian arrangement? If people respond that current outcomes of wealth, income, and power are grossly unequal and unacceptable, Rawls's ethical logic concludes the current system is unjust and should be changed on ethical grounds.

This liberal ethical critique is fully compatible with the realist critique, and it lends additional weight to the case for reversing neoliberal dominance. However, politically, concerns with fairness and equity appear to be second order and trumped by concerns with jobs and economic efficiency. This means that in terms of winning the political argument for change, the realist critique is likely to prove more decisive.

Time for a Great Rebalancing

The last thirty years have been marked by the comprehensive dominance of market fundamentalism and could be labeled the era of Milton Friedman. That dominance shaped globalization and national economic policy and destroyed shared prosperity in the process.

The financial crash and the Great Recession have revealed the disastrous flaws in the market fundamentalist paradigm, and the global economy now confronts the prospect of the Great Stagnation. With hindsight, we can see that when implemented, the neoliberal paradigm undermined the economy's structural balance, producing a range of outcome imbalances that now weigh heavily on the economy.

Escaping the prospect of the Great Stagnation necessitates a great rebalancing. This requires a new set of economic ideas. It is difficult to complete a long journey without a map, and ideas are the map needed for restoring shared prosperity. That is why ideas are so important, and winning the war of ideas is essential. In the words of the Old Testament, "Where there is no vision, the people perish."

The needed rebalancing should begin with the new ideal of a "balanced market economy." Like freedom, balance is something widely valued, and the Great Recession has revealed the huge costs of an unbalanced world. A balanced market economy can be the shorthand counter to neoliberalism's free-market economy.

A first major outcome imbalance concerns wealth and income distribution, which has shifted in favor of society's top echelons. This shift is a bedrock cause of the Great Recession as it forced reliance on debt to sustain aggregate demand and meet living standard expectations. That economic process is unsustainable, meaning income distribution must be rebalanced to ensure demand adequate for full employment.

A second outcome imbalance is the global financial imbalance, exemplified by the U.S.-China trade deficit. Over the last fifteen years, many emerging market economies shifted to export-led growth, which generated large trade surpluses. The United States pursued debt-fueled consumerism that created matching deficits. This configuration is exhausted, requiring a major rebalancing of the global economy based on new modalities of growth. Emerging market economies must shift away from export-led growth to domestic demand-led growth, whereas the United States must switch spending away from imports toward domestic production.

A third outcome imbalance is the worrying long-term budget outlook that confronts the United States and many other countries. Now is not the time for fiscal austerity as it could deepen the slump. However, when the time for rebalancing the fiscal outlook comes, it must be done in a way that contributes to rebalancing society, and not by aggravating existing imbalances. Much of the budget deficit will disappear automatically with economic recovery. Where health care costs are the source of the problem, the production of health care should be reformed. To the extent any remaining deficit is unsustainable, it should be addressed by progressive tax reform that increases the efficiency of the tax system and reverses the neoliberal tilt that has persistently twisted the tax structure in favor of the affluent over the past thirty years.

A fourth imbalance concerns the dominance of speculation over enterprise, which has been repeatedly visible in the Internet stock bubble of the late 1990s, the oil and commodity price bubble of 2008, and the housing price bubble that triggered the Great Recession. Keynes (1936) wrote of this conflict in *The General Theory*: "Speculators may do no harm as bubbles on a steady stream of enterprise. But the position is serious when enterprise becomes the bubble on a whirl-pool of speculation" (p. 159).

A fifth outcome imbalance concerns the relation between the economy and the environment. The problems of pollution and global climate change pose grave dangers and the costs of global warming have been clearly documented in the Stern (2006) report. Moreover, in the United States, there are additional economic and national security costs that come from reliance on imported oil.

These outcome imbalances are the product of fundamental structural imbalances. Behind the worsening of wealth and income distribution lies a shift in the balance of power between capital and labor. Rebalancing income distribution therefore requires rebalancing economic, social, and political power, which has swung in favor of corporations and the wealthy and against workers. That reveals a fundamental conundrum and the depth of the challenge: Rebalancing economic power is the key to rebalancing political power, but rebalancing political power is the key to rebalancing economic power.

The triumph of speculation over enterprise reflects the dominance of finance capital. That dominance extends over both government and nonfinancial corporations. The dominance of finance over government reflects the power of money in the political process, while the dominance of finance over industry reflects the economic ideology embedded in the shareholder value maximization paradigm. The dominance of finance also reflects an ideological imbalance between markets and government that fostered antipathy to government and regulation, one result of which was disastrous excess in financial markets.

Antipathy to government, which is a collective action, is paralleled by abuse of the environment, which is a form of property that is collectively owned within generations and across generations. Overcoming the antipathy to government requires correcting the ideological imbalance between markets and government. Environmental rebalancing requires rebalancing private consumption and private production with the collectively owned environment. Not only are market-government rebalancing and environmental rebalancing needed for sustainable and shared prosperity; they can also spur growth during a period of economic reconstruction via a green public investment agenda that meets important needs.

The preceding list of economic imbalances reveals both the extreme character of the neoliberal era and the momentous challenges it has created. Absent a great rebalancing, shared prosperity will become a relic of the past and the Great Recession will likely evolve into the Great Stagnation. If that happens, it is also easy to imagine a Weimar-style political scenario in which prolonged mass unemployment and economic hardship release the genie of intolerance and hate.

For these reasons a great rebalancing is essential and urgent, but escaping the pull of neoliberalism will not be easy. There exist major political obstacles associated with vested interests and the capture of political parties. Orthodox economists dominate thinking about economics and economic policy, and market fundamentalism has a deep hold on the public's imagination. In part, this hold is because of its rhetoric about freedom and individualism, which resonates especially strongly with U.S. cultural images and values. But it is also because extremes are attractive, offering simple but false certainties.

In contrast, economic perspectives that recognize the need for balance also require judgment, and the exercise of judgment is difficult and challenging, being the ultimate expression of individual responsibility. Ironically, neoliberalism, which touts individualism, avoids that responsibility by its embrace of the extreme. That makes it both dangerous and difficult to dislodge, but, to borrow from Mrs. Thatcher, if we want shared prosperity, there is no alternative.

References

Akerlof, G.A. and R.J. Shiller [2009], *Animal Spirits: How Human Psychology Drives The Economy And Why It Matters For Global Capitalism*, Princeton, NJ: Princeton University Press.

Anand, S. and P. Segal [2008], "What Do We Know About Global Income Inequality?" *Journal of Economic Literature*, 46(1), 57–94.

Arrow, K.J. and G. Debreu [1954], "Existence of an Equilibrium for a Competitive Economy," *Econometrica*, 22, 265–90.

Aschauer, D.A. [1989a], "Is Public Expenditure Productive?" *Journal of Monetary Economics*, 23(2), 177–200.

[1989b], "Does Public Capital Crowd-out Private Capital?" *Journal of Monetary Economics*, 24(2), 171–88.

Baker, D. [2002], "The Run-up in Home Prices: Is It Real or Is It Another Bubble?" Center for Economic Policy and Research, Washington, DC, August.

Baker, D., R. Pollin, T. McArthur, and M. Sherman [2009], "The Potential Revenue from Financial Transactions Taxes," Working Paper 212, Political Economy Research Institute, University of Massachusetts, Amherst, MA.

Barro, R.J. and D.B. Gordon [1983], "A Positive Theory of Monetary Policy in a Natural Rate Model," *Journal of Political Economy*, 91 (August), 589–610.

Bartlett, B. [2007], "Starve the Beast: Origins and Development of a Budgetary Metaphor," *The Independent Review*, 12(1), 5–26.

Bergsten, C.F. [2005], "A New Foreign Economic Policy for the United States," in *The United States and the World Economy: Foreign Economic Policy for the Next Decade*, Washington, DC: Institute for International Economics.

[2009], "The Dollar and the Budget Deficit," *Voxeu*, November 27.

Bernanke, B.S. [2004] "The Great Moderation," Remarks at the Meetings of the Eastern Economic Association, Washington DC, February 20.

221

[2005], "The Global Saving Glut and the U.S. Current Account Deficit," the Sandridge lecture, Virginia Association of Economics, Richmond, VA, March 10.

[2010a], "Causes of the Recent Financial and Economic Crisis," Testimony before the Financial Crisis Inquiry Commission, Washington, DC, September 2.

[2010b], "Monetary Policy and the Housing Bubble," Speech presented at the annual meeting of the American Economic Association, Atlanta, GA, January 3.

Bhagwati, J.N. [2002], "Patents and the Poor: Including Intellectual Property Protection in WTO Rules has Harmed the Developing World," *Financial Times*, September 17.

Bhutta, N. and G.B. Canner [2009], "Did the CRA Cause the Mortgage Meltdown?" available at http://www.minneapolisfed.org/publications_papers/pub_display.cfm?id=4136, March.

Bibow, J. [2008], "The International Monetary (Non-) Order and the Global Capital Flows Paradox," Working Paper No. 531, Levy Economics Institute of Bard College, April.

Bivens, J. [2004], "Shifting Blame for Manufacturing Job Loss: Effect of Rising Trade Deficit Shouldn't Be Ignored," EPI Briefing Paper No. 149, Economic Policy Institute, Washington, DC.

Bivens, J. and J. Irons [2008], "A Feeble Recovery: The Fundamental Economic Weaknesses of the 2001–07 Expansion," EPI Briefing Paper No. 214, Economic Policy Institute, Washington DC, December.

Black, F. and M. Scholes [1973], "The Pricing of Options and Corporate Liabilities," *Journal of Political Economy*, 81, 637–54.

Black, W.K. [2005], *The Best Way to Rob a Bank Is to Own One: How Corporate Executives and Politicians Looted the S&L Industry*, Austin: University of Texas Press.

Blanchard, O.J. [2008], "The State of Macro," MIT Department of Economics Working Paper, August 12, available at http://papers.ssrn.com/sol3/papers.cfm?abstract_id=1235536

Blecker, R.A. [2000], "The Diminishing Returns to Export-led Growth," paper prepared for the Council of Foreign Relations Working Group on Development, New York.

Blinder, A. and R. Reis [2005], "Understanding the Greenspan Standard," Working Papers 88, Princeton University Department of Economics, Center for Economic Studies, August.

Blinder, A.S. and J. Yellen [2001], *The Fabulous Decade: Macroeconomic Lessons from the 1990s*, New York: Century Foundation.

Bradford, C.I., Jr. [2005], "Prioritizing Economic Growth: Enhancing Macroeconomic Policy Choice," G-24 Discussion paper No. 37, April.

Bronfenbrenner, K. [2000], *Uneasy Terrain: The Impact of Capital Mobility on Workers, Wages, and Union Organizing*, Report prepared for the United States Trade Deficit Review Commission, Washington, DC, September.

Bronfenbrenner, K., and S. Luce [2004], *The Changing Nature of Corporate Global Restructuring: The Impact of Production Shifts on Jobs in the U.S., China, and Around the Globe*, Report prepared for the U.S.-China Economic and Security Review Commission, Washington, DC, October.

Buiter, W.H. [2008], "Self-Regulation Means No Regulation," *FT.com/maverecon*, April 10, available at http://blogs.ft.com/maverecon/2008/04/self-regulation-means-no-regulation/

Caballero, R.J. [2006], "On the Macroeconomics of Asset Shortages," NBER Working Paper No.12753, December.

[2007], "Understanding Global Imbalances," Economics at MIT: Research Highlights No. 1.

Calomiris, C.W. and P.J.Wallison [2008], "Blame Fannie Mae and Congress for the Credit Mess," *Wall Street Journal*, Tuesday, September 23, A.29.

Calvo, G. [2009], "Reserve Accumulation and Easy Money Helped to Cause the Subprime Crisis: A Conjecture in Search of a Theory," *Voxeu*, October 27.

DeLong, J.B. [2009], "The Price of Inaction," *Project Syndicate*, April 28, available at http://www.project-syndicate.org/commentary/delong89/English

[2010], "America's Employment Dilemma," *Project Syndicate*, January 27, available at http://www.project-syndicate.org/commentary/delong98/English

De Long, J.B., A. Shleifer, L.H. Summers, and R.J. Waldman [1990], "Noise Trader Risk in Financial Markets," *Journal of Political Economy*, 98, 703–38.

Dodd, R. [2007], "Subprime: Tentacles of a Crisis," *Finance and Development*, 44(4), December, 15–19.

Dooley, M.P., D. Folkerts-Landau, and P. Garber [2003], "An Essay on the Revised Bretton Woods System," Working Paper 9971, Cambridge, MA: National Bureau of Economic Research, September.

[2004], "The US Current Account Deficit and Economic Development: Collateral for a Total Return Swap," Working Paper 10727, Cambridge, MA: National Bureau of Economic Research, August.

Economic Report of the President [2009], United States Government Printing Office, Washington, DC.

[2010], United States Government Printing Office, Washington, DC.

Eichengreen, B. [2004], "The Dollar and the New Bretton Woods System," manuscript, University of California at Berkeley, December.

[2010], "Europe's Historic Gamble," *Project Syndicate*, May 15, available at http://www.project-syndicate.org/commentary/eichengreen17/English

Eichengreen, B. and K. O'Rourke [2009], "A Tale of Two Depressions," *VoxEU. org*, July 3.

Elson, D. and N. Cagatay [2000], "The Social Content of Macroeconomic Policies," *World Development*, 28 (67), 1347–64.

Epstein, G. [2001], "Financialization, Rentier Interests, and Central Bank Policy," manuscript, Department of Economics, University of Massachusetts, Amherst, MA, December.

Evensky, J. [2005], "Adam Smith's Theory of Moral Sentiments: On Morals and Why They Matter to a Liberal Society of Free People and Free Markets," *The Journal of Economic Perspectives*, 19(Summer), 109–30.

Fama, E. [1970], "Efficient Capital Markets: A Review of Theory and Empirical Work," *Journal of Finance*, 25(May), 383–416.

Farmer, R. [2009], "A New Monetary Policy for the 21st Century," *FT. com/Economists' Forum*, January 12, available at http://blogs.ft.com/economistsforum/2009/01/a-new-monetary-policy-for-the-21st-century/

Feldstein, M. [2010], "America's Saving Surprise," *Project Syndicate*, August 31.

Fischer, S. [1997], "Capital Account Liberalization and the Role of the IMF" presented at the seminar "Asia and the IMF" held in Hong Kong, China, September 19, available at http://www.imf.org/external/np/apd/asia/FISCHER.HTM.

Folbre, N. [2001], *The Invisible Heart: Economics and Family Values*, New York: The New Press.

Frank, R., T. Gilovich, and D. Regan [1993], "Does Studying Economics Inhibit Cooperation?' *Journal of Economic Perspectives*, 7(2), 159–71.

Freeman, R.B. [1998], "Spurts in Union Growth: Defining Moments and Social Processes," in Bordo, Goldin, & White (eds.), *The Defining Moment: The Great Depression and the American Economy in the Twentieth Century*, Chicago: The University of Chicago Press.

Friedman, M. [2002], *Capitalism and Freedom*, 40th anniversary edition, Chicago: University of Chicago Press.

[1968], "The Role of Monetary Policy" *American Economic Review*, 58(May), 1–17.

[1961], "The Lag in Effects of Monetary Policy," *Journal of Political Economy*, 69 (October), 447–66.

[1953], "The Case for Flexible Exchange Rates," *Essays in Positive Economics*, Chicago: Chicago University Press.

Friedman, M. and A.J. Schwarz [1963], *A Monetary History of the United States, 1867–1960*, Princeton, NJ: Princeton University Press.

Fukuyama, F. [1992], *The End of History and the Last Man*, New York: Free Press.

Galbraith, J.K. [1954], *The Great Crash 1929*, New York: Houghton Mifflin.

[2008], *The Predator State: How Conservatives Abandoned the Free Market and Why Liberals Should Too*, New York: Free Press.

Gallagher, K. [2010a], "China Crashes CAFTA's Party," *Guardian*, June 5.

[2010b], "Obama Must Ditch Bush-era Trade Deals," *Comment Is Free*, Thursday 1, July, available at http://www.guardian.co.uk/commentisfree/cifamerica/2010/jun/30/obama-bush-us-trade

Glenn, D. [2009], "Notre Dame Plans to Dissolve the Heterodox Side of its Split Economics Department," *Chronicle of Higher Education*, September 16, available at http://chronicle.com/article/Notre-Dame-to-Dissolve/48460/

Godley, W. and G. Zezza [2006], "Debt and Lending: A Cri de Coeur," Policy Note 2006/4, The Levy Economics Institute of Bard College.

Goodfriend, M. [2007], "How the World Achieved Consensus on Monetary Policy," *Journal of Economic Perspectives*, 21(4), 47–68.

Goodman, P.S. [2008], "The Reckoning: Taking a Hard Look at the Greenspan Legacy," *New York Times*, October 9.

Gorton, G.B. [2008], "The Panic of 2007," paper presented at "Maintaining Stability in a Changing Financial System," a symposium sponsored by the Federal Reserve Bank of Kansas City, held in Jackson Hole, WY, August 21–23.

Grabel, I. [2000], "The Political Economy of 'Policy Credibility': the New-Classical Macroeconomics and the Remaking of Emerging Economies," *Cambridge Journal of Economics*, 24, 1–19.

Grantham, J. [2010], "Night of the Living Fed," *GMO Quarterly Letter*, October.

Greenspan, A. [2000], "Technological Innovation and the Economy," Remarks before the White House Conference on the New Economy, Washington, DC, April 5.

[2005], "Consumer Finance," Remarks at the Federal Reserve System's Fourth Annual Community Affairs Research Conference, Washington, DC, April 8.

[2008], "Alan Greenspan: A response to my critics," ft.com/economists forum, April 6, available at http://blogs.ft.com/economistsforum/2008/04/alan-greenspan-a-response-to-my-critics/

[2009], "The Fed Didn't Cause the Housing Bubble," *Wall Street Journal*, March 11.

Greider, W. [2001], "A New Giant Sucking Sound," *The Nation*, December 13.

Group of Thirty [2009], "Financial Reform: A Framework for Financial Stability," Washington DC, report issued January 15.

Gunther, J.W. [2000], "Should CRA Stand for Community Redundancy Act?" *Regulation* 23 (3), 56–60, available at http://www.cato.org/pubs/regulation/regv23n3/gunther.pdfbee

Hasset, K. [2008], "How the Democrats Created the Financial Crisis," *Bloomberg*, September 22, available at http://www.bloomberg.com/apps/news?pid=newsarchive&sid=aSKSoiNbnQY0

Hausmann, R. and F. Sturzenegger [2005], "Dark Matter Makes the US Deficit Disappear," *Financial Times*, December 7, available at http://minerva.union.edu/dvorakt/383/ps/deficit/hausmann%20sturzenegger%20FT.pdf

Hayek, F.A. [1944], *The Road to Serfdom*, Chicago: University of Chicago Press.

——— [1945], "The Use of Knowledge in Society," *American Economic Review*, 35, 519–30.

Heintz, J. [2010], "The Impact of Public Capital on the U.S. Private Economy: New Evidence and Analysis," *International Review of Applied Economics*, (24), 619–32.

Heintz, J., R. Pollin, and H. Garrett-Peltuer [2009], "How Infrastructure Investments Support the U.S. Economy: Employment, Productivity and Growth," Political Economy Research Institute, University of Massachusetts, Amherst, MA, January.

Hirsch, B.T. and D.A. Macpherson [2003], "Union Membership and Coverage Database from the Current Population Survey: Note," *Industrial and Labor Relations Review*, 56(January), 349–54.

Husock, H. [2008], "The Financial Crisis and the CRA," *City Journal of the Manhattan Institute*, October 30, available at http://www.city-journal.org/2008/eon1030hh.html

International Monetary Fund [2006], "People's Republic of China: Staff Report for the 2006 Article IV Consultation," Washington, DC.

——— [2007], *World Economic Outlook Update*, July, available at http://www.imf.org/external/pubs/ft/weo/2007/update/01/index.htm

Jensen, M.J. and W.H. Meckling [1976], "Theory of the Firm: Managerial Behavior, Agency Costs and Ownership Structure," *Journal of Financial Economics*, 3, 305–60.

Johnson, S. and J. Kwak [2010], *13 Bankers: The Wall Street Takeover and the Next Financial Meltdown*, New York: Random House.

Keen, S. [1995], "Finance and Economic Breakdown: Modeling Minsky's Financial Instability Hypothesis," *Journal of Post Keynesian Economics*, 17(4), 607–35;

——— [2006], "The Recession We Can't Avoid," Steve Keen's Monthly Debt Report, November.

Keynes, J.M. [1931], "The Pure Theory of Money: A Reply to Dr. Hayek," *Econometrica*, 11(November), 387–97.

——— [1936], *The General Theory of Employment, Interest, and Money*, London: Macmillan.

——— [1973], *Collected Writings* Vol. 13 (The General Theory and After, Part I, Preparation).

Kotlikoff, L. [2010], "How Greece Can Devalue without Devaluing," *FT. com/Economists' Forum*, February 18, available at http://blogs.ft.com/ economistsforum/2010/02/how-greece-can-devalue-without-devaluing/

Kristof, N.D. [2006], "China and Sudan, Blood and Oil," *New York Times*, April 23.

Krueger, A. O. [1974], "The Political Economy of Rent-seeking Society," *American Economic Review*, 64, 291–303.

Krugman, P. [2009], "How Did Economists Get It So Wrong?" *New York Times*, September 6.

[2010a], "CRE-ative Destruction," Conscience of a Liberal Blog, January 7, available at http://krugman.blogs.nytimes.com/2010/01/07/cre-ative-destruction/

[2010b], "Taking on China," *New York Times*, March 14, available at http://www.nytimes.com/2010/03/15/opinion/15krugman.html

[2010c], "Now and Later," *New York Times*, June 20, available at http://www.nytimes.com/2010/06/21/opinion/21krugman.html

[2010d], "Samuelson Memorial," Conscience of a Liberal Blog, April 20, available at http://krugman.blogs.nytimes.com/2010/04/11/samuelson-memorial/Cited

Makin, J.H. [2009], "A Government Failure, Not a Market Failure," Commentarymagazine.com, July/August.

Malanga, S. [2009], "Obsessive Housing Disorder," *City Journal*, 19(2), available at http://www.city-journal.org/2009/19_2_homeownership.html

Mankiw, N.G. [2009], "It May be Time for the Fed to go Negative," *New York Times*, April 18, available at http://www.nytimes.com/2009/04/19/business/economy/19view.html

Manova, K. and Z. Zhang [2008], "China's Exporters and Importers: Firms, Products, and Trade Partners," unpublished manuscript, Department of Economics, Stanford University, CA, June.

Markowitz, H. [1959], *Portfolio Selection*, New York: Wiley.

Masters, M.W. and A.K. White [2008], "The Accidental Hunt Brothers: How Institutional Investors are Driving up Food and Energy Prices," Special Report, July 31, available at www.accidentalhuntbrothers.com

McLuhan, M. [1964], *Understanding Media: The Extensions of Man*, New York: McGraw Hill.

Merton, R.C. [1973], "Theory of Rational Option Pricing," *Bell Journal of Economics and Management Service*, 4, 141–83.

Milanovic, B. [2007], *Worlds Apart: Measuring International and Global Inequality*, Princeton, NJ: Princeton University Press.

[2009], "Two Views on the Cause of the Global Crisis – Part 1," *YaleGlobal Online Magazine*, May 4, available at http://yaleglobal.yale.edu

Minsky, H.P. [1992, 1993], "The Financial Instability Hypothesis," Working paper No. 74, The Jerome Levy Economics Institute of Bard College,

New York, and published in Arestis P. and Sawyer M. (eds.), *Handbook of Radical Political Economy*, Aldershot: Edward Elgar.

Miron, J.A. [2010], "Less Policy Means More Jobs," *New York Times*, June 24, available at http://roomfordebate.blogs.nytimes.com/2010/06/24/can-obama-create-more-jobs-soon/#jeffrey

Mishel, L., J. Bernstein, and S. Allegreto [2009], *The State of Working America 2008/2009*, Ithaca, NY: Cornell University Press.

Lago, I., Duttagupta, R. and R. Goyal [2009], "The Debate on the International Monetary System," Strategy, Policy, and Review Department, International Monetary Fund, November 11.

Munnell, A. [1990], "Why Has Productivity Growth Declined? Productivity and Public Investment," *New England Economic Review* (September/October), 11–32.

[1992], "Infrastructure Investment and Economic Growth," *Journal of Economic Perspectives*, 6(4), 189–98.

Niskanen, W.A. [1971], *Bureaucracy and Representative Government*, Chicago: Aldine-Atherton.

Obstfeld, M. and K. Rogoff [2007], "The Unsustainable U.S. Current Account Position Revisited," in ed. Richard Clarida, *G7 Current Account Imbalances: Sustainability and Adjustment*, Chicago: University of Chicago Press.

OECD Observer [2003], "China Ahead in Foreign Direct Investment," No. 237, May.

Ostry, J.D., A.R. Ghosh, K. Habermeier, M. Chamon, M.S. Qureshi, and D.B. Reinhart [2010], "Capital Inflows: The Role of Controls," Research Department, International Monetary Fund, February 19, available at http://www.imf.org/external/pubs/ft/spn/2010/spn1004.pdf

Palley, T.I. [1998a], *Plenty of Nothing: The Downsizing of the American Dream and the Case for Structural Keynesianism*, Princeton, NJ: Princeton University Press.

[1998b], "Building Prosperity from the Bottom Up: The New Economics of the Minimum Wage," *Challenge*, 41(July–August), 1–13.

[1998c], "The Minimum Wage and Low Wage Labor Markets: A Wage Curve Analysis," Technical Working Paper T011, Department of Public Policy, AFL-CIO, Washington, DC, March.

[2000], "The Economics of Globalization: A Labor View," in eds. Teich, Nelson, McEnaney, and Lita, *Science and Technology Policy Yearbook 2000*, American Association for the Advancement of Science, Washington, DC.

[2001a [2002a]], "Economic Contradictions Coming Home to Roost? Does the U.S. Face a Long Term Aggregate Demand Generation Problem?" Working Paper 332, Levy Economics Institute of Bard College, June 2001, and *Journal of Post Keynesian Economics*, 25 (2002), 9–32.

[2001b], "Destabilizing Speculation and the Case for an International Currency Transactions Tax," *Challenge* (May/June), 70–89.

[2001c], "The Economic Case for Labor Standards: A Layman's Guide," *Journal of Global Law and Business*, 2(Fall), 183–95.

[2002b], "Domestic Demand-Led Growth: A New Paradigm for Development," in *After Neoliberalism: Economic Policies That Work for the Poor*, in eds. Jacobs, Weaver, and Baker, *New Rules for Global Finance*, Washington, DC, and also published as "A New Development Paradigm: Domestic Demand-Led Growth," *Foreign Policy in Focus*, September 2002, http://www.fpif.org/

[2003a], "Asset Price Bubbles and the Case for Asset Based Reserve Requirements," *Challenge*, 46(May–June), 53–72.

[2003b], "Export-led Growth: Evidence of Developing Country Crowding-out," in eds. Arestis et al., *Globalization, Regionalism, and Economic Activity*, Cheltenham: Edward Elgar.

[2004], "The Economic Case for International Labor Standards," *Cambridge Journal of Economics*, 28(January), 21–36.

[2005a], "The Questionable Legacy of Alan Greenspan," *Challenge*, 48(6), 17–31.

[2005b], "Labor Standards, Democracy and Wages: Some Cross-country Evidence," *Journal of International Development*, 17, 1–16.

[2005c], "Chilean Unremunerated Reserve Requirement Capital Controls as a Screening Mechanism," *Investigacion Economica*, 64 (January–March), 33–52.

[2006a], "Sabotaging Government: How the Right Shifted from a Small Government Stance to a Radical Anti-government One," *Mother Jones*, January 10, available at http://motherjones.com/politics/2006/01/sabotaging-government

[2006b], "The Weak Recovery and Coming Deep Recession," *Mother Jones*, March 17.

[2006c [2007/8]], "The Fallacy of the Revised Bretton Woods Hypothesis: Why Today's System is Unsustainable and Suggestions for a Replacement," Public Policy Brief No. 85, The Levy Economics Institute of Bard College, 2006. Also published in *International Journal of Political Economy*, 36(Winter), 36–52.

[2006d], "Why Dollar Hegemony is Unhealthy: The World's Dangerous Dependence on the U.S. Dollar Risks Hurting All," *Yale Global Online*, June 20, available at http://yaleglobal.yale.edu/content/why-dollar-hegemony-unhealthy

[2007a], "Seeking Full Employment Again: Challenging the Wall Street Paradigm," *Challenge* 50 (November/December), 14–50.

[2007b], World Asset Prices: What's Really Going On?" January 1, available at http://www.thomaspalley.com/?p=61

[2008a], "America's Exhausted Growth Paradigm," *The Chronicle of Higher Education*, April 11, 2008.

[2008b], "Financialization: What It Is and Why It Matters," in eds. Eckhard Hein, Torsten Niechoj, Peter Spahn, and Achim Truger, *Finance-Led Capitalism: Macroeconomic Effects of Changes in the Financial Sector*, Marburg: Metropolis-Verlag, 2008 and Working Paper 04/2008, IMK Macroeconomic Policy Institute, Dusseldorf, Germany.

[2008c], "Demythologizing Central Bankers," *Asia Times Online*, April 8, available at http://www.atimes.com/atimes/Global_Economy/JD08Dj06.html

[2009a], "America's Exhausted Paradigm: Macroeconomic Causes of the Financial Crisis and Great Recession," New American Contract Policy Paper, New America Foundation, Washington, DC, July 22.

[2009b [2011a]], "A Theory of Minsky Super-cycles and Financial Crises," IMK Working Paper 2/2009, Institute for Macroeconomics, Dusseldorf, Germany and *Contributions to Political Economy*, forthcoming.

[2009c], "Rethinking the Economics of Capital Mobility and Capital Controls," *Brazilian Journal of Political Economy*, 29(July–September), 15–34.

[2010a], "The Limits of Minsky's Financial Instability Hypothesis as an Explanation of the Crisis," *Monthly Review* (April), 28–43.

[2010b], "Global Core Labor Standards are More Important than Ever" 2010 edition of the *United Nations Global Compact International Yearbook*.

[2011], "The Fiscal Austerity Trap: Budget Deficit Alarmism Is Sabotaging Growth," *Challenge*, 54(1), 6–31.

Peters, G.P., J.C. Minx, C.L. Weber, and O. Edenhofer [2011], "Growth in Emission Transfers Via International Trade from 1990 to 2008," Center for International Climate and Environmental Research, Oslo, Norway, March 29.

Piketty, T. and E. Saez [2004], "Income Inequality in the United States, 1913–2002," manuscript, available at http://elsa.berkeley.edu/~saez/piketty-saezOUP04US.pdf

Polanyi, K. [1944], *The Great Transformation: The Political and Economic Origins of Our Time*, New York: Farrar & Rinehart.

Pollin, R. [2010], "Austerity Is Not a Solution: Why the Deficit Hawks Are Wrong," *Challenge*, 53(6), 6–36.

Pollin, R. and D. Baker [2010], "Reindustrializing America; A Proposal for Reviving U.S. Manufacturing and Creating Millions of Good Jobs," *New Labor Forum*, 19(2), 17–34.

Pollin, R., D. Baker, and M. Schaberg [2003], "Security Transactions Taxes for U.S. Financial markets," *Eastern Economic Review*, 29 (4), 527 – 558.

Pollin, R. and S. Luce [2000], *The Living Wage: Building a Fair Economy*, New York: The New Press.

Popper, K.R. [1959], *The Logic of Scientific Discovery*, New York: Basic Books.

Posen, A. [2007a], "Don't Worry about U.S. mortgages," *Welt am Sonntag*, April 12, available at http://www.iie.com/publications/opeds/oped. cfm?ResearchID=729

[2007b], "A Drag, not a Crisis," *Welt am Sonntag*, September 27, available at http://www.iie.com/publications/opeds/oped.cfm?ResearchID=812

Posner, R.A. [2009], "Capitalism in Crisis," *Wall Street Journal*, May 7.

Rajan, R.G. [2005], "Has Financial Development Made the World Riskier?" Paper presented at the Jackson Hole Conference of the Kansas City Federal Reserve Bank, available at http://www.kc.frb.org/publicat/ sympos/2005/PDF/Rajan2005.pdf

[2010], *Fault Lines: How Hidden Fractures Still Threaten the World Economy*, Princeton, NJ: Princeton University Press.

Rawls, J. [1971], *A Theory of Justice*, Cambridge, MA: Belknap Press.

Roach, S. [2004a], "Why We Ought to Be Thanking the Chinese," *Fortune Magazine*, March 22.

[2004b], "Twin Deficits at the Flashpoint?" Morgan Stanley Global Economic Forum, August 16.

[2010], "Blaming China Will Not Solve America's Problem," *Financial Times*, March 29.

Rogoff, K. [2008a], "The World's Runaway Train," *Project Syndicate*, July, available at http://www.project-syndicate.org/commentary/rogoff44/ English

[2008b], "No More Creampuffs," *Washington Post*, September 16, available at http://www.washingtonpost.com/wp-dyn/content/article/2008/09/15/ AR2008091502532.html

Roubini, N. and B. Setser [2005], "Will the Bretton Woods 2 Regime Unravel Soon? The Risk of a Hard Landing in 2005–2006," paper prepared for a conference organized by the Federal Reserve Bank of San Francisco, February, p. 5, available at http://www.frbsf.org/economics/ conferences/0502/Roubini.pdf

Seguino, S. and C. Grown [2006], "Gender Equity and Globalization: Macroeconomic Policy for Developing Countries," *Journal of International Development*, 18(8), 1081–104.

Sen, A.K. [1982], *Poverty and Famines: An Essay on Entitlements and Deprivation*, Oxford: Clarendon Press.

[1999], *Development as Freedom*, Oxford: Oxford University Press.

Sharpe, W. [1964], "Capital Asset Prices: A Theory of Market Equilibrium under Conditions of Risk," *Journal of Finance*, 19, 425–42.

Shiller, R.J. [2005], *Irrational Exuberance*, 2nd edition, Princeton, NJ: Princeton University Press.

Siegle, J.T., M.M. Weinstein, and M.H. Halperin [2004], "Why Democracies Excel," *Foreign Affairs* (September/October), 57–71.

Smith, A. [1784 [1976a]], *An Inquiry into the Nature and Causes of the Wealth of Nations,"* ed. W.B.Todd, based on 1784 edition. Volume 2 of *The Glasgow Edition of the Works and Correspondence of Adam Smith*, eds. D.D. Raphael and A. Skinner, Oxford: Clarendon Press.

[1790 [1976b]], *The Theory of Moral Sentiments*, eds. D.D. Raphael and A.L.Macfie, based on 1790 edition. Volume 1 of *The Glasgow Edition of the Works and Correspondence of Adam Smith*, eds. D.D.Raphael and A. Skinner, Oxford: Clarendon Press.

Soros, G. [1987], *The Alchemy of Finance*, New York: Simon and Schuster.

Stern, N. [2006], *Stern Review on the Economics of Climate Change*, London: Her Majesty's Treasury.

Stigler, G.J. [1971], "The Theory of Economic Regulation," *Bell Journal of Economics and Management Science*, 2(1), 3–21.

Taleb, N.N. [2007], *The Black Swan; The Impact of the Highly Improbable*, New York: Random House.

Taylor, J.B. [2007], "Housing and Monetary Policy," NBER Working Paper No. 13682, December.

[2009], "How Government Created the Financial Crisis," *Wall Street Journal*, February 3, A.19.

Thatcher, M. [1987], Interview for *Woman's Own*, September 23, available at http://www.margaretthatcher.org/speeches/displaydocument. asp?docid=106689

Tobin, J. [1958], "Liquidity Preference as Behavior towards Risk," *Review of Economic Studies*, 25(February), 65–86.

Tobin, J. and W. Brainard [1968], "Pitfalls in Financial Model Building," *American Economic Review*, 58(May), 99–122.

Triffin, R. [1961], *Gold and the Dollar Crisis*, New Haven, CT: Yale University Press.

[1968], *Our International Monetary System: Yesterday, Today and Tomorrow*, New York: Random House.

Tullock, G. [1967], "The Welfare Cost of Tariffs, Monopolies, and Theft," *Western Economic Journal* (now *Economic Inquiry*), 5, 224–32.

Tzioumis, K. and R. Gomez [2007], "What Do Unions Do to CEO Compensation?" Center for Economic Performance Discussion Paper No. 720, available at http://papers.ssrn.com/sol3/papers. cfm?abstract_id=1032796

Wicks-Lim, J. [2006], "Mandated Wage Floors and the Wage Structure: New Estimates of the Ripple Effects of Minimum Wage Laws," Working paper No.116, Political Economy Research Institute, Amherst, MA, June.

Zakaria, F. [2008], "There Is a Silver Lining," *Newsweek*, October 11.

Index